Money

A Mirror Image of the Economy

J.W. Smith

The Institute for Economic Democracy Press

Published by: the Institute for Economic Democracy
313 Seventh Ave., Radford, VA 24141, USA
888.533.1020 / www.ied.info / ied@ied.info

In Cooperation with the Institute on World Problems
www.worldproblems.net

Library of Congress Cataloging-in-Publication Data

Smith, J. W., 1930-
Money : a mirror image of the economy / J.W. Smith.
p. cm.
Includes bibliographical references and index.
ISBN 0-9624423-8-0 (hbk. : alk. paper) -- ISBN 0-9624423-4-8 (pbk. : alk. paper)
1. Money. 2. Capital. 3. Equality. 4. Economic policy. 5. Distributive justice. I. Title.
HG220.A2S62 2005
332.4--dc22

2005025522
The above were provided by The Library of Congress
6. Henry George 7. Public Commons 8. World Federation

Book cover designed by John Cole, www.johncolegrf.com

This book is printed on acid free paper.

THE INSTITUTE FOR ECONOMIC DEMOCRACY PRESS

BOOK CATALOGUE
FALL, 2006

IED Press is dedicated to publishing high quality, scholarly books dedicated to transforming our economic and political world order to one of peace, freedom, prosperity, and sustainability

Have your library order books you feel are important.

Publicity Release information with each title.

Send requests for titles to review to ied@ied.info or call 888.533.1020

More information on the order blank

Dr. Smith clarifies the basics of that most mysterious and powerful of human inventions—money. – Professor Richard Heinberg, author, *Oil, War, and the fate of Industrial Societies.*

Dr. J.W. Smith Leaps the Ob fuscations and makes the operations of money easily understandable. – William Kotke, author *Final Empire*

Only a handful of great books, brief and highly focused, have moved civilizations significantly forward. This is one of those rare books. – Professor Glen Martin, author, *Millennium Dawn*

An analysis of the simplicity of creating or destroying money tells us that all inflations and an occasional deflation are planned events.

Utilizing a currency valid only within their borders, a dual currency system, an allied developing world can create money to build infrastructure and industry.

Applying Henry George's philosophy across the economic spectrum transposes monopoly rent values into equally-shared use-values. Quality of life increases as working hours drop by half.

Henry George's principles applied to world money systems is the lever to eliminate monopolies worldwide. Fully 60% of those huge blocs of capital disappear. Not only were they never necessary, their collection under the current monopoly structure reduces economic efficiency by fully 50% or more. That those monopoly funds can be replaced by a few computer strokes is the secret that banking monopolists will never share.

For 500 years rights to the commons were forcibly taken away from the people. Everyone knew this was theft of the rights and millions were slaughtered in the struggle to protect those rights. The last 200 years of that 700 plus year struggle private ownership of public wealth became accepted as normal. Some of what we know as "the classics" were not even philosophies, they were only justifications for the inefficient rule of law being put in place.

Economy & Politics – Money July 2006
0-9624423-4-8 (pbk) $28 – 0-9624423-8-0 (hbk) $50 – 200 pages

Dr. Smith charts a clear and brilliant path away from war and terrorism towards a peaceful and prosperous world economy. -- Alanna Hartzok, UN ECOSOC NGO Representative

Henry George would fully approve of Dr. J.W. Smith applying his philosophy (restructuring *exclusive titles* to nature's resources and technologies to *conditional titles*) across the economic spectrum. -- Ole Lefmann, a writer for 60 years on the exclusive title principles of Henry George.

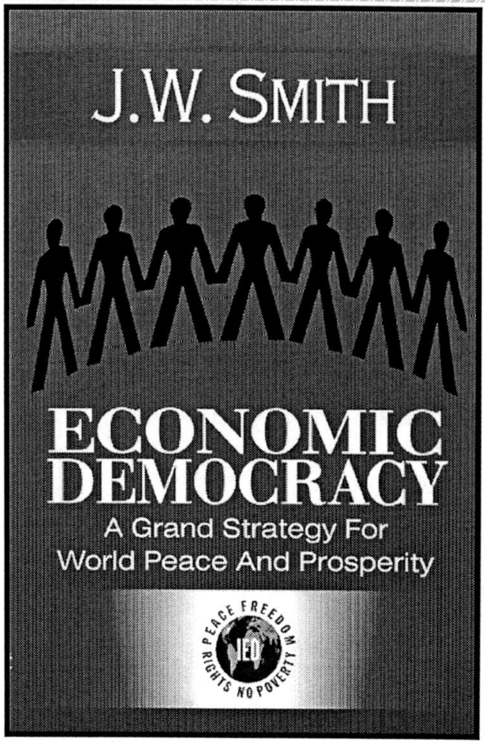

The West spent 700 plus years establishing capitalism. That *rule of law* was little more than the old aristocratic system (*exclusive title* to nature's resources and technologies) hiding under a benign name. Identical to aristocracy, capitalism's *rule of law* laid claim to—or wasted—at least half the wealth produced by productive labor.

This exposes classics on economics—reverently taught in today's classrooms—as nothing more than justifications for unequal and unjust rules of law being put in place

During that same timespan, *plunder by trade* became the norm in world commerce. Impoverished nations poised to take control of their resources and destiny threatens to collapse that trade structure. Such a collapse of trade norms will shatter capitalism's internal economies.

That would be the opportune moment to replace monopoly capitalism's *rule of law* with Henry George's economic principles which has the potential of eliminating poverty in 10 years, providing a quality life for all within 50 years, and all while reducing the workweek to 2 to 3 days per week.

Once Henry George's principles have been applied to an economically viable nation or region, the classics on economics, reverently taught in today's classroom, will stand exposed as justifications for the unequal and unjust *rules of law* put in place the past 700 plus years, not philosophies for efficient economic systems. -- The Author

Economy & politics July 2006

1-933567-03-1 (pbk) $32 1-933567-02-3 (hbk) $65 – 490 pages 2

A collection of articles and essays on how cies address problems of poverty, the wealt and resource wars.
Forthcoming, 2007

The Earth Belongs to Everyone

A Collection of Articles and Essays
by Alanna Hartzok

Themes include: Democracy, Earth Rights and the Next Economy; Sharing Our Common Heritage; Land for People, Not for Profit; Financing Local to Global Public Goods; Women, Earth and Economic Power; Restructuring Economic Relationships.

Endorsements:

More and more people are convinced that the only way to a just, prosperous and ecologically sustainable future is to share the value of Earth's resources more fairly. One of the many merits of Alanna Hartzok's collection of writings is to ground that conviction in practical proposals. She inspires us to do something about it. - **James Robertson**, author, *The New Economics of Sustainable Development*, co-founder, The Other Economic Summit and the New Economics Foundation, consultant, European Commission, London

Alanna Hartzok has deeply researched tax issues with equity and ecological-sustainability firmly in mind. This book is a storehouse of wisdom and insights on these and many broader issues relating economics to the larger planetary ecology. - **Hazel Henderson**, author, *Beyond Globalization* and *Building a Win-Win World*, member, President's Commission on Sustainable Development, founder, Ethical Markets TV

There are many of your articles which I dearly want to publish at www.stwr.net. The *Share the World's Resources* audience is vast and certainly your message through your articles will be most welcome by our readers and members around the world. - **Mohammed Mesbahi,** Chair and Founder, *Share the World's Resources*, London

Alanna Hartzok is one of the top experts describing new economic ethics and policies that can create a fair distribution of wealth and protect the earth. In this collection of articles she shows us how fairly sharing the earth can build a culture of peace and justice. She must be heard if we are to avoid further crises and chaos in our world! - **Anne Goeke (de la Bouillerie),** co-director, Earth Rights Institute, author, Global Greens Coordinator, international peace and political activist, sustainable living consultant, Santa Monica, California

Alanna Hartzok is a United Nations NGO Representative, Co-Director of Earth Rights Institute, and a former Green Party candidate for US Congress.

Millennium Dawn

The Philosophy of Planetary Crisis and Human Liberation

by Glen T. Martin

Millennium Dawn is a complete examination of our human situation in the light of the global crises at the dawn of the twenty-first century.

It examines the philosophical, spiritual, political and economic conditions under which we live and illuminates the basis for human liberation on planet Earth within the twenty-first century.

Glen T Martin is Professor of Philosophy at Radford University in Virginia, President of International Philosophers for Peace and Secretary General of the World Constitution and Parliament Association. He is author of several books and dozens of articles on global issues, political philosophy, and human spirituality

Contents

1. Humanity at the Crossroads
2. Between Liberation and Self Destruction
3. A Planetary Paradigm: Unity in Diversity
4. Deep Nonviolence: Compassion, Critical Theory, and Nonviolence
5. Religious and Spiritual Maturity in the 20th and 21st Centuries
6. Spirituality and Mysticism
7. Stages of Human Development toward Ethical and Spiritual Maturity
8. An Ethical and Spiritual Foundation for Socialism
9. The Maturing of Critical Theory
10. The Nightmare of Capitalism
11. Transformative Spirituality
12. The Principle of Unity in Diversity and democratic World Government
13. Practical and Revolutionary Implications of the Constitution for the Federation of Earth
14. A Paradigm Shif to Universal Peace, Freedom, and Prosperity
15. Barcelona Reflections on Transformative Praxis for the 21st Century

0-9753555-1-1 (pbk) $20

0-9753555-0-3 (hbk) $60 – 445 pages

In this book, Glen T. Martin traces the historical development of the concept of law from Ancient times to the present. He shows the development of the concept to the present as the development of the ideas of democratic law, the universality of law, and human rights.

Dr. Martin then examines contemporary philosophy of law to show both its current limitations and contradictions and its place in the development of Democratic World law. In doing so, Martin allows us to see real hope in our current intellectual milieu and the possibility of a positive future for humanity.

CONTENTS

I. Introduction: Ascent to Freedom

II. The Democratic Foundations

1. The Modern World System
3. The Moral Foundations of Democracy
4. What is Political Legitimacy?
5. Sovereignty of the People of Earth
6. The Current System of AInternational Law@
7. The Concept of AWorld Law@

III. Principle of Unity in Diversity

IV. Philosophy of Law Foundations: The Ancients to Rousseau

V. Philosophy of Law Foundations: Kant to Contemporary

VI. The Philosophy of Law

1. Historical development of the concept of law
2. The tradition of natural law
3. The nature of law
4. The failure of legal positivism

VII. The Ecological Foundations

VIII. The Justice and Human Rights Foundations

IX. The Peace and Nonviolence Foundations

X. The Economic Foundations

XI. The Earth Constitution as the foundation of democratic world law

Bibliography

Index

Philosophy & Law Forthcoming October 2006

1-933567-05-8 (pbk) $30
1-933567-06-6 (hbk) $60 p. 250

EMERGING WORLD LAW

Key Documents and Decisions of the World Constituent Assemblies and Provisional World Parliament

Edited with Commentary by

Eugenia Almand
Glen T. Martin

This book is a compendium and an account of the immense work that has been accomplished by the World Constitution and Parliament Association and thousands of world citizens since 1958. It details the creation of the Constitution for the Federation of Earth through four Constituent Assemblies from 1968 to 1991.

It also contains the collection of extraordinary provisional world law passed by the Provisional World Parliament (under the authority of the Earth Constitution) in its first nine sessions from 1982 to 2006.

CONTENTS

Chapter One: Introduction (by Glen T. Martin)
Chapter Two: A History of the World Constitution and Parliament Association, the Provisional World Parliament, and the Global Constituent Assemblies by Terence Amerasinghe
Chapter Three: Manifesto of the Earth Federation
Chapter Four: Analytical Commentary on the Constitution for the Federation of Earth by Eugenia Almand
Chapter Five: The Constitution for the Federation of Earth
Chapter Six: Resolutions and Declarations of the Provisional World Parliament
Photo plates from the sessions of Parliament
Chapter Seven: Commentary on Provisional World Law by Terence Amerasinghe
Chapter Eight: Legislative summaries of the acts of the PWP
Chapter Nine: Legislation from the first and second sessions
Chapter Ten: Legislation from the third and fourth sessions
Chapter Eleven: Legislation from the sixth session
Chapter Twelve: Legislation from the seventh session
Chapter Thirteen: Seventh session continued
Chapter Fourteen: Seventh session continued
Chapter Sixteen: Legislation from the eighth session
Chapter Seventeen: Legislation from the ninth session
Chapter Eighteen: Where do we go from here?
Chapter Nineteen: The Provisional World District Court System
Chapter Twenty: An Overview of Democratic World Government
Charts and diagrams of the Earth Federation
Index (including websites)
Bibliography

Philosophy & Law Forthcoming October 2006
1-933567-07-4 (pbk) $45 1933567-08-2 (hbk) $90 900 pages

Contents

1. Introduction: The Supreme Act of Civil Obedience
2. Declaration of the Rights of People to Create and Ratify a World Constitution and Sessions of the Provisional World Parliament
3. Manifesto of the Earth Federation
4. The Constitution for the Federation of Earth
5. Summary and Analysis of the Earth Constitution
6. Essays on the Promise and Necessity of World Law

"The only truly practical road map for human survival on Earth"
T.P. Amerasinghe

6.1 The Philosophy of Anarchism versus the Philosophy of Democratic World Government
6.2 The Earth Constitution and the Question of Sovereignty by T.P. Amerasinghe
6.3 The Roots of Terrorism in Sovereign Nation-States and the Path to a Secure World Order
6.4 Are We Unteachable? By Errol E. Harris
6.5 World Legal Revolution by Eugenia Almand
6.6 The Philosophy of Nonviolence and World Revolution Through World Law
6.7 The Principles of Ecology and the Earth Federation

7. Conclusion: Pledge, Resolution, and Revolution
7.1 The Pledge of Allegiance to the Earth Federation
7.2 Resolution for Introduction to National Parliaments
7.3 Conclusion: World Revolution Through World Law

Appendix: The Development of a World Parliament: A Brief History
Selected Bibliography and Works Cited
Index

Philosophy, Government, & Law — October 2006

0-9753555-2-X (pbk) $17.95 -- 0-9753555-3-8 (hbk) $60 – 300 pages

World Revolution Through World Law

Basic Documents of the Emerging Earth Federation

by Glen T. Martin

This book presents four key documents from the emerging Federation of Earth along with extensive commentary and analysis situating the Earth Federation Movement within our contemporary global crisis situation

Glen T. Martin is Professor of Philosophy and Religious Studies and Chair of the Peace Studies Program at Radford University in Virginia.

As President of International Philosophers for Peace, and Secretary General of the World Constitution and Parliament Association, he has lectured and traveled in many countries of the world in the service of world peace and a prosperous future for everyone on Earth. He is author of *From Nietzsche to Wittgenstein: The Problem of Truth and Nihilism in the Modern World, Millennium Dawn: The Philosophy of Planetary Crisis and Human Liberation,* and dozens of articles on a variety of topics in political commentary, comparative philosophy, the spirituality of human liberation, economic democracy, democratic world government, and global social issues.

EARTH FEDERATION NOW!
Tomorrow is Too Late

Errol E. Harris

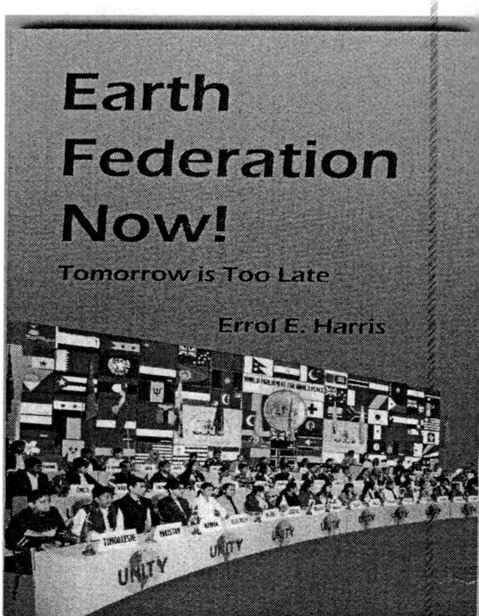

This book examines our planet's increasing political and ecological problems and offers cogent arguments for a comprehensive global approach to these problems in the form of a democratic Earth Federation.

Professor Harris argues that the Establishment of a civil Earth Federation, democratically operated and empowered to enforce World Law, is the one truly practical approach. He discusses alternative approaches and examines the proposed *Constitution for the Federation of Earth* in detail.

Errol E. Harris is John Evans Professor of Moral and Intellectual Philosophy (Emeritus) at Northwestern University, Honorary Research Fellow at the Center for Philosophy and the History of Science, Boston University, and a former President of the Hegel Society of America. He is author of some 30 books and dozens of articles in scholarly journals. Among his books are: *Nature, Mind and Modern Science, Formal, Transcendental & Dialectical Thinking: Logic and Reality, The Survival of Political Man, Annihilation and Utopia, Cosmos and Anthropos, Cosmos and Theos, and Apocalypse and Paradigm: Science and Everyday Thinking*

THE EARTH BELONGS TO EVERYONE, By Alanna Hartzok

"The abolition of the claim to sovereign independence is now the precondition of any effective measures against the ominous threats of catastrophe that we face today, because the root-source of the reluctance of governments to take effective measures to remove the perils now facing the peoples of the world, or to agree to concerted action where (as to remedy global warming) it is indispensable, is their exercise of national sovereignty. If the prevailing international anarchy is to be brought to an end with the maintenance world-wide of the Rule of Law, the one feasible means is the establishment of a federal world government constitution on sound democratic principles"

From Errol E. Harris' Introduction: "Are We Unteachable?"

Contents

Are We Unteachable?

1. The State of the Planet

Threats to Survival
Population
Agriculture
Fishery
Industry
Mining
Energy
Hazardous Waste
Cities
Tourism

2. Cautionary Tale

Interrelation of Problems
The Necessity for Species Diversity
Deforestation
Desertification
Atmospheric Pollution
Taking Stock
Conditions of Success
Resistance to Change
Cautionary Tale

3. 21st Century Crisis

September 11, 2001
Weapons of Mass Destruction
Global Terrorism
The Economic Scene
International Flashpoints
Persistent Perils
Obstacles to Amelioration

4. Sovereignty and Power

Aim of the Discussion
Sovereignty
Security and Vital Interests
The Balance of Power
Treaties
Disarmament
International Law
Power Politics

5. Impracticable Choices

Has Anything Changed?
Proposals for Change
United Nations Reform
Peace Through Law
International Civil Society

6. Federalism

7. The Precedent

8. World Union

9. Efforts for Ratification

A Constitution for the Federation of Earth

0-9753555-5-4 (pbk) $28

Philosophy & Government

May 2006

0-9753555-4-6 (hbk) $60 – 215 pages

All wealth is processed from resources so why are resource-rich countries poor and resource-poor countries rich? The answer: *plunder by trade* as learned in the city states of Europe a millennium ago.

Every major advance in civilization and every economic success that increased the world's wealth was due to cooperation. Competition intensifies the struggle but destroys much more, many times more, than it produces.

Peaceful competition and cooperation in place of battling over resources and the wealth producing process is many times more productive.

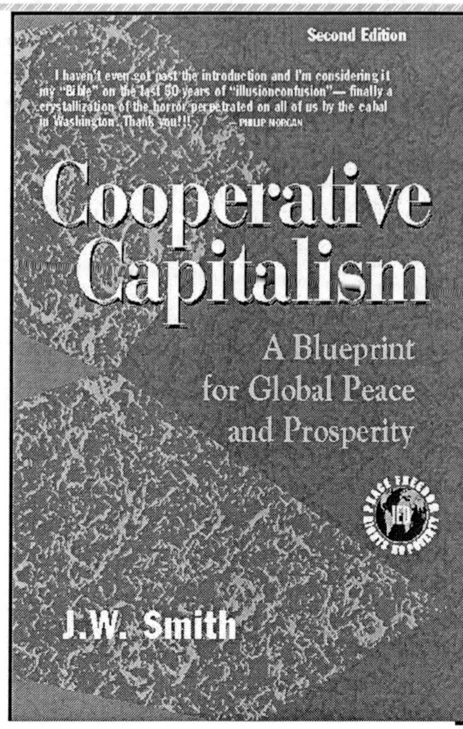

Cooperation instead of competitive struggles increases economic efficiency equal to the invention of money, the printing press and electricity. Power brokers know this, used it to restore war shattered Europe and Japan, the Asian Tigers used it, and China is copying that development plan

Instead of utilizing this knowledge to eliminate poverty throughout the periphery of empire, powerbrokers utilize the IMF/World Bank/GATT/NAFTA/WTO/GATS/FTAA/military colossus to impose residual-feudal *exclusive* property rights, the very heart of their system of theft.

The secret:, first learned almost a millennium ago, establish exclusive property rights (monopolies) through raiding parties destroying the primitive industries of the countryside. Those people then had to sell their resources to the city to be processed into products to be sold within the city and back out to the countryside.

Those city states became countries, some of those countries became empires, and the militaries of today's *imperial centers of capital* are for the same purpose as those raiding parties throughout the Middle Ages, enforcement of *plunder by trade*.

A modern commons in land, technology, and money (nature's freely-offered wealth properly shared by all) eliminates *exclusive feudal property rights* even as it expands and ensures *use rights*, individualism, competition, and personal property rights—Henry George's philosophic principles.

Economy & Politics September 2005

0-9753555-9-7 (pbk) $20 0-9753555-8-9 (hbk) $60 – 220 pages 11

Why the terrorist attacks on America? The answer: *plunder by trade.* Though neither will acknowledge it, for 1,300 years Christians and Muslims have battled over control of the *wealth producing process.* The Christians won. defined the borders of rulers of Muslim countries throughout the Middle East and Africa, and have been laying claim to the wealth of those regions ever since..

Today's massive military build ups are for the same purpose as the raiding parties sent out from the City States of Europe 800 years ago—to control resources, control the *wealth producing process*, and claim the wealth produced.

Where would America's wealth be if Mexico controlled Texas and Oklahoma, Japan controlled California, England the Northeast, Spain the Mississippi valley, and the rest of the country was divided into small emirates?

Resource wealthy nations are poor and resource-poor nations are wealthy because wealth appropriation greatly increases or decreases as wage differentials increase or decrease. If one nation's equally-productive labor is paid 20% that of the nation they trade with (a 5-times differential), they retain one unit of wealth while the well-paid nation retains 25 units of wealth (a 25 times differential). At a 10-times wage differential, the low-paid nation retains one unit of wealth while the well-paid nation retains 100 units of wealth. (a 100-times differential).

Terrorism will disappear if all have equal rights within the *wealth producing process.* Turning half the current expenditures on arms towards world development would alleviate poverty in 10 years and develop the world to a sustainable level in 50 years.

Today's massive military build up is for the same purpose as the raiding parties sent out from the City States of Europe 800 years ago—to control resources and the *wealth producing process.*

Utilizing only a small part of the enormous potential efficiency of Henry George's philosophy of full and equal rights is how the war-shattered Germany, Japan, the Asian Tigers, and now China developed.

Economy & Politics October 2005

0-9753555 7 0 (pbk) $28 0-9753555 6 2 (hbk) $60 – 2225 pages

Students in my 'Ethics and Society' classes were enthused by the clarity of the causes of war, terrorism, and poverty. The sensible and practical approaches to peace and prosperity for all people and all nations made a deep and lasting impression. – Dr. Glen T. Martin, Professor of Philosophy.

I feel that this scholarly work will be viewed in the future as a milestone of the new Millennium. It is a rare work that turns the corner from the mode of thinking of one era to the mode of thinking in the nest. – William Kotke, author Final Empire

This book created a little earthquake in the Indonesian University system and, it seems, they named their "Centre for Economic Democracy Studies" after this book. In the six years since we put this up on the Internet for all to read, the entire world has become conscious.

The most important aspect of regaining rights to modern commons is that private ownership and individualism is retained and competition increases as monopolists disappear. Wealth and *use values* within a modern commons are distributed through fully-productive labor and fully-productive capital.

GNP and the average workweek would fall by half even as average living standards rise. Money would no longer flow through low-productive monopolies providing a high living to those not producing. – The author

This book constitutes an incisive review and analysis of the post-war political economy. J.W. Smith carefully integrates geopolitical, strategic, institutional, and human rights issues into the understanding of post-war economic change and transformation. – Michel Chossudovsky, University of Ottawa, Professor

Smith's exposure of how conscientious professors and reporters are the unwitting carriers of disinformation, and thus unwittingly misinform their students and audience, provides researchers with invaluable tools for unearthing truth. – Ralph McGehee, originator of the database CIABASE and author of *Deadly Deceits: My 25 years in the* CIA

Economy & Politics October 2005

1-933567-01-5 (pbk) $32 – 1-933567-00-7 (hbk) $65 500 pages

THE INSTITUTE FOR ECONOMIC DEMOCRACY PRESS

ORDER FORM

Order toll free: 888-533-1020 (leave message); Fax: 623-547-5392; E-mail ied@ied.info Mail to 9936 W Camden Ave, Sun City, AZ 85351; We highly recommend the simplicity and security of ordering through PayPal on our webpage: www.ied.info.

Reviewers, please note below.

TITLE	hbk pbk	ISBN #	PRICE	QUAN	TOTAL
Subtotal					
Discount 20% two or more books					
S & H $5, $1.50 per additional book; $9 overseas, $3 per additional book					
Total					

Reviewers: email: (ied@ied.info) is the preferred method to request review copies.

Or 888-533-1020, please leave message, we will call you.

Or list books you would like to review in the above order blank.

Person requesting review copies____________________

Publication requesting review copies ____________________

Purchasers/reviewers please fill in below

Name________________ Reviewers________________

Address____________________

City/State/Zip________________ Daytime phone________________

Email________________ Signature________________

☐ **Check Enclosed** ☐ **American Express** ☐ **VISA** ☐ **Master Card** ☐ **Discover**

															Card#					**Exp.Date**

To request *review copies* please call 888-533-1020, email us at ied@ied.info or use the order blank

The Institute for Economic Democracy Press is a cooperative publishing house within the Institute for Economic Democracy dedicated to publishing high quality books how to attain world peace, sustainable development, establishment of permaculture and eco-housing, eliminating poverty, and an earth federation providing a quality life for all the world's citizens.

Our books provide all the arguments and details necessary to eliminate the global war-system of sovereign nation-states and create a peaceful, federated world order based on the common good of all human beings.

Progress is being made in economics as well. When we placed our research on the web six years ago, it did not seem like many people understood the financial, economic, and covert wars which kept the world in bondage.

When our *Economic Democracy* books reached the university system of Indonesia it created a little earthquake. They quickly understood, a lecture on the subject made the front page of a major Indonesian newspaper, and it seems they named their 'Centre for Economic Democracy Studies' after that book.

We will never know how much our research had to do with the current worldwide populist revolution about to burst upon us but the shakeup in Indonesia indicates it did have substantial influence. Now most on the periphery of empire understand how the international trading game is played and are again demanding their freedom with full and equal rights.

Few books are researching the beating heart of monopoly capitalism as we are doing. We have all read read the 500-year history of taking the commons away from the masses. But no where else do you read that this was only the first stage of a 700-plus-year process establishing current *rule of law* or that the economic classics produced the last 200-plus years were little more than justifications for that violent and inefficient economic structure. Abandoning that imposed *rule of law* will quickly eliminate poverty. Abandoning the system of sovereign nations for a *rule of law* of full and equal rights governing all nations can quickly eliminate war and bring world peace.

Have your library order Books you feel are important.

The Institute for
Economic Democracy Press
9936 W Camden Ave.
Sun City, AZ 85351
Address Correction Requested
www.ied.info

Table of Contents

Foreword vi
Introduction........ 1
Monopoly Capitalism's Rule of Law Versus Henry George's Rule of Law.... 3
1. Henry George's Rule of Law: A Modern Money Commons 14
From Barter to Commodity Money 14
From Commodity Money to Coins of Precious Metal 14
From Gold, to Gold-Backed Paper Money, to Fiat Paper Money........ 15
Paper Money, to Checkbook Money, to Computer Money........ 16
Credit or Trust Money........ 17
The Different Meanings of Money........ 17
Money is a Contract against another Person's Labor........ 17
Money Productively Contracting Labor 18
Money Unproductively Contracting Labor........ 18
Learning the Secret of Bank-Created Money........ 20
Primary-created money and Circulating Money 21
Testing the Assertions that, under Required Reserves, Private Banks Create Money........ 25
The Fed's Open Market Operations hide the Simplicity of Money Creation 26
Accumulation of Capital under Henry George's Inclusive Rule of Law........ 30
A Money Commons:........ 34
The Theory of Interest as Usury........ 40
2. Henry George's Rule of Law: A Modern Land Commons 43
Land is Social Wealth........ 43
Pride in Ownership must be maintained........ 45
The Feudal Origins of Land Titles 45
Private Ownership of Social Wealth moves to America........ 47
Saleable Land Titles permitted the Mobilization of Capital........ 49
Profound Thinkers Who Believed in Society Collecting Resource rent........ 50
Commercial Land 52
Farm Land 53
Home Sites 53
If Society Collected Resource rents, other Taxes could be Eliminated........ 55
3. Henry George's Rule of Law, A Modern Technology Commons 59
Capital Destroying Capital........ 61
Labor should employ Capital 62
Efficient Socially-Owned Capital........ 64
Efficient Privately-Owned Capital........ 66
Fictitious Capital........ 66
Invention, a Social Process 68
Capitalizing Actual and Fictitious Values 70
The Ever-increasing Efficiencies of Technology 72
A Nation's Wealth is Measured by, and Siphoned to Titleholders through, Capitalized Values 77

The Financial Structure to Harvest the Profits of Subtly-Monopolized Patents 78
Market Bubbles and Crashes 80
Options, Futures, and other Derivatives are Gambling Chips in a Worldwide Casino 82
Bringing the World's Markets under Control 84
Restructuring Patent Laws 84
4. Secondary Monopolies Disappear under Henry George's Rule of Law 89
Insurance 90
Law 92
Health Care 94
Welfare 96
Agriculture 97
5. Henry George's Rule of Law: a Modern Information Commons 100
Efficient, cheap, Communications may Eliminate Monopolization 103
Communication Eliminates Intermediaries and Reduces Trading Costs 104
Big-ticket, Infrequently-Purchased Items 105
Inexpensive, Small, Frequently-Traded Items 108
Shopping as a Social Event entails a Cost 108
Reserving TV Time for New Products 108
Music, Sports, Movies, and Game Shows 109
Investment and Job Opportunities 110
Education 111
Inspired Teachers for Every Student 115
Parents Interacting closely with their Children's Education 115
Better Institutions for Socialization 115
Maintaining Curiosity, Creativity, and Love of Learning 116
Once Borderline Teachable Graduating at the Top of Their Class 116
Culture and Recreational Learning 117
Minority Cultures 117
Foreign Cultures 118
Local Television 118
Elections 118
A Socially-Owned Banking System Paying for WiFi 119
6. Capitalism's Mighty Economic Engine: Henry George's far more Powerful Engine 120
7. Summary 123
8. Conclusion: Henry George's Rule of Law Creating World Peace and Prosperity 138
Appendix I: Myths in Monetary Theory 169
Appendix II: A Practical Approach for Developing Poor Nations & Regions 171
About the Author 185

Acknowledgements

The greatest acknowledgement and thanks must go to Henry George. Through his books he taught me the basics of economics and moving his thesis across the full economic spectrum, as is done in this work, is what I feel he would have spotted as extensions of land monopolization were he studying today's economy. The other monopolies we address as extensions of the principles of land monopolization were either in their infancy or had not yet formed.

Special thanks go to the authors of the 50 to 60 books on money which provided the foundation for my understanding of that mystery. Specifically I have proven the validity of William F. Hixson's book title, *It's Your Money*. William Krehm of COMER, Professor Mieczyslaw Dobija's research revealing that money originated as an accounting unit of productive labor on the stone tablets of Sumer 5,000 years ago is priceless. Discussions with Steve Zarlenga (*Lost Science of Money*) triggered the writing of this book.

William H. Kötke, author of the impressive *Final Empire*, Jana Paripovich Dr. Ekema Manga, our webmaster Anup Shah, Bernie Maopolski, Jeff & Diana Jewell, and Mike Masters were especially helpful.

Special mention must be made for the great help and advice of Mochamad Effendi Aboed of Indonesia. Crucial support was provided by Phil Hawes, Keith McHenry (FoodNotBombs), Alanna Hartzok, John Leonard, Michael Mityok, David Aronson, and many more.

The advice and support of Professor Glen T. Martin of International Philosophers for Peace (www.ippno.org) and the Institute on World Problems (www.worldproblems.net) has been crucial. I thank Ms. Sudha Menon for her proofreading. The advice of William Krehm of COMER was priceless. Ole Lefmann 36-year study extending Henry George's principle of monopolies being based on exclusive titles provided great support.

As always, I wish to dedicate this book to my children, Betty, Ada, Patti, and Cynthia, and grandchildren Sam C., Will, Stephan, Mathew, Sam O, and Suzie. It is hoped that this work will contribute to their understanding of the world.

Foreword

Books describing the violence, environmental destruction, and pending cataclysms of today's world abound. Books calling for the revitalization of democracy, for an end to economic globalization, and for an abstract peace with justice are not difficult to find.

But nowhere can there be found books that offer a clear and comprehensive path forward for our world. Dr. J.W. Smith's present book is quite unique in this respect. In the face of a world of cynicism and despair, it offers a clear, common-sense path to a decent world order.

It is not that the ideas presented here do not appear in Dr. Smith's earlier works such as *The World's Wasted Wealth* and *Economic Democracy: The Political Struggle of the Twenty-First Century*. But here they are extrapolated from these larger texts and compacted like a laser beam. The result is a masterpiece of power and clarity.

Critically aware people know that much of the ideology of "free enterprise," disseminated, for example, by the Neoliberal propaganda originating in the United States, is meant to justify and cover up the unjust appropriation of the wealth created by the true producers of the world. But few have been able to see that we need not throw out the baby with the bath water.

Through simple common-sense changes that bring us to the creative, productive, and innovative heart of capitalism, we can create a just and prosperous world order for everyone. As Smith's magnum opus, *Economic Democracy*, points out, the final struggle if we are to have real democracy on Earth is the struggle to make capitalism democratic. The propaganda claiming this is already so is meant to protect "*exclusive titles* to nature's wealth and technologies," the system—as Georgist Ole Lefmann has been writing on for 36 years—for siphoning the wealth created by hard-working producers into the hands of non-producers.

Over the centuries only a handful of great books, often brief and highly focused, have moved civilization significantly forward. I believe *Money: A Mirror Image of the Economy* is one of these rare books. It is a powerful, concise statement of both the next step for human civilization and how to take this step.

Glen T. Martin
Professor of Philosophy, Radford University
Author, Millennium Dawn – The Philosophy of Planetary Crisis and Human Liberation
Secretary-General, World Constitution and Parliament Association

Money
A Mirror Image
of the Economy

Pulling this research together alerted us that roughly 60% of America's huge blocs of capital were little more than capitalized values of unearned wealth and elimination of those monopoly values would double economic efficiency permitting each to live a quality life while reducing working hours by half.

This led us to another realization: Economic classics are not philosophical works on efficient economies. They are instead justifications for a monopoly system put in place by powerbrokers the past 700 plus years. Though it is getting more difficult every day, those classics and their descendents are still justifying their inefficient and unequal "*rule of law.*"

Egyptians spending their labor and resources building pyramids had nothing on modern capitalism (properly named *subtle monopoly capitalism*) whose waste is just as massive. Powerbrokers were able to get away with the fraud, first because ever-improving technology was so enormously efficient that all would gain even though the "*rule of law*" being established was enormously inefficient and, second, enormous amounts of wealth was being appropriated from the periphery of empire and distributed as honest earnings. The citizenry—working hard every day—were unaware half their efforts were wasted and thus unaware that much of their wealth had been *unnecessarily* appropriated from other societies.

Quite simply, if any country or region successfully gained their freedom, eliminated monopolization within their internal economies, and achieved economic efficiency—as we demonstrate is possible—the impoverished world will notice and the monopolization game will come to an end.

The legal structure of a non-monopolized capitalist economy is very simple—full and equal rights for all through *conditional titles* to nature's wealth and technologies. Under that "*rule of law*," designed by Henry George over a century ago, the massive blocs of monopolized capital—previously buying and selling appropriated values—are transposed into *equally-shared use-values.*

Socially-owned banks under social control fulfill any need for finance capital through creating essentially debt-free money for social infrastructure (all payments, including interest, paid goes right back into essential services). The wealth built and produced are the values which back both *primary-created money* and circulating money, those circulating symbols of value we spend and are paid with every day.

Within an economy, circulating money covers most needs. If a shortage of finance capital develops, money can be created. If there is an excess of money in an economy (inflation caused by too much money chasing too few goods), it is a simple matter to increase required reserves and destroy that surplus.

The efficiencies of modern banking, land, technology, and communications commons will create a highly-productive society and a quality life for all with each working outside the home only 2 to 3 days per week.

Introduction

> The surface of American society is covered with a layer of democratic paint, but from time to time one can see the old aristocratic colours breaking through
>
> ---- Alexis de Tocqueville:

As products and services are paid for with money, its flow as the mirror image of an economy is easily understood. It is accepted as a given that a nation's banking system collapses when a nation's economy crashes. This is only true of "private" banking which takes care of private interests while a *socially-owned* banking system, properly structured and operated, stays open taking care of both public and private interests.

When an economy is booming, a private banking system appears to operate smoothly and efficiently. But, at some level, it is understood that private bankers—caring for their private interests—corrupt the economy and cause economic collapses. What is not understood is that a *socially-owned* banking system, caring for the needs of all, would have—measured in steadily advancing qualities of life—created a more robust economy than private banking in its best years.

More important, an economic crash under private banking can be stopped in its tracks and the economy quickly rebuilt by restructuring to a *socially-owned* banking system and utilizing its inherent powers. Those powers are denied society under private banking because the bankers are caring for their interests and that of powerbrokers, not that of the citizenry as a whole.

Henry George was the economic philosopher who gave us the tools to understand that. Before they go on to their final reward, most economists of high standing will say that "Henry George had it right." What he had right was that no one produced land, it was produced by nature, all are entitled to their share of the wealth produced by nature, and that can be efficiently accomplished through social collection of resource rents.

His philosophy of social collection of resource rents converts *exclusive title* to nature's wealth to *conditional title*. Those resources were produced by nature, not by anyone's labor. Thus the wealth it produces is properly shared by all and social collection of resource rents operating governments and caring for other social needs accomplishes that goal.

Henry George's philosophy required "converting *exclusive titles* to land with its private tax (land rent) to *conditional titles.*" Through social collection of resource rents, its expenditure on social needs, and the disappearance of most other taxes, each citizen receives their share of nature's wealth.

Land titles, being first issued by governments as "patents," acknowledge that patented mechanical and chemical technologies are a part of nature. They are, like natural resources, waiting to be discovered. By applying Henry George's principles of social collection of resource rents and rights of all citizenry to their share—in this case paying inventors well and placing all technology in the public domain—the wealth produced by technology is equally shared through at least a 50% drop in the price of consumer products.

Georgists recognize that taxi medallions (licenses) in New York City having a rental (capitalized) value of $200,000 as being a monopoly identical to land monopolization, land has rental (capitalized) value and so do taxi medallions. The connection between them, as studied by Georgist Ole Lefmann for the past 36 years, is that their values were not produced by labor but by *exclusive title* (monopolization) which gives them rental values. Like taxi medallions, banking, insurance, law and health care are all technologies (a part of nature that must be discovered) licensed within a monopoly system and that legal structure gives them monopoly rental values. Land has tangible value but it is produced by nature. Banking and insurance are social technologies and their licenses within a monopoly system give them monopoly values. There are no tangible values produced by labor. Healthcare and law have tangible labor values (years of study), but their market prices are primarily monopoly values—created by their license—far above that created by labor. Patents have some tangible labor values (produced by labor) but the much greater monopoly values double the cost of production, possibly 80% of the overcharge is wasted overseeing these monopolies and possibly 20% is banked as monopoly profits.

It is not the licenses per se which have monopoly value; they are a necessity and are proper. It is the ad hoc expansion of the monopoly system within which they were issued. Those same licenses are issued within other social structures that do not limit their use and they do not develop monopoly values. The ad hoc manner in which the superstructure operating these social technologies formed required enormous labor costs which were factored in as normal. A hundred years later those technologies are well understood and that same unnecessary and wasted labor is now battling for market share for what is now recognized as a necessity and thus should be a right. Converting those marketing rights (banking, health care, insurance, etc.), for a few to a human right would eliminate battles for market share and drop costs by half. The resulting full and equal rights, eliminating most legal battles, are part of that cost savings.[a]

---

[a] We use the term full and equal rights throughout this book. This would be the fulfillment of Henry George's goal of restoring "to all their natural and equal rights in the common heritage."

Monopoly Capitalism's Rule of Law Versus Henry George's Rule of Law

Money is a social technology discovered over 5,000 years ago. Banking is an extension of money technology learned over the centuries. By restructuring private banking to a *socially-owned* banking system, one has applied Henry George's principle that—as such technologies are only a part of nature waiting to be discovered and have few, or no, tangible values produced by labor—each citizen has a right to their proper share of the wealth produced.

Over the centuries—to protect and increase their wealth and power—powerbrokers have extended the principle of monopolization of land through *exclusive titles* to include banking, patents, communications, insurance, health care, the legal system interpreting those rights for us, and other more minor sectors of the economy (run an Internet search for "rent seeking"). To both protect their system of wealth appropriation and lay claim to even more wealth, this system of unequal rights is being imposed upon the rest of the world. Our earlier research christened unique aspects of that process *plunder by trade.*

Propaganda as to the high efficiency of an economy operating at half its potential is not only hiding inequalities, violence, and lack of democracy, it is hiding the fact that monopoly capitalism's fundamental property rights evolved from aristocratic law and were designed at its earliest beginnings to appropriate the wealth of the politically weak and less fortunate.

Aristocracy fought for centuries to retain their superior rights and a large share of violence and wars today is financial aristocracy battling to retain, actually expand, the same *exclusive titles* to nature's wealth and technologies—in only slightly adjusted form—as under aristocratic law. Those principles are still with us and the battle against unequal rights is still being fought.

How is it possible to have "free thought," "free thinking universities," and a "free press" and not be aware of this process? Think of the centuries the common people were trained to look up to and worship aristocracy. The first books can only have supported them; they were the only ones who could read and write. When education spread to the common people, literature still had to glorify aristocrats, for powerless people to have attacked them in books in any way would have led to very unpleasant consequences.

This system of control held as the bourgeoisie gained rights and power. The common people still did not have rights and their masters had disciplinary power. Thus the classics supporting the system of theft being put in place as *rule of law* were allowed but none seriously attacking the system were permitted. This was firm control of what was taught. For a century or two, there was really nothing else out there. Bourgeoisie *rule of law* was taught then and now as maximally efficient full and equal rights while all others were, except on the margins, taught as dictatorial and inefficient.

Marx's philosophy is one such *belief system* on the margins which gained traction and gained large numbers of followers. Powerbrokers spent trillions of dollars, slaughtered tens of millions, spent billions on propaganda (through funding authors and their books, through the media, and in the universities), to relegate that philosophy back to the margins. Marx is now marginalized and that control process is still with us today. The classics and derivative works were taught as the only viable philosophies and simultaneously it was taught that all were free to think as they wish and encouraged to do so. But those who did were immediately ostracized to the margins, just as all challenging thought had been for centuries, and that scene is replayed over and over. Those marginalized understand it, the rest believe such people are a threat to their freedoms and rights, that they are radicals not to be listened to, or whatever. Meet any mainstream professor today and you will find them totally sincere, wanting to do good, and unaware their thoughts are as firmly under control as 500 years ago.

Note the complexity of classical and neoliberal economics. Note the simplicity of eliminating poverty and providing a quality life for all we will be laying out, note its solid logic, and note the certainty that it will be rejected by those locked within the "system." However, when circumstances are right, that control will be thrown aside and one who parrots the old beliefs will be hard to find.[a] The waste and violence of the current system is so enormous—fully as much wasted, destroyed, and production forgone as that consumed—we must hope that day will be soon.

Citizens within what are touted as full democracies, but in reality are only *representative* democracies, are subject to laws decided upon by others—primarily corporate lobbyists, whose bosses claim far more than their fair share.

For each to attain their rightful share, full and equal rights for each citizen must be enshrined in a constitution. The justice of those rights will be evident through each both producing and consuming their fair share. The essentials of such a constitution are laced throughout this treatise.

Once such a foundation is in place, laws covering disputes and changing circumstances can be decided upon by either participatory or direct democracy as opposed to today's representative democracies. Such laws voted on by a citizenry—as referendums are now approved or disapproved, utilizing eye or thumbprint scans to assure honesty—is very viable. With direct citizen approval of important laws and constitutional changes, and though not perfect, Cuba and possibly Libya are the only such democracies today.

As opposed to a full democracy, the laws Western nations are subject to are the unequal legal structures designed by their predecessors over the past 700 plus years, generally addressed as "*rule of law*." They are not a steadily advancing legal system with equality and justice in mind. Even though it is an

---

[a] During the Vietnam War, except for those "radicals" protesting publicly, those against that war were hard to find. When those protestors proved their point and shut down that war, everyone I talked to firmly let me know they were always against that war.

unequal legal system, individuals can make decisions and society can advance. That often-pointed-out reality fails to mention that societies could advance much faster and more equally if those laws were designed for full and equal rights.

Through the greater share of those 700 plus years, little consideration was given to the rights of the common person. Laws were written by the powerful for protection of their wealth and power and for attaining more wealth and power. Thus the extension of *exclusive* titles to land under the enclosure process, which started formally in England under the Statute of Merton of 1235, created massive wealth for the powerful few and colossal poverty for the many. See chapter 1 of *The Earth Belongs to Everyone*, 2006, by Alanna Hartzok. She goes much further into the privatization of the commons as a system of theft of wealth properly belonging to all and how that and the ongoing privatizations yet today are the fundamental *rules of law* governing monopolization.

Aristocrats created those first monopoly laws and the very principle of aristocracy was *exclusive* title to nature's wealth, those huge blocs of land they controlled. Those *exclusive* titles, enclosing the commons, were only aristocratic privileges (monopolization) masquerading as modern law.

The *rule of law* being established dealt with rights but only in the sense of superior and inferior rights. As the masses slowly gained more rights, they were given the opportunity to purchase land (resources). Quietly and slowly this "*rule of law*" spread in step with the increased wealth produced by ever-increasing efficiencies of technology. The elite—with their excessive rights (they were the only ones educated, they held all the positions of power, and they created all the laws)—poured out philosophies of high economic efficiency under the *rule of law* as structured (exclusive title to nature's wealth and technologies) and we hear that claim repeated in almost every classroom today. In later laws, those superior/inferior rights were continually extended.

Those superior rights, assured by *exclusive* titles to nature's wealth, had a hidden secret: Aristocracy proper was to disappear, but the principles of aristocracy—still protecting wealth and power—lived on in those *exclusive* titles to nature's wealth and technologies. At that time, it could not have been anticipated that the common people would ever own a part of the earth upon which they lived and worked. When the bourgeoisie—and later the common people—were brought into the flow of money to purchase land, the fortunate now had—once that purchase was paid for—a share of the superior rights that aristocracy once had. This book exposes that hidden secret, *exclusive title* to nature's wealth and technologies as the very foundation of today's monopoly system being imposed upon the world. By giving each a chance, most a small chance, the system is—like every game of chance—very seductive.

Let's address that hidden secret deeper. If you were accosted and robbed, that is obviously a criminal act outside the *rule of law*. If your legislature passed a law giving an advantage to a group or an individual which amounted to they pocketing unearned income (it happens all the time, run a search for "rent seeking") that would be within the *rule of law* but would be easily recognized as creating inequality through granting excess rights to a fortunate few.[a]

The British Enclosure Acts addressed above, assigning exclusive land titles to lords of the land and forcing the serfs into the city to survive in breadlines, is easily analyzed as *rule of law* giving excessive rights to a few and taking away rights from many. That injustice was justified by philosophical treatises (known today as classics) stating that those unemployed workers were necessary to work in the factories coming on stream at the start of the Industrial Revolution.

This is a clear example of the need to philosophically justify inequality structured into the *rule of law*. Today we know that every factory ever built in either a poor country or a rich country is always overwhelmed by applications for employment. The reason is obvious; those employed can purchase more of the amenities of life. As labor has always been available in long-established, heavily-populated societies, the need to dispossess people from the land to create a labor force was only a justification, not an honest philosophical analysis.

With continued philosophical justification (the classics), rights to the commons were forgotten and *exclusive* title to nature's wealth and technologies became the accepted norm. We hear those justifications yet today; "this is the most efficient legal structure." Even when its imperfections are recognized it is still justified: "this is a really bad system except that it is better than all others." Through demonstrating the enormous efficiency a modern commons would have under Henry George's *rule of law*, we prove that such alibis have little relevance to reality.

What those rationalizations were hiding was simple theft of other people's wealth through unequal *rules of law*. Those evicted from the commons knew they were losing rights and the landlords were gaining rights. But, just as today, the only voices heard were those justifying that theft. Over time, former rights were forgotten and current *rules of law* were accepted as normal.

An attempt was made to establish British aristocratic law in America. But the expanse of land was so vast that those intended as serfs simply squatted on "empty" land (that is empty after genocidal slaughters), claimed it, and retained 100% of what they produced as opposed to half or less that a serf would retain. At that time, and as the Industrial Revolution was forming, the American Revolution gave more rights to the common person, primarily in the same form as aristocracy, *exclusive title* to land. Through the French Revolution, other crises, and with the new freedoms and rights in America blowing back onto Europe, the suppressed serfs of that continent also attained more rights.

Over time, the theft of wealth throughout the colonial world, and a need for a loyal citizenry to provide the military to enforce that piracy, permitted (dictated) a further sharing of wealth with internal labor (See this author's si-

---

[a] Every law that lays claim to wealth beyond the value of labor expended is an extension of the principle of *exclusive title* to nature's wealth and technologies established over the past 700 plus years.

multaneously released *Economic Democracy: A Grand Strategy for World Peace and Prosperity*).

With wealthy citizens throughout Western Europe and America, the acquisition of wealth beyond anyone's dreams only three generations ago is taught as justification for what is obvious to many as an unequal and unjust system. But the above noted source and this treatise proves *subtle monopoly capitalism* (misnamed capitalism) is inefficient to the extreme. Massive wealth is being appropriated from society's own labor and from the periphery of empire. Half that wealth is ground up through the offices and staff overseeing those monopolies and in the military forces required to protect what is little more than a racket.

As addressed in earlier research, Southeast Asia's industrialization was an accident of history; Western powers were seeking allies in their desperate effort to prevent honest and moral *rules of law* from emerging to challenge their unequal and unethical legal structure. The conclusion will address how that accident of history—a highly industrialized Southeast Asia—will likely overthrow the unequal legal structure the West has spent 700 plus years establishing.

As much of the world now understands the fraud imposed upon them for the past half millennium, those *exclusive titles* to nature's wealth—the very essence of monopolization—has the possibility of disappearing into history to be replaced by a peaceful, prosperous, sustainable, federated world with a quality life for all. Contrary to those 700 plus years of justifications, there was never a need for *exclusive titles* to nature's bounty to accumulate finance capital and avoidance of that unequal legal structure through utilizing Henry George's mighty economic and financial engines would have doubled economic efficiency and eliminated poverty as fast as new technologies were invented.

Exclusive title to nature's wealth and technologies is a system of theft and, as proven by the 500 year struggle against it, was recognized as such when first being imposed. But philosophical justifications—taught in the universities and through the media—have erased that reality from the social mind. To bring up the possibility of such inequality and inefficiency in either polite society, in an academic setting, or in this book, is to create total shock. Such is the totality of the *belief systems* imposed upon us to hide the reality of a system designed from its origins to lay claim to others' wealth.

Placing Henry George's principle of restructuring *exclusive titles* to nature's wealth and technologies to *conditional titles*, point by point, alongside the *rule of law* of any economic philosophy serves as a template to judge whether that philosopher is unwittingly parroting justifications of the current unequal and unjust system or whether he or she has truly produced a philosophical work that will provide full and equal rights to all, eliminate poverty, and all while conserving our resources and protecting the environment.

Comparing the rights, equality, and economic efficiencies under Henry George's *inclusive rule of law* will expose inefficiencies and inequalities which are the result of a long history of injustices within other societies. Example: The caste system, now outlawed in India but still having substantial impact, is a system of rights (entitlements, *rule of law*) established centuries ago. The principles are the same, superior rights for some and inferior rights for others. Excessive rights are easy to spot in such a system and thus easily condemned. The superiority of the Western system of inequality is hidden so deep in custom, in *rule of law*, and protected by philosophical justifications (classical and neoliberal) through the educational system and the media, that it is not only considered normal and just, but it is also deemed, and taught, as essential.

Social scientists must look closely. Currently large parts of the world are accepting Western *rule of law* as one of equal rights and maximum economic efficiency. As we will be thoroughly addressing, that is not true. Capitalism's mighty economic engine and the *belief system* societies are encased in hide the enormous inefficiencies and violence of this *rule of law* imposed over the past 700 plus years. The first imposition of unequal rights under capitalism's rule of law was by violence as the commons was privatized. Classics then justified the imposition of that system of theft. Later impositions of the belief in the justice of those thefts of others wealth were through the university systems teaching those classics. The *belief system* was in place so tight, these professors were unaware those classics were only justifying a system of theft being imposed for centuries and being imposed yet today. One of the assumptions of this book is that, in their struggle for full and equal rights, a large share of the world is breaking out from under that *belief system* protecting Western culture's *rule of law*, currently being imposed upon the world.

Henry George pointed the way out from under this system of theft. Production of wealth is, at every turn, a utilization and transformation of nature's wealth. This treatise addresses how restructuring property rights in land, technologies, money, and communications—all wealth of, or technologies of, nature—from *exclusive* titles to *conditional titles* (society shall collect rent values or it shall be legislated as a right) would increase economic efficiency equal to the invention of money, the printing press and electricity. That process would give full and equal rights (economic and political) to everyone.

We are primarily addressing the internal economies of today's hegemon, America—it is their system of *exclusive title* to nature's resources and technologies, creating wealth and power for a few and the impoverishment of many, being imposed upon the world.

The proof that Western *rules of law* are systems of inequality and inefficiency will be the disappearance of fully 60% of the finance capital within a monopolized economy and the simultaneous rapid increase in real wealth relatively equally shared when one restructures those *exclusive titles* to resources and technologies to Henry George's *inclusive* principles of *conditional titles.*

That condition: society should collect rental values on all natural resources, in the case of technologies eliminate those monopoly values through paying inventors well and placing that technology in the public domain, and, in the case of monopolization through licenses, legislate those crucial services as a right. There will then be no need for fully 60% of the huge blocs of capital currently operating the American economy. They appear to be necessary but in reality they are only buying and selling the capitalized values of wealth appropriated through *exclusive titles* to nature's wealth and technologies.

There are simpler and cheaper ways to accumulate finance capital. Those appropriations of wealth through *exclusive titles*—no matter where or how they are invested—engender a continual appropriation of more wealth. The owners of those unearned funds—searching for a safe place to invest—typically settle for buying treasuries issued to cover the costs of the federal government or bonds to build schools, sewers, water systems and other crucial infrastructure. Citizens, from whom that wealth was appropriated in the first place, pay taxes to pay off that principal, plus interest. As those debt instruments are paid off, that money is reinvested. The same citizenry, through either taxes or the purchase of products and services at roughly double the necessary charges, again pay off those debts. And that *impoverishing cycle* goes on in perpetuity, interrupted only by economic collapses due to too much wealth in the hands of the few and too little buying power in the hands of the many.

It is the potential of doubling or tripling economic efficiency through *conditional titles* to nature's wealth and technologies and eliminating all appropriation of others' rightful wealth which tags those continual repayments of appropriated wealth as "*impoverishing cycles*." Those inefficiencies under the founding principles of classical economics alert us that they were only justifying a system of excessive rights; they were not laying out principles of an efficient economy. Those justifications—trying to rationalize *rules of law* within classical and neoliberal principles—are pouring out yet today.

Just as customs of ancient cultures are huge obstacles for their societies to evolve efficiently, residues of *exclusive* feudal property rights in Western cultures severely restrict the potential efficiency of capitalism. Inefficiencies are not perceived because modern technologies are so efficient that the huge gains are visible and admired while the even greater gains possible under *inclusive* property rights remain unknown. This work is an attempt to bring those potential gains out into the open for all to see and restructure their laws and economies to gain the benefits of Henry George's *inclusive rule of law*. It is that recognition of economic efficiency and full and equal rights which led respected economists to say that Henry George, the philosopher rightfully credited with the clearest presentation of this philosophy, had it right.

The basic principles of monopolization under feudalism were never abandoned. Citizens living within the *belief systems* of *subtle monopoly capitalism* have full rights only in the sense that each has a chance at becoming a wealthy monopolist. But only a calculable few can attain those *residual feudal* rights.

These inequalities are not visible to Americans and Europeans because of the large percentage with a high standard of living and thus appearing to have full rights. But—unrealized by the citizenry and most in academia—that high standard of living is only through massive thefts of wealth from the periphery of empire. The powerful today are fighting to retain and expand their monopoly property rights—*exclusive titles* to nature's wealth and technologies—just as feudal powers fought for centuries to maintain their *exclusive titles* to land which is, of course, the same wealth of nature that is being fought over today.

As the enormous wastes within a banking system cannot be eliminated without elimination of all other monopolies, we will address deeply the four primary monopolies (banking, land, technology, and communications) and—with the principles of *exclusion* and *inclusion* within *rules of law* well established—summarize the secondary monopolies (insurance, law, health care, etc.). This being primarily a book on money, we will address that first.

Money is a social technology, hence a part of nature's wealth, discovered over 5,000 years ago. That a banking system is properly owned by society is demonstrated by outlining the enormous efficiencies of full and equal rights under that banking structure. Each social unit (a federation of nations, each nation, each region within a nation, each state, each community, each business, and each individual) should have a *constitutional right* to their share of created money and savings (investment capital). Though credit cards approach this ideal for consumption purposes, such full and equal rights have never in the history of private enterprise been applied to investment.

The elimination of monopolization does away with the need for those huge blocs of unearned capital—roughly 60% of all finance capital. Contrary to that capital being necessary, its elimination would be a blessing. So long as there are available resources and labor, money can be created to build social infrastructure and industrial capital. As social infrastructure (governing structures, roads, railroads, harbors, communication systems, water systems, sewers, etc, any natural monopoly) they are properly owned by society and should be built with *primary-created money* up to the level monetary balance is maintained. Through adjustments of required reserves, that balance point between building with created money or savings can be moved. Through payment on bonds originally funded with created money cycling right back into infrastructure, that balance can be further extended across the economy.

History is replete with creating money for wars. The populists of the late 19th century advocated printing money to loan to farmers. Surely the Germans and Japanese rapid buildup of industry in the early 20th century was financed with created money. Most money theory is silent on the enormous potential for created money funding infrastructure and crucial social needs. Stephen Zarlenga, in his classic *The Lost Science of Money,* pp. 665-66, suggests creating money for infrastructure, housing, environmental cleanup, communications, Social Security, and universal health care. Not having read all his work, as yet I do not know if he is aware of the necessity to continually increase required reserves to soak up the increased money supply and, at this point in time, I have not seen him address the huge blocs of capital created by appropriating the rental values of nature's wealth and technologies which properly belong to all. Unless that unearned wealth is addressed as per Henry George, any banking system established must either finance those monopolies or drive them out of business. If driving them out of business is the route chosen, then the entire economic structure collapses, you are dealing with the same collapse as this monetary thesis assumes and, I trust but have not yet read it is so, his answers in quickly recovering from that crash will be the same as ours, an economy powered by Henry George's powerful economic and financial engines.

Such *primary-created money* building infrastructure circulates within communities, regions, nations, and federations to provide the citizenry with food, fiber, and shelter. As industrial capital is justly privately owned, industries are built by savings (financial capital) with any shortages balanced by creating money to loan for such productive purposes and any excess circulating money rebalanced by destroying (by higher mandatory reserves) any surplus that arises.

Balancing an economy under a modern banking commons within an *inclusive* society with full and equal rights for all would be simplicity itself. Financial capital would then be the total savings of all, balanced by *primary-created money* to fill any shortfall, or its destruction through higher required reserves to eliminate any surplus. Such full and equal rights would eliminate inflation and deflation and assure a quality life for all (see footnote, p. 23).

Eliminating offices and staff operating, and the wars generated protecting, those monopolies eliminates half the economic activity of a monopoly system even as poverty disappears.

Those *exclusive titles* to nature's wealth (primary monopolies) and those secondary monopolies further structured into the *rule of law* (typically by license) are consuming over half the financial capital flowing through America's current banking system. Those wasteful flows of money can only be shut off by eliminating all residue of *exclusive* feudal monopolization (primary monopolies) and modern methods of monopolization (secondary monopolies) firmly entrenched within Western economies.

Societies do not change incrementally, they change in revolutionary leaps. The appearances of current changes are only potentials. The actuality is that the poor of both the wealthy economies and the less developed world are getting poorer as the rich get richer and only under extreme crisis will the rights of the politically weak be considered.

The necessary restructuring can only happen when the current system collapses. As it has always done so before, it will do so again. When it does we must be ready to provide the philosophical foundation for restructuring unearned values, currently capitalized into massive blocs of unearned capital, into roughly *equally-shared use values.*

Those efficient economic principles should be applied to the developing world. The infrastructure necessary for them to be efficient appears expensive. But that is only true if built by outside contractors. All costs above resource rent values are labor costs and we thoroughly document that most resources are within their borders and such rents properly go into the social fund. Machinery and infrastructure built by a region's own companies and trained labor creates wealth equal to the price of that labor (which is their own), interest on industrial capital (which is stored labor and those factories should be built with local labor), and resource rent (which comes from their regional resources). As labor spends wages for living and governments spend resource rents to run governments and essential services, all except that spent for imports are a region's circulating buying power.

Train labor, build industries to scale for a region, build construction equipment with those industries, build that infrastructure, and the cost to a region is primarily the cost of importing modern tools for those factories.

Those undeveloped regions have most the world's natural resources and all manufactured wealth is processed from natural wealth. So, although it is necessary that the banking system be socially owned, an economic region must form an alliance. As developing a region is primarily creating money to train and employ a region's labor force to build the necessary infrastructure, their currency must have no value outside their borders (a dual currency system). That infrastructure and the wealth produced backs the circulating created money and surpluses are easily destroyed by increasing required reserves. Current *exclusive titles* to nature's resources and technologies and the many other monopolies copied after those original excessive rights *structured in law* denies that simplicity to the world.

Though we broaden out to describe an *inclusive* world banking system with full and equal rights for all, our examples of current *exclusive* property rights within banking systems are primarily within America. Our readers are asked to use these tools to visualize and analyze property rights and banking systems throughout the world and within all economic systems.

That the world will abandon its current struggles over who will control resources and the *wealth producing process* and peacefully and rapidly eliminate poverty—we describe in depth that it can be done—is not likely. But such revolutionary leaps have happened before and modern communications and the current disastrous foreign policy of America, the hegemon currently blocking such changes, has cost them the moral high ground and greatly increased, and may have assured, the potential of another such leap.

Our concluding chapter is a theoretical example of restructuring a collapsed capitalist economy, the world breaking free and then rapidly developing—both using Henry George's mighty economic and financial engines. As a banking system has to fund them, leaving monopoly *rules of law* in place while creating a theory of either money or economics is an exercise in self delusion.

The theoretical elimination of these monopolies brought to light many deep secrets of money. That fully 60% of America's huge blocs of capital is appropriated wealth lowering economic efficiency by at least 50%, that inflations are conscious decisions, that money can be created for any crucial purpose and yet the money supply kept stable by calculated increases in required reserves, that the patent system is central to denying the rest of the world their freedom and rights, and that a currency only valid within a newly developing region permits printing money for both infrastructure and industry are only some of those secrets.

We must firmly point out: the chance that the world will peacefully eliminate the monopoly system imposed upon the world as per this thesis is unlikely to happen. But eliminating those monopolies will be revolutionary and the only way to address those many obstacles to peace and prosperity was to assume it as a revolution in progress. So, the improbabilities aside, it is one of the possibilities and that is the way we addressed it.

That modern communications will revolutionize the world is well understood. That a worldwide populist revolution is in progress is recognized by many. We hope to alert these same people that Western *rule of law* was designed from its origins as a system of appropriating wealth produced by others; that the capitalized value of these annually claimed unearned values is capitalism's mighty engine which wastes or forgoes production of half the wealth potential; and that the much smaller—yet twice as powerful—economic engine under Henry George's philosophy will eliminate that waste, will eliminate wars, will eliminate poverty, and will provide a quality life for all within 50 years.

The exposure that *exclusive titles* to nature's wealth and technologies is the very essence of *subtle monopoly capitalism* was so important that we included it in our simultaneously published primary work, *Economic Democracy: A Grand Strategy for World Peace and Prosperity*. Apologies on the duplications but the exposures were of such importance we feel we owed it to those readers.

A maximally efficient economy with full and equal rights will have elements of capitalist, socialist, and communitarian principles within it. The *inclusive rules of law* of Henry George blend the essential principles of all three and adds one more, society should collect resource rents. Though crucial elements of other philosophies are involved, expanding the principle of society collecting resource rents across the full economic spectrum tags this work as an expansion of Henry George's thesis.

Searching for other monetary theories that could be tied into this theory, Steven Zarlenga's *Lost Science of Money* is the closest but all were written within the *rule of law* carefully put in place the past 700 plus years. That *rule of law*, accepting monopolists appropriating value (wealth) produced by others, is the centerpiece of Western capitalism's monopoly system.

Henry George's philosophy, the elimination of appropriation of wealth through *exclusive titles* to nature's wealth and technologies, creates a totally new framework for monetary theory. Those huge blocs of capital—created through capitalizing annually appropriated values—power the famous engine of capitalism which becomes the justification for confiscation of wealth produced by others. Henry George's economic engine is half the size, twice as powerful, permits all to retain the wealth they produce, and operates flawlessly as it expands across the world whereas monopoly capitalism's mighty engine invariably appropriates too much wealth, flounders, and collapses.

Every thesis has its challengers. As most monetary theories assume monopolies do not exist, the only intellectually valid challenge will be one first addressing their elimination. We start with the first one that must be eliminated, money and banking.

1. Henry George's Rule of Law: A Modern Money Commons

Everybody uses money and instinctively understands how it works. Thus it would be possible to outline an easily-understood honest banking system in a few pages. But such a simple book would be ignored by money theorists. So, along with the elimination of monopolies we are told do not exist, we will first go through the ritual of outlining the history of money. Those versed in the subject will quickly spot where our views of a modern banking system diverge sharply from the classics.

From Barter to Commodity Money

Before the widespread use of money, trading involved the simplest form of commercial transaction—barter, an exchange of two or more products of roughly equal value. This limits most trading to persons possessing equally valuable items. Eventually cattle, tobacco, salt, tea, blankets, skins, and other items were used as a form of money. Such commodities were the most desirable because they were durable, portable, readily exchangeable, and had the most recognizable common measure of value.

Products intended for consumption typically have 1 to 3 owners on their way from producer to consumer. Those that are used as money may have dozens or even hundreds of owners. Whether a product is used for exchange or consumption distinguishes it as money or a commodity. The products listed above were imperfect as a medium of exchange, and their limited usefulness limited trade. They also created problems of storage, transportation, protection, and not everyone could use these commodities.

From Commodity Money to Coins of Precious Metal

Only highly desirable, useful items could become money. No one would accept a piece of paper, brass, or copper in trade for what he or she had worked so hard to produce. Such a trade would effectively rob one of hard-earned wealth.

Gold and silver have been highly esteemed and accepted as money in most cultures. The first known coin, the shekel, was minted in "the temples of Sumer about 5,000 years ago," and coins of measured value have been routinely minted from precious metals ever since.[1] Except for scarcity values, the labor required to produce a given amount of gold, silver, or precious stones was roughly equal to the labor required to produce other items this treasure could buy. As accustomed as we are to viewing gold as money, it is still commodity money: desirable, useful, and requiring roughly equal labor to produce.

Inequality of money values is only inequality of exchanged labor values. Often when rulers became strapped for cash (usually because of war), they resorted to debasing their currency by lowering the gold or silver content and replacing it with inexpensive metals such as copper. The labor value represented by these debased coins was less than the labor value of the items purchased. Assuming the labor cost of gold was 300 times that of copper, each day's production of copper substituted and traded as gold would confiscate the value of 300 days of labor spent producing useful items. It was the universally recognized value of precious metals that became the first readily acceptable money.[2]

With gold (or any precious metal) divisible into units of measurable value, a trade could be made for any product. As it was only with handy universally accepted money that commerce could flourish, this convenience fueled world trade. However, as these precious metals had to be located, mined, delivered, stored and protected before society could have money, trades were still clumsy.

From Gold, to Gold-Backed Paper Money, to Fiat Paper Money

The use of gold as money was handicapped by its weight, bulk, and the need for protection against debasement. These problems were eventually eliminated by printing paper money that could be redeemed for a stated amount of gold or silver (the gold standard). As this paper money was backed by gold, there remained the complication of finding, mining, smelting, and storing this valuable commodity.

The next step in its evolution was the use of pure fiat (by government decree) paper money—almost universally resorted to in revolutions, although it usually had little value once the banking systems returned to the gold standard. Benjamin Franklin had proposed fiat paper money, and, while it was used less successfully in the New England colonies, it was used productively in the middle colonies in promoting production and commerce while controlling deflation. The powerful of Britain recognized the threat to their control of trade and outlawed the printing of money in the colonies. This effectively dictated control of commerce, determined who would profit, and was a contributory cause of the American Revolution.[3]

World War I and WWII weakened the old imperial nations and eroded the subtle monopoly of the gold standard.[4] As most of their gold had been traded for war materiel, these countries had to keep printing money to rebuild their shattered cities and industrial plants. To return to money backed by gold would have left their economies to the mercy of U.S. bankers. Thus the subtle monopoly of the gold standard was partially broken in these countries. The arms race that followed WWII almost totally eliminated gold-backed money as nations continued to print money wastefully for war.

Once freed from its bondage to gold, paper money *represented* rather than possessed value. Printed at little cost, it could be traded for as much wealth as its stated value. Society now required only one product to make a trade. Those who sold their labor in the form of products produced or services rendered received in return the paper symbols of value and needed only save this money form of wealth until they wished to buy products produced by others. Fiat paper money, used productively and not backed by gold, was true money.

Paper Money, to Checkbook Money, to Computer Money

As simple and light as paper money was, it was still too clumsy for most trades. Most of these units of value called money were deposited in a bank (just as gold had been) and trades were then consummated with checks. These were more efficient than cash because each check was a symbol that the signer had produced, saved, or borrowed that much wealth and that its money form—safely deposited in the bank—was now being traded for equal value in other products or services. Family, business, corporate, and international trades use these symbols of deposited savings, checks, drafts, notes, bills of exchange, etc.

Commodity money (hides, tobacco, etc.) had dozens, possibly hundreds, of owners before this trading medium returned to its status as a commodity to be consumed. Gold (still commodity money) retained the status of money much longer and had thousands of owners. Gold-backed paper money traded more conveniently and passed through the hands of many tens of thousands of owners. Reserve deposit money, traded by check—via bank debits and credits—can have an endless number of owners as this representation of value keeps moving from owner to owner. Modern computer money (still reserve deposit money) is but a blip on a computer drive that can be instantly debited from one account and credited to another. Though tied closely to the principle of checkbook money, this is the ultimate in efficient fiat money.

Paper money and checks are familiar to everybody. Even a child learns quickly what they are and how to use them. When most of the historical and ideological mystiques are eliminated, money is easy to understand. The banking system collects all production (symbolized by money), completes society's trades through debits and credits, lends the surplus production (savings) to those who—at any particular moment—have capital or consumer needs greater than their savings, and—through borrowing from the Fed to expand their reserves and increase their loan capacity (or the Fed creating, and the government spending, money for infrastructure)—creates more money for an expanding economy. Money is no more complicated than this.

What makes money appear mysterious is that the powerful have always controlled it. Its secrets are protected by governments, bankers, and—in the ethereal world of high finance—subtle finance monopolists of every shade trying to siphon to themselves others' wealth.

Credit or Trust Money

People accept money because they trust that the value represented can be replaced by equal value in another commodity or service. Credit (pure trust) is both the oldest and most modern currency. When credit is given, nothing is received for the item of value except a promise. Each month, families and businesses are provided with products or services (value) and then billed. This is a procedure based on trust. Cash money is also based on the trust that it can be redeemed for equal value.

If money is controlled with equality and honesty, there is trust. Money then exchanges freely and is easily understood. We are describing money and banking in the everyday language that would apply if all were equally paid for equally-productive labor and if they had full and equal rights to a productive job and to finance capital.

The Different Meanings of Money

Money is correctly referred to as a unit of accounting, savings, stored value, a measure of value, a standard of value, a receipt for value, a system of accounting, a deferred payment, a transferable claim, a lien against future production, an IOU, an exchange value, and an information medium. At a fundamental level, money represents the value of the final product of combining the elements of production—land, industrial capital, and labor. In a properly structured society, money represents the value of labor, profits on stored labor (capital), and a share of the costs of running society represented by land rent being paid to society as outlined in the following chapter on land.

To the layperson, money is normally explained as a medium of exchange. This is true. However, a medium of exchange implies equality and it is precisely the *inequality of exchanges* that is the greatest problem. To understand these inequalities, we must have a better explanation of money.

Money is a Contract against another Person's Labor

Money is first, and foremost, a contract against another person's labor. Except for wealth produced by nature, value is properly a measure of the time and quality of all labor spent producing a product or service. If the difference between the payment received for productive labor and the price paid by the consumer for a product or service is greater than fair value for expediting that trade, either the producer was underpaid, the final consumer was overcharged, or both. When intermediaries underpay producers or overcharge consumers, they are siphoning away the production of the labors of one or the other, or both. This process is seen in the notorious and once common practice of forced shopping at the company store. The underpaid workers' meager wages were further reduced by their compulsory purchase of overpriced merchandise.[5]

Savings implies that something has been produced and not consumed. But even if a commodity is produced for consumption, it is properly understood as capital until sold to the final consumer. It then becomes his or her wealth for consumption and is no longer capital. (Some commodities, such as a meal, are consumed in minutes and some, such as homes, are consumed in decades or even centuries.) Products are sold, production expenses are paid, any surplus is deposited in a bank, and that deposit is credited at the Federal Reserve as an expansion of the depositing bank's reserves. Banks lend that in excess of mandated reserves to others for investment or consumption. The parties who labored to create the value represented by that money are only lending their surplus production in its money form (finance capital) with the promise to be repaid, plus interest, for what their stored labor produced. Interest is the money form of wealth produced by that stored labor (capital).

Money Productively Contracting Labor

Because money is always controlled by those who rule, revolutionaries resort to printing money to finance their insurrections. Successful revolutionary wars, like those of the United States,[6] France, the Soviet Union, and China, were fought for freedom, were productive expenditures of labor, and were all fought with paper money.[7] Every battle for freedom requires large expenditures. Most labor is donated, but much of the weaponry, clothing, food, and medicine must be paid for with money. Money is thus a tool for mobilizing society's labor to produce great things—in this case freedom.

Examples of money properly employing labor are seen every day in farming, in the creation of consumer products, and in the building of homes, roads, schools, shopping centers, and factories. The rebuilding of Europe after WWII was a productive use of labor employed—in part—by U.S. capital, as was the industrialization of Southeast Asia.

Money Unproductively Contracting Labor

An efficient economy has been judged as requiring only $3 of speculation for every $1 invested in the real economy yet currency speculation for financing world trade alone in the year 2000 was 55 times the real economy. The massive profits from this unnecessary speculation are charges against other stakeholders within the world economy.

To use one's *earned* money for speculation is properly one's privilege. But borrowing society's money capital for speculating on, gold, silver, commodities, already issued stock, derivatives, or currency, (the ethereal world of high finance) is an attempt to intercept social production by speculating with society's savings; there is no intent to actually produce. For example: On March 5, 2006, CBS News stated that 1/3 of the price of oil is accounted for within the buying and selling of oil contracts. Other commodities will have similar costs attached through speculations in the market. The massive profits earned in those speculations show up in higher prices. To quote William Krehm of COMER (Committee on Monetary and Economic Reform), in that process "the real economy is rapidly being reduced to the part of a bit player.

The uses of society's savings for corporate takeovers usually are battles between the powerful for control. Whether the takeover is successful or not, these unproductive uses of social capital continually milk money from the economy. All this unnecessary activity diverts money capital from its true purpose, production and distribution. More appropriately, massive speculation beyond that needed for an efficient economy is an exercise in social insanity. By taking the easy way out, society is being irresponsible.

An even more nonproductive use of money occurs when labor is contracted to destroy others' capital (war), or to work at endeavors from which neither the present generation nor its descendants will benefit. In 1800, Robert Owen, manager of a family textile mill in Scotland, began his famous social experiment of paying workers well, giving them decent housing, educating their children, and doing all this profitably. He calculated that this community of 2,500 persons (workers and families) was producing as much as a community of 600,000 did less than 50 years before.

Owen wondered where the wealth from such a large increase in efficiency was going. He concluded it was being consumed by the petty wars continually fought by aristocracy.[8] The mill workers were being underpaid for their work, the customers were being overcharged for their cloth, and the production of their labor, in its money form, was being siphoned away and used to contract materiel and labor for war. Labor was being paid to fight because this generated the greatest rewards for those who controlled the use of money. This was wasteful to the rest of society—nothing useful was produced when that confiscated wealth was spent on wars and much of what existed was destroyed.

In the 15th century, "about 70% of Spanish revenues and around two-thirds of the earnings of other European countries" were employed in these wars.[9] Most of this revenue was siphoned away from a country's own citizens. The treasure pillaged from the Americas was but a small share of the wealth destroyed in European wars:

> Until the flow of American silver brought massive additional revenues to the Spanish crown (roughly from the 1560s to the late 1630s), the Habsburg war effort principally rested upon the backs of Castilian peasants and merchants; and even at its height, the royal income from sources in the New World was only about one-quarter to one-third of that derived from Castile and its six million inhabitants.[10]

The powerful today are wasting massive wealth battling over the world's wealth, identical to Robert Owen's analysis 200 years ago.

Learning the Secret of Bank-Created Money

The secret of creating money was first learned by goldsmiths. Others' gold was deposited with them for safekeeping. They learned that deposits were usually left for a substantial period and they could safely make loans in the form of receipts for gold. These receipts circulated as money with the gold remaining on deposit. On balance, loans were paid off faster than the gold was reclaimed. Loans issued for several times the amount of gold on deposit became created money.[11]

Whenever Rothschild or other early bankers loaned 10 certificates of gold at 10% interest, for every unit of gold they owned or held for safekeeping, each year their personal net worth would increase equal to all gold on deposit. When private banks printed their own goldbacked currency, its creation of money and its profits—between collapses—were identical to that of goldsmiths.

One hundred years ago there were no federally required reserves in American banking. A prudent bank with $1 million in gold that decided to maintain its fractional reserves at 10% could print $9 million in banknotes, $8 million of that would be bank-created money. All goes well until some banks go far beyond reasonable loan to reserve ratios leading to runs on banks and economic collapses.

Viewing the Federal Reserve required and controlled fractional reserve system as one bank, which any mandated reserve banking system is, a private bank today with $1 million on deposit and a 10% mandated reserve could initially make only $900,000 in loans. As the money was spent and redeposited, it could loan 90% of each new reserve deposit and eventually would loan out $9 million, the same as the prudent banker 100 years ago with self-imposed reserves of 10%. In contrast, assuming a sound economy and *prudent bankers*, the money created in a modern economy—as it circulates productively contracting land, labor, and industrial capital—is backed by the wealth produced.[a]

Here we must detour: Instead of money actually circulating, no checkbook or credit card money ever leaves a banking system. It is only transferred from one account to another. Just as goldsmiths loaning certificates of gold 200 years ago, all that is circulating in each case are promises to pay. There was no increase in gold when certificates of 10 times that in safekeeping were loaned and there is no increase in money when 10 times or 33 times (as is possible under 3% reserves) the original *primary-created* money is loaned. However, gold

---

[a] The difference between no central bank (a Federal Reserve) to clear trades between banks (private banks creating money) and clearing through a federal reserve (with the central bank creating money) is that private banks cannot go beyond a mandated reserve to loan ratio. Actually the ratio between loans and reserves (the money supply) can be controlled, as both Australia and Canada does, by simply limiting or increasing the money supply. But required reserves are so easy to understand we will follow that model.

to repay a debt can be obtained anywhere in the world while money to repay a debt can be obtained only by debiting another account within the banking system. Nor do those promises to pay (checks) circulate. When that promise is cashed, it is transferred back to the signer. Even though nothing is actually circulating, all theorists say it does, loaned cash does circulate in this manner, and it is easier to visualize, so we will continue with the story of creation of money using that faulty terminology.

The 13 American colonies printed money to fight the Revolutionary War but this power of government to create money was not used by the United States again in any great measure until President Lincoln printed greenbacks to finance the Civil War. Though the alert will have spotted this efficiency potential of banking, as soon as that war was over, the U.S. government ceased creating money and started pulling those greenbacks out of circulation. This destruction of money caused bankruptcies to soar for the first 10 postwar years as wealth was again consolidated within the hands of entrenched wealth.[12]

There was no need for those bankruptcies. If those greenbacks had been allowed to stand, and—so long as there were unemployed resources, unemployed labor, and consumer needs—that money would have continued to circulate freely combining labor and industrial capital with America's immense natural resources, creating even more wealth. A healthy, wealthy, economy requires the creation of money to create wealth, not its destruction. Those greenbacks were withdrawn because their creation encroached upon private bankers self-appointed rights to create money.

As those greenbacks were being withdrawn, conservative bankers required $33.60 of gold or gold-backed currency in reserve for every $100 on deposit (as it was gold-backed, it was bank-created money). This privately managed policy changed and the next 40 years recorded greedy bankers loaning 20 to 50 times their reserves or even more. Banks pooled funds to cover runs on banks but those runs would spill over onto strong banks. With their depositors' money loaned out operating the economy and thus not immediately collectable (illiquid), perfectly sound banks would go under and bankrupt many farms and businesses with them.

Primary-created money and Circulating Money

America reined in wildcat banking in 1913 through the establishment of the Federal Reserve[13] Since that act, U.S. banks that were members could not loan above a set multiple of their reserves. The reserve requirements of state chartered nonmember banks varied for the next 67 years. In 1980, all U.S. banks were brought under the Federal Reserve System and creation of money has ever since been regulated by the Federal Reserve. The error that private banks create money is that they control the Federal Reserve, create all the money they need protecting their monopoly system, and ignore the enormous efficiency potentials we demonstrate are possible within a banking system.

Modern Money Mechanics (MMM),[14] an out of print publication of the Federal Reserve, very clearly backs up this description of the creation of money under fractional reserve banking. At various points below we will address what that document says and occasionally point out what it fails to say.

Two failures are misnaming a loan as both created and circulating money. A loan does not create money and nothing circulates. A loan is debited from one account and credited to the loan account, a check against that account is given for a purchase, that promise to pay is deposited by the second party, that amount of money is debited from the borrowers account and credited to the sellers account, and the check is returned to the borrower. Money under one person's control has been traded for value and that trade was consummated by debiting one account and crediting another. Nothing circulated except the check and that promise to pay went from the borrower, to the seller, to the bank and back to the borrower. But the faulty terminology does not damage the integrity of the theory and is easier to visualize, so we will use it also.

MMM recognize deposits, until they are loaned, as "excess reserves." In Section three, it states that since "lending banks *expect* to lose these deposits—and an equal amount of reserves—as the borrowers' checks are paid, they will not lend more than their excess reserves." That acknowledges loans are made from excess reserves. Both the Fed and money theorists stating that "each loan is balanced by a deposit somewhere" is also an acknowledgment that money is debited from one account within a bank, credited to the borrowers account, and transferred to other deposit accounts within the banking system as promises to pay (checks) are honored. In the process, money has been accounted for but it has not been created.

Primary money in the historic circulation of money is first created by the Federal Reserve/Treasury (government) purchasing debt instruments from the public, primarily banks, through crediting a bank's reserves without debiting anyone's account. Those reserves are loaned out, spent, and return to a bank to be again credited to their reserves. By recording the debiting of one account and crediting another, then loaning 90% back out, private banks are only in the business of accounting for money, they are not in the business of creating money.

The Fed calls the reserves they created, the reserves deposited as that money circulates, and currency in circulation as "high-powered money." Among those three categories, money created by the Fed is especially powerful, unique, and—for the sake of clarity—needs a name. We call it "*primary-created money*" because that and currency/coin is the only real money in existence in a fractional reserve banking system. Deposits of circulating money are only the original loaned excess reserves (base money) moved from one account to another within the banking system. "*Primary-created money*" is not a noun phrase used in MMM. But, since—as we prove—it is that original created money which is in continuous circulation (actually only debited from one account and credited to another but we are using their words), they should be so termed.

Though judgments are being made on credit worthiness, private banks are not—by the act of making a loan—creating money. Yes—through their control of the Fed—private bankers create all the money they need (want), and excess profits are made on loaning out those reserve deposits. But—in federally mandated fractional reserve banking—only the Fed can credit one account without debiting another and expand those reserves (create money). Only in the sense that private bankers control the Fed do private banks create money. What some money theorists call creation of money by private banks as money circulates is really only an accumulative accounting of whose hands money passes through as it circulates.

If a bank makes a $10,000 loan and credits a borrower's account with that money, some money theorists insist this is the creation of money. But that is not so. In federally required fractional reserve banking supervised by a central bank (the Federal Reserve), and assuming mandated 10% reserves, that private bank must have $11,000 in excess reserves before that loan can be made.

When that $10,000 loan is withdrawn, spent, and redeposited into the receiver's reserve account, the original 10% reserve and the latest deposit exactly match the original $11,000 reserve deposit. Ninety percent of that 2nd deposit is loaned out, spent, and returns to the banking system as a 3rd reserve deposit. The 10% in reserve backing the first two loans and the 3rd reserve deposit again exactly equal the original $11,000 reserve deposit.[a] One person's spent loan is quickly redeposited as another person's reserve deposit. Never is money in two people's hands at the same time. Beyond the initial creation of money by the Fed, there is only an accounting of whose hands that *primary-created money* is in at any one time. That accounting accurately measures economic activity.

At 10% required reserves for a $10,000 loan issued from a reserve deposit, when the cycles (anywhere from 30 to 50 in ever smaller increments) of the

---

[a] Checks drawn on other banks are cleared at the Fed. Every two weeks each bank sends an accounting of their reserve deposit balances to the Fed. Only the Fed can create money. By removing bankers from the helm and keeping the money supply in balance, a Federal Reserve overseeing required reserves is pure gold to an economy. Not only can an economic collapse be stopped in its tracks and brought back to health, a developing region utilizing a currency viable only within its borders (a dual currency system) can create money for both infrastructure and industry. Calculated increases in required reserves will maintain a stable money supply and prevent inflation due to too much money chasing too few goods. (Prices rising due to infrastructure, human, and environmental investments by governments, or that due to equal pay for equally productive labor as suggested throughout our research, requires all society adjusting to those higher prices. See William Krehm's analysis of "the social lien." *Price in the Mixed Economy: Our Record of Disaster,* Thornwood Publications, 1975) Once a region is developed, mandated reserves can be lowered and industry and most infrastructures will be financed from savings or recycling payments on previously issued bonds. So long as it is designed to reach productive elements of society, primarily labor, money creation and calculated levels of required reserves can quickly restart and restructure a collapsed economy.

acclaimed circulation of money is complete, a total of roughly ten times that original loan will have been accounted for. Though $100,000 in trades has been accounted for ($330,000 if considering actual current required reserves of 3%), no more money beyond that first $11,000 deposit will have been created. That $100,000 is only an accounting of the committed (loaned) reserves circulating (loaned, deposited, and reloaned) 30 to 50 times in ever-smaller increments. The reserves backing those multiple deposits—or loans if you are looking at the other side of the double entry bookkeeping ledger—are, at all times, the original $11,000 created by the Fed/Treasury.[a]

Not one cent beyond the original *primary-created money* (or gold, or certificates of value if that is the value kept in reserve) has been created. When that first loan is made, 90% of the original unit of value is only starting its circulation, it continues to circulate in ever-smaller increments, and eventually trades equaling roughly 10 times the original loan will have been accounted for, roughly 33 times if considering actual current mandated reserves of 3%.

Under fractional reserve banking, only when a banking system is viewed as one bank does a bank create money and even then it is still the Fed that creates it through crediting a bank's reserves without debiting another account. Private bankers do control the Fed and banks do collect the substantial difference between interest paid depositors (or the Federal Reserve) and that collected from the borrowers. But, in a fractional reserve banking system—mandated and overseen by a central bank—individual banks do not create money.

If one had been using diamonds (commodity money) or for that matter printed $100 bills, they too would have gone from hand to hand—first as a loan and returning as a reserve deposit—each time it circulated that value would have been counted as an increase in the money supply, but—when that circulation began, throughout its circulation and when that circulation was complete—there was at all times only the same number of diamonds or $100 bills. Money will have been accounted for in different hands at different times but none will have been created.

If the receiver of what is commonly, and wrongly, referred to as "bank-created money" puts it under the mattress instead of into a reserve deposit, money circulation stops. But as soon as that person spends that money, where it is eventually deposited into a reserve account, again 90% is loaned back out (that money is then committed and there is no surplus to loan until it is again deposited), and the money continues to circulate. In the act of being counted each time it changes hands, the money totals increase and these increasing totals within double-entry bookkeeping (each debit has a balancing credit) make it appear that money has been created. But each trade of money for value has only been counted; money has not increased.

---

[a] At this time, time deposits do not require reserves. Though 80% of capital formation is through pension funds, mutual funds, insurance companies, security dealers, and finance companies, those funds are credited and debited within the banking system, are part of the money supply in motion, and are affected by required reserves.

Unless one can trade paper for value, which America has done for decades in overseas trades, money in a monopolized economy does not increase until values increase. When those values increase (land and businesses gain in value, meaning monopolists have claimed a larger share of real wealth), money must be created by the Fed to buy and sell those monopoly values.

When loaned money is spent and redeposited, utilized reserves and excess reserves remain at the original combined level. There has been no increase in money. The fact that a bank short on reserves must borrow overnight funds from surplus banks again proves that loans are made from reserves. Every two weeks, each bank sends their balanced accounts to the Federal Reserve which dutifully records that bank's loans and reserve balances. That accounting of all banks' reserves adds up to the original *primary-created money* (base money) because it is, and always was at every point, that same money.

A bank could have bought a bond, a business, or a vacation for its entire staff instead of making a loan and it would have had exactly the same effect. The check written would have returned to the bank as another deposit ready to loan out or to spend.

Testing the Assertions that, under Required Reserves, Private Banks Create Money

Money theorist's assertions are very clear, "money is first created through making a loan and deposit of that money into an account comes second." Let's follow that money trail. A private bank makes a loan for $10,000. They are creating that money by crediting it to the borrowers account and must have 10% that amount in reserve ($1,000) to back that creation. That $10,000 is spent, circulates within the economy, and is deposited back into a reserve account. In short, money is not loaned from accounts. Money is created when loaned and then returns as other accounts which add up to $11,000 ($1,000 in reserve and the $10,000 deposited after that first loan of created money was spent).

Money theorists cannot have it both ways. If that first $1,000 in reserve backs a $10,000 loan (since we have required reserves, that is their reasoning), that secondary deposit of $10,000 into a reserve account becomes excess reserves for a $100,000 loan. That $100,000 is spent, circulates back to the banking system as a $100,000 reserve deposit (cycle two) which in turn will back a $1,000,000 loan which too is bank-created money, and which too returns (cycle three) as $1,000,000 in reserve deposits. Cycle four would create $100 million, cycle five would create $1 billion, and two more cycles would reach $1 trillion.

No theorists are claiming money creation of that magnitude, but they do claim that banks are creating money by making loans. Their own words say it correctly: "Every last cent of the net increase in capacity of the system to make loans came from the Fed. None of it came from deposits of legal tender by the public or the deposits of checks by the public." Then another page will say in error: "through the process of making loans, private banks create money."

For private bank creation of money theorists to be right, they have to prove that America's banks own the money they created, which, except for excessive interest earned, they can't. Interest becomes profits and payments, on balance, replace accounts debited to make that loan.

Actually the term required reserves is a matter of semantics. Neither Australia nor Canada have required reserves, reserves are not required for a large share of America's banking deposits, and all three countries create money the same way, their central banks credit individual bank's accounts without debiting another account within the circulation of money. Different words are used but their meaning and the process are the same and, except to the extent that private bankers control their central banks, individual private banks do not create money.

What is important is that the bankers and politicians (the powerstructure) of each are careful to retain control of the money creation process. With modern communications and computers, money creation and control is so simple that its effective use would replace the greater share of today's immense blocs of capital. Before that can happen, those monopolies must be eliminated. To not do so, would leave money creationists and money monopolists battling over funding the economy. Through denying society knowledge of this simplicity, money monopolists have won hands down.

The Fed's Open Market Operations hide the Simplicity of Money Creation

To maintain the mystery of how simple money creation really is, bankers conceived the Fed's devious Open Market Operations. The profits made being returned to the U.S. Treasury (see below) leaves no other conclusion than the Fed being an arm of the government.

Money is created when the Fed buys debt instruments. The reserve accounts of the bank where that check is cashed being credited with the amount of the sale with no debiting of another reserve account creates what we have, for the sake of clarity, labeled "*primary-created money*" available for loans. That and currency and coin (circulating) is the only "real" money within fractional reserve banking.

Once the limit of circulation of money is reached yet there are legitimate entrepreneurial endeavors to fund, any further increase in the money supply requires private banks borrowing from the Federal Reserve (credited but no account debited so it is created money) or the Federal Reserve purchasing more bonds in the market (no bank's reserves are debited as that banks reserves are credited, so again money is created.[15]

Private bankers may derive great benefits from money created and they certainly are the ones that decide when money is to be created and how much. But only the government (the Treasury in cooperation with the Federal Reserve and both are arms of the government) has title to *primary-created money* when first created. Once the government spends that newly-created (real) money, it ends up in a business' or individual's account and is accounted for as owned by that party.

So, with checkbook money, all that is circulating are promises to pay. The money moving from person to person (account to account) remains what it was at all times, *primary-created money* with a part sitting in a reserve account waiting to be loaned and another part as a reserve for depositor's money already loaned. Even though checkbook money never leaves the bank, we have no problem following the crowd and calling it circulating money. The principle is the same: The accounting of that money moving from person to person keeps adding up but it was at all times nothing more than the original *primary-created money* owned at different times by different people.

Lowering or raising reserve requirements—through increasing or decreasing the number of times money will circulate—does increase or decrease the money supply but does not increase or decrease total reserve deposits.

It would be transparent and much simpler for the Fed to purchase treasuries directly from the Treasury. But that would expose the obvious; the government owes that money to itself. To avoid the exposure of that simplicity, the Fed purchases debt instruments on the open market. The Fed's check is cashed, the banking system returns the check to the Fed for clearing and—without debiting another account—the Fed credits the bank in which its check was deposited with an increase in reserves equal to the face value of the check. By the Feds purchase of treasuries with created money, the bank has been reimbursed for funds it had paid to the Treasury to purchase those bonds.[a]

The interest paid by the U.S. Treasury on Fed-purchased T-bills goes to the Fed, which annually returns all that plus a part of other profits (other bonds, currency trading, priced services to banks, etc.) to the Treasury. Thus in 1994 the Fed received $19.247 billion from the U.S. Treasury as interest on bonds and paid to the Treasury $20.470 billion, or $1.223 billion more than it received in interest.[16]

That the Fed is privately owned is a shell game. The unpaid principal and interest on those Fed-purchased—and thus government-owned—bonds are simply credits and debits on the Fed's and Treasury's books. Both are government agencies and when interest is paid to the Fed by the Treasury that interest and other profits are promptly returned to the Treasury, thus proving there never was a debt. The Treasury/Fed could have openly created that money without any debt. But the simplicity of creating money would be visible to all and maintaining that secret is the very purpose of the whole charade.

Member reserve banks control but do not own the Fed. If they really did, the Fed would pay taxes and the owners would be receiving the interest on Fed-owned debt instruments. In 1994, as discussed above, member banks re-

---

[a] We ignore creating money through printing currency and minting coins. Bank's purchase of that currency comes out of reserves so that is only a trade of reserve deposits for currency. Unless it is loaned by a central bank or used to purchase securities from a private bank, it is not a creation of money.

ceived $212 million in dividends and $283 million for their mysterious "surplus fund," which only means the government, the owner, should have received $20.965 billion instead of $20.470 billion.[17]

Operation costs are paid for by charges to banks, the Fed reports to Congress, and the payment of 97% of the profits of the Fed to the Treasury is proof that bankers know well that the Fed is an appendage to the Treasury and both are arms of the federal government.

However private bankers do control Fed policy. That they do not have the courage to distribute amongst themselves the profits from those Fed-owned bonds proves they know they do not own the Fed. That part of the national debt owed to the Federal Reserve can be eliminated by simply writing it off. After all, one cannot owe money to oneself. Besides owning stock certificates, the only other sense in which private banks own the Federal Reserve is that it is they who receive most of the interest on that created money. This is accomplished through the rate spread between the interest paid the Fed and depositors and that charged the borrowers. Obviously, as we will be addressing in full later, society should buy up those stock certificates and openly take control of the Federal Reserve.

A growing economy requires more money which banks obtain by selling debt instruments to the Federal Reserve.[18] To pay for these securities, when the Fed's check comes back to itself for clearing, the Fed simply credits the selling bank with that number of dollars without debiting from any reserve account; it is *primary-created money*. That money is deposited into the reserves of the bank that sold those bonds; that bank can now loan 90% of that money, it circulates, it returns as a deposit, it is reloaned in ever smaller increments, and that cycle continues until 10 times the created money has been loaned. When loans are being repaid faster than money is borrowed, money accounted for (known as the money supply) disappears from an economy by the same multiple.

In a steady state economy, value is being destroyed (by consumption and depreciation) as fast as it is created (by production) or, if you prefer, created as fast as it is destroyed. To put it another way, consumption and production are in balance. The circulation of money does this naturally while the Federal Reserve oversees the primary creation of money. However, they fail to create money for the right purposes and they control inflation primarily through increasing interest rates rather than required reserves. Pointing created money towards the ethereal world above the real economy, towards war, and the failure to fully utilize the power of mandated reserves in balance with that creation, seriously lowers economic efficiency.

America had the good fortune of sincere bankers—tired of the multiple crisis of wildcat banking—establishing in 1913 super-efficient fractional reserve banking overseen by the Federal Reserve. Then they had the misfortune of corrupt bankers taking over the beautiful system they had designed.

Though by law fractional reserve banking had to be practiced, those selfish few prevented the widespread use of the unique and efficient creation of debt-free money for building economic infrastructure (post offices, roads, railroads, water systems, sewer systems, electric systems, schools, parks, museums, etc.). You and I easily analyzing increasing mandated reserves as the most efficient method of controlling inflation means bankers have always known this efficient tool was there but chose to fatten their profits by controlling inflation through higher interest rates even if it meant savaging the economy.

We are very conservative in outlining how, under fractional reserve banking owned by society, there would never be a shortage of finance capital. At first look it appears building economic infrastructure with created money would create inflation. But a proper level of circulating money (the money supply) can be maintained by increasing required reserves. Through elimination of monopolies and full and equal rights for all—as addressed in the Conclusion—money circulating back to the government in the form of resource rents and bank profits will fund governments and money created should be limited primarily to financing economic infrastructure, some without debt and some through financing bonds. That which requires minimum investment accountability—water systems, sewers, ports, parks, roads, railroads, and communication systems (all natural monopolies)—can be built without debt. If financial accountability, spacing out of construction capacity, or simply social habit requires bonds financing construction, payments cycling right back into infrastructure is effectively the same as no debt. Those payments replace funding through taxes or creation of more money.

Why did private bankers derail the potential efficiencies of government creation of money? It is because the massive funds generated through monopolies (*exclusive title* to nature's wealth and technologies as we address in depth) needed a secure place for investment and bankers—over the centuries—have always chosen loans to governments as that safe haven.

Unrealized by most, including economists, the tax system is paying both principal and interest on what we are addressing as wealth appropriated from its rightful owners, the ones paying off those bonds. The annual values appropriated are capitalized by 10 to 30 times, sold, those unearned profits loaned to governments and otherwise invested, and those values are now, in the form of those bonds, a debt to be repaid by the same people from which it was appropriated. Those payments are recycled into more bonds or investments and those appropriated values are repaid, either through taxes or consumer purchases, over and over in perpetuity.

The only thing preventing that compounding of appropriated wealth from quickly claiming all wealth is the rapid increase in the efficiencies of technology creating more wealth along with the steady impoverishment of the periphery of empire from whom a part of the wealth of an imperial center is appropriated. Even then too much wealth is eventually pulled to a few people, too little buying power is left in the hands of consumers, and economic crises occur.

Monopoly values created through *exclusive titles* to nature's wealth and technologies and bought and sold on the markets, are also money creation processes. The proof is in the instant creation of capitalized wealth through *exclusive titles* which requires that money be created to finance sales and purchases. The quick disappearance of those appropriated values under *conditional titles* (full and equal rights), their reappearance as relatively *equally-shared use values*, and the enormous economic efficiencies (a workweek of 2 to 3 days per week with no loss of food, fiber, shelter, or recreation) that are quickly realized proves the existence of those monopolies.[a] Such an increase in free time requires a total restructuring of society (see conclusion).

Since, in a *socially-owned* banking system, any financial need at any time not covered by savings can be covered by creating money, roughly 60% of those huge blocs of capital we are taught as crucial for investment capital were never needed. The powerful throughout history have instinctively known both their power and unearned wealth will disappear under full and equal rights. So they protected their superior rights through short circuiting the potential efficiencies of the Federal Reserve to create what is essentially debt-free money (payments on bonds cycling right back into essential social needs). Once created and used for the right purposes, that money circulates forever.

Very little has to be done for society to reclaim their full and equal rights to finance capital. Simply buy up those privately owned shares in the Federal Reserve system, remove those bankers from their undemocratic positions of power, put trained professionals in their place, mandate the creation of money for social infrastructure bonds (up to a balance point between creation of money and savings, adjustable through higher or lower required reserves), and run the Federal Reserve efficiently with all regions, all states, all communities, and all individuals having full and equal rights to finance capital. .

Accumulation of Capital under *Henry George's Inclusive* Rule of Law

Chapters 1 through 5 address the enormous capital accumulations of the various privatized commons. The enormous unearned profits of these *exclusive titles* to nature's wealth and technologies require a place to be safely invested where it will not devalue those already overbuilt sectors of an economy. This accounts for the export of finance capital buying up overseas investments. We have the anomaly of wealthy nations with too much money and impoverished nations with too little—almost no—money.[b]

---

[a] Market charges above *use values* are monopoly values appropriated through exclusive title or license. The larger share is wasted through monopolies' superstructures. What remains are profits (capitalized annual appropriated values), those huge blocs of capital.

[b] A large share of the surplus funds we are addressing being wealth appropriated from the periphery of empire is the subject of this author's primary work, *Economic Democracy: A Grand Strategy for World Peace and Prosperity*. In short, wealth is appropriated both internally and from the periphery of empire.

All borrowers (consumers of the moment) are borrowing the deposits of all producers (savers of the moment). (One may be borrowing from oneself, either from a checking account or out of pocket, and expecting to replenish the bank account or pocket change [both are savings]). The banking system keeps an account of these trades between people. Many are equal trades—in a month, or year, most people earn roughly what they spend—but the unequal trades (more produced [earned] than spent, or more consumed [spent] than earned) are balanced by lending and borrowing deposited savings residing in banks' reserve accounts.

It is possible to be paid but not produce value. If the purchasers think they are receiving value, in the current monetary system that is tantamount to real value. However, if money contracted only productive labor and full values were paid for that labor, money would represent real value and would become a symbol of actual wealth. Money would then be only a tool, a symbol for the trade of productive labor, which is the mechanism that functions when we describe the economy increasing equal to the invention of money, the printing press, and electricity once those monopolies and their huge blocs of appropriated wealth are eliminated.

Under conditions of equal rights (when each person is fairly paid for his or her fully productive labor and each has rights to his or her share of the remaining productive jobs), money lent combines land, labor, and industrial capital to produce full value in needed goods and services. A society can be fully productive only if each of its citizens is fully productive. Neither money nor the economy can become truly efficient until all nonproductive siphoning of wealth through unequal trades (in both internal and world trade)—as opposed to producing and trading equal value—is eliminated. Likewise, every contracting of labor for nonproductive use must, on final analysis, be paid for by appropriating value from other stakeholders' productive labor.

Powerful bankers thousands of miles away have no concept of local needs and no loyalty to local people. Farmers, homeowners, and small businesses are strapped for finance capital as their locally produced wealth is siphoned thousands of miles away to stock speculators, merger and takeover artists, currency speculators, and other gamblers in the worldwide market casinos.

Do away with the casino aspect of both money and stock markets and local needs can be easily financed. It will be a simple matter to calculate finance capital needs and assign a surcharge to all loans to go into a *socially-owned* capital accumulation fund kept in, and loaned from, local banks. Capital needs of each region of the world, each nation, each state, each county, and each community can be calculated. So long as there are surplus labor and resources and real value is to be produced, finance capital can be obtained through printing money. But once the capital accumulation fund is established, it will largely replenish itself through loan repayments and interest rates high enough to cover loan losses.

A quick analysis of the simplicity of a *socially-owned* capital accumulation fund makes it clear that wealth accumulated in the past through *exclusive titles* to nature's wealth and technologies has gone for many other things besides society's finance capital needs—primarily buying and selling the capitalized values of appropriated wealth (speculation) and for extravagant living.

Every alert entrepreneur knows that the big profits end up with those who call the tune with their money. With a *socially-owned* capital accumulation fund replacing those huge blocs of capital destined for obsolescence under the full and equal rights of Henry George's *inclusive rule of law,* citizens with sound ideas—but no capital—would have the opportunity to realize the profits from their abilities and accumulate capital in their own names. As talent is broadly diffused, wealth, accumulated by true producers would quickly diffuse itself relatively equally throughout the population.

Just as each individual has rights, regions, nations, regions within nations, states, communities, and entrepreneurs should have rights to their share of the world's *primary-created money* and finance capital. Denying social funds for speculation in the worldwide gambling casino (but permitting it for new speculative enterprises) and giving rights to finance capital as described above, would guide lending into productive channels, the real economy as opposed to the ethereal world of high finance battling to lay claim to wealth produced by others.

Consumer credit (within limits) should be a right instantly available, just as it has been pioneered by computerized credit cards. Using artery, vein, eye pattern; thumbprints, and signature scanning (procedures now in use), along with a credit check, risks will be almost nonexistent. Each person's right to credit would be tempered by being subject to standards much as they are now, and the local credit union—an integrated member of the banking system—would be in a position to know a member's creditworthiness. Local bankers should best know the needs of the region and the trustworthiness of those who borrow to build and produce for that society. If not, they should not be bankers.

The economies of prosperous nations are dynamic due to the hopes and dreams of their citizens. These hopes are the motivation for the millions of small businesses springing up. The economic health of a nation requires that those with ideas, talents, and energy have access to finance capital. With rights to credit, a nation's talented can bring together land, labor, capital, and technology at the right time and in the right place to fulfill society's needs. If there is a shortage of finance capital for productive use, and the resources are available and can be used without destroying the environment, a nation's Treasury/Federal Reserve can easily increase reserves (create money).

Only individuals operating under free enterprise and competition (partially so under *subtle monopoly capitalism* but fully expressed under the *inclusive philosophy* of Henry George) can develop the millions of ideas necessary for the progress of science, industry, and society. In order for citizens to fulfill these visions and provide their special expertise, it is necessary that they have access to credit. With entrepreneurs having rights to finance capital and banking personnel trained to be generous, yet careful, innovation in production by business and industry (productive speculation) would be unhampered

Credit is currently rationed by the simple method of checking track records and lending up to a certain percentage of a borrower's equity—a great rule for monopolists. "Loans are made in a very impersonal way—everything depends on 'track record,' and if you don't have a 'track record' [or equity], as most young people do not—you can forget it."[19] Access to investment capital should be a right based on productive merit as well as collateralized equity. Thus credit for productive people in their first ventures and those with a vision for productive expansion would be easier to obtain.

With employees of a banking authority trained to be alert to productive investment requests, these loans would be quite simple. When a loan request was received, an evaluation would be made of its potential productive and financial success. If it looked reasonable, the loan would be approved. This is precisely how loans in America were made for the first 15 to 20 years after WWII. After the boom years were over, banks reverted primarily to loans against equity.[a]

With the disappearance of monopoly values, smaller loans will be backed by a smaller, secure, true value and those values will be matched by the savings of fully-productive labor and entrepreneurs within a much more efficient economy. A loan would, of course, require financial accountability by the borrower just as it does now.

Through regional capital accumulation funds charging higher interest to cover risk, loan institutions can fund new projects. It is not necessary to lend strictly to owners who would then hire workers. Those with insight need only prepare a prospectus describing the product or service, market potential, profit expected, financial requirement, and labor needs. The loan institution would study the proposal and—assuming the ideas were sound and beneficial—would approve the loan. Workers would study the prospectus, and agree to 10-20% of their wages being deducted as payments for 60-80% of the stock. Those who planned the productive endeavor would own, and be responsible for paying for, 20-40% that industries value.

With workers owning a share of an industry and a share of their wages being used to pay off the loan, those owners of capital would be true producers. Society would receive useful products or services and the nation's savers and national treasuries (providing *primary-created money* if necessary) would be fully paid for their finance capital.

With these triple benefits to society, bankers should be taught to pay close attention to requests for investment credits; they are the sinews of capitalism. Most workers would stay on the job, but, once a new business was secure and their new stock had capitalized value, the talented ones would search out an-

---

[a] With the elimination of appropriated values in the various monopolies, there will not be those monopoly values against which to lend. But neither will money capital be needed to purchase these fictitious values. To understand restructuring from the current inefficiencies of subtle monopoly capitalism, one must keep in mind the roughly 60% of finance capital created to buy and sell appropriated values, the needs of which simply disappear when the monopolies' capitalized values are eliminated.

other prospectus, help develop another business, train more workers, gain more capitalized value, and move on again.

Labor would be both mobile and highly productive just as capital is now and the most productive of those workers would be the accumulators of capital. This would be mobilization of labor without the dispossession that has been so typical of past capitalization processes. Labor would have the same rights to gains in efficiencies of technology as investors now have. The talented would be in high demand by the developers of industry.

Besides collateral protection, there are three flows of money that make those loans secure—resource rents, profits, and a share of wages. Every success increases the *use value*, and thus the rental value, of land. As they are sharing in those profits, society's collection of resource rent (see below) could, and should, permit it to accept its share of the risks of new entrepreneurs.

. With these restructured borrowing rights, many more people would qualify for investment capital than under equity loans. If successful, they and their workers would own that capital honestly, as opposed to the current custom of capitalizing values through *exclusive titles* to nature's wealth and technologies laying claim to values produced by others.

Those searching for a higher return—and confident they have found good investments—could directly employ their capital. Those with the opportunity to lend their savings at a higher rate would be free to do so. But they could no longer obtain high profits by bidding on *exclusive titles* to nature's wealth and technologies and, through that monopoly structure, laying claim to wealth produced by others. The huge blocs of accumulated capital confiscated from productive labor would disappear under these proposed *conditional titles* to nature's wealth and technologies.

Once restructured, a society will have to address what nature offers to all through increased economic efficiencies and the increased efficiencies of technology. They must reduce labor time and share productive jobs. If this is not done, new mini-monopolizers—in the form of excessive job rights—will emerge. If all are guaranteed a productive job, each could work outside the home 2 to 3 days per week with—considering a total restructuring of society (see conclusion)—no loss of living standards.

A *socially-owned* capital accumulation fund within a modern financial commons will eliminate the centers of power created through *exclusive titles* to nature's wealth and technologies laying claim to wealth produced by others.

Japan operated just such a capital accumulation fund and utilized it with a vengeance to reach its current position in world trade. We do not suggest a nation's international trade capital accumulation fund be that aggressive but it would be great protection against others' predatory trade practices.

A Money Commons:

People unproductively attached to the arteries of commerce, either for making a living or making fortunes, see only their momentary self interest and will not permit the necessary legal and social changes to eliminate those wasted labors. Because of the *belief systems* (spin, *frameworks of orientation*) created by think tanks established and funded by the power structure and perpetuated through the university system and the media, only under extreme crisis can change be imposed upon them.[20] For the sake of precision and clarity, and recognizing that only small changes are likely and then only under severe crisis, we are outlining a reconstructed banking system that avoids monopolization while providing rights to money and finance capital to all relative to efficient productive needs.

The key to understanding an honest banking structure is that money and banking are only social technologies, beyond a little brick and mortar there is nothing there to own. Just as taxi medallions (a license to operate) in New York City develops a value of $200,000 due to the profits guaranteed by that piece of paper, a license to operate a bank develops a value of hundreds of millions, or even hundreds of billions, of dollars due to the profits guaranteed by their monopoly structured into current *rule of law*. In each case there are no tangible values created by labor, only monopoly values.

This author's first writings documented that competition did not eliminate monopolization. Instead, those competitors consumed enormous amounts of resources and labor battling over market share and—in most cases—doubled the cost of services or products. As elimination of the monopoly system meant elimination of those huge blocs of unearned wealth and the owners of that monopolized capital controlled governments, at no time was society—either within the wealthy world or on the periphery of their empire—given the opportunity to restructure to efficient social and economic structures.

This is why we have heard all our lives, and still hear, about the horrors and waste of governments and the dictatorships and violence of societies breaking free. Monopolists understand well that they disappear if ever the citizenry figure out that an economy controlled by a truly democratic government would double in efficiency and halve their working hours.

That efficiency can only be when society—not monopolists—collect resource rents; when society shares roughly equally the *use values* produced by the ever-increasing efficiencies of technology as opposed to monopolists appropriating and capitalizing those values and buying and selling them on the markets; when all members of society have full and equal rights to *primary-created money* and finance capital as opposed to its current monopolization; and when the remaining secondary monopolies are also eliminated. We will be addressing all that but first we will analyze money a little deeper.

Let's assume that an economically viable, highly educated population emigrates and starts up a new economy in virgin territory and was planning to manage it honestly, equally, and efficiently. There are no *labor-created* values in this virgin territory but this population brings with them basic industrial tools and has the knowledge to run an economy and create a new nation. These modern Pilgrims arrive with the papers already prepared to establish fractional reserve banking to create money and keep account of this new nation's trades.

Their newly established Treasury/Federal Reserve is empowered to create debt-free money to combine their industrial tools (industrial capital) and labor with their resources to produce basic infrastructure, roads, railroads, post offices, schools, water systems, sewers, communication systems, more Industrial tools, etc. (we agree with Henry George, these natural monopolies should be socially owned, *Protection or Free Trade*, pp. 304, 309).

So long as there is surplus labor, unused resources, and a social need not cared for through the current circulation of money, a nation's, or a region's Treasury can create (print) more debt-free primary money. Through creation of money and raising or lowering required reserves, a society can design the proper balance between money creation and money destruction.

The process is rather simple: If reserve requirements are doubled, loanable funds (circulating monies) are reduced 50%. If *primary-created money* simultaneously doubles reserve deposits, the money supply (loanable funds) remain the same. Thus, an increase in mandated reserves from America's current 3% rate to possibly 4% (or to whatever level is necessary) would dampen any threat of inflation due to too much money to purchase too few goods. When that threat is over, money creation and required reserves return to normal. This simple inflation control option alerts us that inflations are power structures' planned events.

Creation of money must be planned within the earth's resource capacity and its ability to absorb society's wastes without ecological destruction. In a nation's early development stage—so long as there are surplus labor, resources, and industry—debt-free primary money can be created to build schools, roads, electric power, water systems, sewer systems, post offices, communication systems, etc. In the very early stages—remembering that balance in the money supply can be retained by increasing reserve requirements—even industry can be built with created money. Those options are only viable if that region's currency has no value outside its borders (see Conclusion for dual money systems in operation) and private investments and infrastructures which require financial accountability should not be debt free. [a]

Basic infrastructure makes society far more efficient and the greater wealth produced as this *primary-created money* circulates backs both the newly-created money and the debts incurred as that circulating money is loaned out to produce more wealth.

---

[a] There are other ways besides financial accountability to assess use of and conserve resources. When built with created money, water, electricity, and natural gas can have very low charges up to a proper amount for an efficient home, higher charges above that, and very high charges for higher usages.

When first industrializing in the late 19th and early 20th centuries, and again when rebuilding after WWII, the Japanese government covered possibly two-thirds the cost. Newly developing regions will develop much quicker following the trail that they—and others—blazed for rapid industrialization.

When *primary-created money* is spent for development, society owns what is built or has a mortgage against that created wealth. Investment accountability requires debts be incurred on most, but not all, infrastructure. Those payments circulate back into a nation's infrastructure lowering the need for future creations of money. To the extent there are unemployed workers, unused resources, unused industrial capital, and unmet human needs—and taking into consideration the capacity of the earth to recycle wastes to protect resources, ecology, and environment for future generations—it is only necessary for a nation's Treasury/Federal Reserve to create the money to employ that labor, utilize those resources, and meet those needs.

It is crucial that we understand how close fractional reserve banking already is to a modern money commons: Through "Revolving Reserve Accounts," total deposits and loans of each individual bank should be accounted for just as they are now through banks debiting and crediting customer reserve accounts and the Fed debiting and crediting bank reserves. Reserve requirements should be regulated just as now but, in place of increasing and decreasing interest rates, mandated reserves should be managed much more aggressively. Banks should be collectors and loaners of the nation's savings, just as now. All loan institutions should be under mandated reserves just as now. All money needed beyond the revolving reserves (circulating money) would be created by the Treasury/Federal Reserve, just as now.

There are two more differences: (1) this is a *socially-owned* banking system with no intermediaries (private banks) claiming unearned profits. Instead, those much smaller profits (from both smaller finance capital needs and smaller interest charges) go to society to fulfill social needs with the differential (current excess profits) and the values once appropriated through monopolization remaining with the citizenry. (2) As the appropriation of the labor and wealth of others will have been eliminated—so long as they are honest—it matters little whether this *socially-owned* banking system is run by bankers or public servants.

The Fed can lower reserve requirements where loan needs are high (poorer regions which need development, regions of natural disaster, etc.) and holding steady, or even increasing, reserve requirements in booming sectors of the economy. The affluent sectors of the economy awash in funds are thus rebalanced with the undeveloped sectors previously deprived of finance capital.

With banking rights held in common, there would be *local rights to finance capital.* Each region, each nation, each region within a nation, each state, each community, and each bank would have a constitutional right to their share of finance capital (*primary-created money* and savings), but only a national, regional, or federated world Treasury/Federal Reserve could create that money.[a] That creation of money would be—by a formula established by law and adjustable to the deficits or surpluses of a region—automatically distributed. There would be neither control by an elite nor control by politics. It would be a formula of

[a] In *Protection or Free Trade*, p. 322, Henry George, foresaw the day Governments would create money. On p. 331 he hints to the future federation of the world.

world regional, national, state, local, and individual rights to *primary-created money* and savings (finance capital).

The success of local currencies proves that regions, localities, and individuals are denied their full rights to finance capital. But local scrip is enormously labor intensive and it is neither legal tender nor universally accepted, thus it is limited in circulation. With banks attuned to take care of those needs, each locality would, in the form of rights to finance capital, effectively have a local currency and—because it is legal tender and can be spent anywhere—it would be much more efficient than enormously labor-intensive, local currency schemes—LET Systems, Ithica Hours, Time Dollars, etc.[a]

Honest money, such as we are proposing in a modern commons, is efficient locally, nationally, and internationally. Efficient means they are instantly acceptable anywhere and accounting costs are infinitesimal. The money itself is the accounting system and those costs are reduced to a fraction of the accounting under subtle monopolization.

The Populists of late 19th century America studied banking reform and their agenda

> became a sourcebook for political reforms spanning the next fifty years: a progressive income tax; federal regulation of railroads, communications, and other corporations; legal rights for labor unions; government price stabilization and credit programs for farmers.... The populist plan would essentially employ the full faith and credit of the United States government directly to assist the "producing classes" who needed financing for their enterprises. In effect, the government would *circumvent the bankers and provide credit straight to the users.... The government would provide "money at cost," instead of money lent by merchants and bankers at thirty-five or fifty or a hundred per cent interest.* [21]

There have been many reforms since those days of blatant extortion by the owners of finance capital, but "the money creation system that the [American] Congress adopted in 1913 [and reformed during the Great Depression] ... preserved the private banking system as the intermediary that controlled the distribution of new money and credit."[22]

That exorbitant interest rates are unnecessary was demonstrated by early Scottish bankers whose thrift is so well known that even today a person careful with his or her money is called "Scotch." In the 19th century, the universal practice of Scottish banks was setting interest on loans from 1-2% above that paid depositors. Their innovative practices are still considered a model of banking stability.[23] With the proper banking service charge having been well established at 1-2% for small-volume banking using expensive hand accounting, 1% would be a proper service charge for large-volume banking using inexpensive computerized accounting.

During the stable years following WWII, the real rate of interest in the United States (allowing for inflation) hovered around 1-2%. Previously, the

---

[a] An Internet search will locate these local currencies and more. Tom Greco, *Understanding and creating Alternatives to Legal Tender* (White River JCT, VT: Chelsea Green Publishing, 2001) is one source.

normal world rate had been 2-3%.[24] Although the real rate of interest in the United States during what were considered the best years the world economy has ever known was under 2% we will allow the highest long-term average real rate of interest, 3%, as a fair rate. With subtle monopolization and the waste it engenders eliminated, with workers fully paid for their fully productive labor, and with true interest at the high end of historical norms, both capital (stored labor) and current labor would be well paid. People would save and those savings would be available for productive investments.

Savings accounts would pay—by law—3% interest. The tendency of many people to spend any money in their pocket would require paying interest on checking accounts at half that on savings or even none. Rights to *primary-created money* and savings (finance capital) would eliminate money market instruments and the attendant wasted labor competing for deposits. Detractors may decry this as a loss of their rights. But the only right lost is that of the powerful to intercept the production of others' labor, especially those pure gamblers whose wagers in the world's market casinos amount to 50 to 100 times the investment, labor, and commodity, activity in the real economy. An honest banking, production, distribution, and consumption economy will have adequate entrepreneurial speculative funds but not the massive blocs of capital consisting of the capitalized value of wealth appropriated through *exclusive titles* to nature's wealth and technologies. Though a large share ended up in productive investments where they create immense problems in restructuring to an honest economy, their original purpose was buying and selling those appropriated values.

In a banking system—with the exception of money created and that destroyed (bankruptcy for example)—total debits and credits will balance (withdrawals equaling deposits). With a fully integrated banking system, any deviation from that balance could be quickly corrected. The visible flow of funds would be the economic pulse of a community, a region, a nation, a world region, and the entire world. Any unexplained deficit in a bank, community, or region could be immediately looked into while normal deficits are balanced by others' normal surpluses.

To provide an adequate living standard for all people and still protect the world's resources and environment, a balance between a respectable living standard and the capacity of the earth's resources and ecosystems would have to be reached. Assuming *centers of capital* could no longer siphon the world's wealth to themselves and then waste it battling over that wealth (the thesis of this author's simultaneously published *Economic Democracy: A Grand Strategy for World Peace and Prosperity*); societies throughout the world could then progress calmly.

Every trade financed by money capital that moves between two banks creates a change in bank reserves at the central bank for that currency. If that central bank does not honor a transaction in its currency through suspending targeted banks' access to their reserves, those banks funds are frozen. In November 2001, President George W Bush threatened to suspend rights of disbursing or accepting dollars for any bank in the world that does not cooperate in the search for those who are funding terrorist attacks on America.

Theoretically other countries can control their currencies but this is true only of countries that are economically powerful. The power to discount currencies of weak nations gives powerful nations effective control over other countries' currency values and thus control over their ability to create money.

Nothing is more important for a nation's or an economic region's economy than productive use of created money and savings, its finance capital.

The Theory of Interest as Usury

Working on a bill to submit to the Eighth Session of the Provisional World Parliament, Professor Glen Martin of Radford University expanded upon the Biblical and Koranic principles that it is wrong to charge interest. As money and banking are social technologies understood for thousands of years and ownership is only proper for items built by one's labor or purchased with funds earned by one's labor, and banking systems are neither, so they are properly *socially owned.*

What caught Professor Martin's attention was that, if properly structured, the elimination of the waste of monopolies and the attaining of full and equal rights through sharing the remaining productive jobs (each working only 2 to 3 days per week and equally paid for equally-productive labor) equalizes the earnings of all relative to their productivity and does away with the huge accumulations of money formerly confiscated through *exclusive title* to nature's wealth and technologies.

Beyond application, approval, accounting, and brick and mortar costs—less than 1% of loan values—there is no one within a banking system applying anything other than normal mental or physical labor. Therefore—though all are entitled to be well paid—no one is entitled to the unearned profits earned through 6-24% interest charges.

No interest buffs and socialists here is an opening to expand your philosophies. Roughly 60% of the values bought and sold within America are primarily monopoly claims to wealth produced by—and properly belonging to—all citizens. It is possible to structure an economy with very low debts, public and private.

By raising required reserves in step with the creation of money, it is possible to create debt free money for all except consumer needs and speculations. However, as savings (honestly earned finance capital) is but stored labor we hold that those who did the mental or physical labor to produce that wealth (both finance capital and industrial capital) deserve to be paid. For that reason, even with Professor Martin's pointing out that an economy can run efficiently without paying interest, we have changed our description of an efficient banking system as laid out in our earliest works only to the extent of who besides well-paid banking labor and depositors are entitled to the values that interest represents. Depositor's savings are properly owned. They are entitled to interest on their stored labor and society is entitled to banking profits.

Saving should be rewarded and we do so through—as outlined above—the payment of interest on savings at the high end of long term averages, 3%. The key is what is done with the greater interest earned by banks. No one's labor is involved beyond that of well-paid managers, accountants, and clerks within the banking system and we have deemed monopolies structured through *exclusive titles* to technology (licenses) are the heart of the current monopolized banking system, so—beyond brick and mortar—there are no tangible, labor-created, values to own. Thus the proper recipient of bank interest—above operational costs—is society itself.

With society collecting banking profits, those charges go right back to the citizenry in the form of essential services. Effectively there is, just as preached in the Bible and Koran, no interest. Society has simply taxed the loan structure in the form of an annual percentage on outstanding loans (the differential between the 3% paid savers and the 4-10% charged borrowers, well under current interest charges). [a]

Once the impoverished world is developed to a sustainable level—as we demonstrate in the Conclusion can be done—the wealthy world will have repaid the struggling world for 500 years of slavery and plunder through which the massive wealth of the imperial nations was accumulated. At that point interest and resource rents should (except for those protecting against resource depletion and environmental degradation) be reduced to the level required to operate a *peaceful federated world.* To not federate means continual war. To federate means peace for all time. [25]

The elimination of banking monopolies through *socially-owned* banking—with society collecting the profits—engenders an economic efficiency gain equal to the invention of the printing press. This increased efficiency would require democratic, communitarian oversight to conserve the earth's resources and protect the environment (see Conclusion).

Analyzing Henry George's philosophy, restructuring *exclusive title* to land to *conditional title* (though he did not always use those words), exposes *exclusive titles* to nature's wealth and technologies as the *rule of law* for all monopolies. Monopolization of banking, technology, communications (with land, the four primary monopolies) and the secondary monopolies (insurance, health care, law, etc.) all are understandable as monopolization of nature's resources and technologies.

We now turn to Henry George's *inclusive rule of law* with society properly collecting resource rents which—written in 1879—provided us the tools with

---

[a] We wish to alert you to Stephen Zarlenga's outstanding book *The Lost Science of Money: The Mythology of Money – the Story of Power.* This is arguably the deepest study of money out there; thoroughly demolishing many common errors in monetary theory and possibly creating a couple errors of his own.

which to understand all monopolies. He laid the foundation for this expansion of his philosophy across the full economic spectrum.

---

[1] Joel Kurtzman, *The Death of Money* (New York: Simon and Schuster, 1993), p. 11.

[2] William Greider, *Secrets of the Temple* (New York: Simon and Schuster, 1987), p. 335.

[3] John Kenneth Galbraith, *Money* (Boston: Houghton Mifflin, 1976), pp. 62-70.

[4] Ibid, pp. 167-78; Greider, *Secrets of the Temple*, pp. 228, 282.

[5] Philip S. Foner, *From Colonial Times to the Founding of the American Federation of Labor* (New York: International Publishers, 1947), p. 67.

[6] John Kenneth Galbraith, *Money* (Boston: Houghton Mifflin, 1976), pp. 62-70.

[7] S. P. Breckinridge, *Legal Tender* (New York: Greenwood Press, 1969), chapter 7; Galbraith, *Money*, pp. 72-75.

[8] *Carl Cohen, Editor, Communism, Fascism, Democracy* (New York: Random House, 1962), pp. 13-14; Paul Kennedy, *The Rise and Fall of Great Powers* (New York: Random House, 1987), p. 53.

[9] Galbraith, *Money, pp. 18-19.*

[10] Paul Kennedy, *The Rise and Fall of the Great Powers. New York: Random House,* 1987, p. 53.

[11] E.K. Hunt, Howard J. Sherman, *Economics* (New York: Harper and Row, 1990), pp. 491-93, 505-508.

[12] Thoren and Warner, *Truth in Money*, pp. 120-24.

[13] William F. Hixson, *Triumph of the Bankers: Money and Banking in the Eighteenth and Nineteenth Centuries* (Westport, Conn: Praeger, 1993), chapter 23; William F. Hixon, *It's Your Money* (Toronto, Canada, COMER, 1997), chapter 5.

[14] MMM, http://landru.i-link-2.net/monques/ mmm2.html.

[15] Hixon, *Triumph*, chapter 5.

[16] Ibid.

[17] Ibid

[18] Greider, *Secrets of the Temple*, pp. 61-62.

[19] Robert Swann, *The Need for Local Currencies* (Great Barrington, MA, E.F. Schumacher Society, 1990), p. 6.

[20] J.W. Smith, *Economic Democracy: A Grand Strategy for World Peace and Prosperity* (Radford, VA: The Institute for Economic Democracy, 2006), chapter 6.

[21] Greider, "Annals of Finance," *The New Yorker,* November 16, 1987, pp. 72, 78, emphasis added.

[22] Ibid, pp. 72, 78.

[23] George Tucker, *The Theory of Money and Banks Investigated* (New York: Greenwood Press, 1968), pp. 219, 255.

[24] Michael Moffitt, *The World's Money* (New York: Simon and Schuster, 1983) p. 197; John H. Makin, *The Global Debt Crisis* (New York: Basic Books, 1984), p. 162.

[25] Errol E Harris, *Earth Federation Now: Tomorrow is too Late* (www.ied.info: the Institute for Economic Democracy, 2005; Glen Martin, *Basic Documents of the Emerging Earth Federation* (www.ied.info: the Institute for Economic Democracy, 2006).

2. Henry George's Rule of Law: A Modern Land Commons

Land and other aspects of nature's wealth are subtly monopolized by a society's total tax structure. Before going on to their final reward, almost every economist of high standing will say that Henry George's *Progress and Poverty*, describing the simplicity, efficiency, and justice of society's collection of resource rents replacing all other taxes, outlines the most efficient and just tax structure.

Although this tax structure has been proposed by various highly respected thinkers for 300 years, America's preeminent economic philosopher, Henry George, was undoubtedly the leading authority on the subject. This chapter is his 1879 primary work—*Progress and Poverty*—condensed and simplified.[1]

The subtle monopolization of social wealth started centuries ago as the powerful structured superior rights into ownership of land. As British Prime Minister Winston Churchill said, land is "by far the greatest of monopolies—it is a perpetual monopoly, and it is the mother of all other forms of monopoly."[2] Later monopolization of industrial and social technologies, through patents and licenses, are structured along the principles of those same *rules of law.*

If you feel threatened by such a simple solution for maximum economic efficiency as offered by Henry George, keep in mind that when society collects its full due in resource rents all private-property *use rights* will be retained. Ownership of land for homes, businesses, and production will be both easier and cheaper. Considering taxes abandoned would equal the value of resource rents collected, sites for homes and businesses would cost nothing. With resource rent being paid out of cash flow being slightly cheaper than paying interest on current land purchase contracts, r*emoval of subtle monopolization would not only increase your right to land and the profits from its productive use, it would ensure those rights.*

Land is Social Wealth

If a person were born with fully developed intelligence, physical ability, and judgment—but without social conditioning—one of the first confusing realities he or she would face is that all land belongs to someone else. Before one could legally stand, sit, lie down, or sleep, he or she would have to pay (or have the implicit permission of) whoever owned that piece of land. This can be shown to be absurd by reflecting on the obvious: land, air, and water nurture all life and each living thing requires, and is surely entitled to, living space on this earth. No person produced any part of it, it was here when each was born, and its bounty is everybody's common right.

By observing title claims in action, earlier economic philosophers were able to deduce that the essential factor in accumulation of wealth was the appropriation of a useful part of nature by claiming *exclusive* private title to land and—unless they pay land rent (a private tax)—alienating all others from its use. All other monopolies follow these principles:

> The first man who, having enclosed a piece of ground, bethought himself as saying "this is mine," and found people simple enough to believe him, was the real founder of civil society. From how many crimes, wars, and murders, from how many horrors and misfortunes might not any one have saved mankind, by pulling up the stakes, or filling up the ditch, and crying to his fellows: "Beware of listening to this impostor; you are undone if you once forget that the fruits of the earth belong to us all, and the earth itself to nobody."[3]

Jean Jacques Rousseau, in *A Discourse on the Origins of Inequality*, was outlining the injustice of one person having unrestricted ownership of another's living space. This practice is only customary. It is part of social conditioning (spin, "*frameworks of orientation*") that locks society within *belief systems*. Being thoroughly conditioned, and having never experienced or imagined anything else, few realize that under *exclusive* private ownership of land (and other aspects of nature's wealth including mechanical and social technologies) they do not have all their rights. Instead, the possibility of *eventually owning* one's piece of land (or a license to practice within a monopolized structure—banking, insurance, law or other social technologies) is viewed as full rights. Being conscious of the not-so-distant past when common people did not have even those rights, citizens view and celebrate these limited rights as full rights.

Mark Twain recognized that appropriation of nature's gifts in unrestricted private title by one person means alienation and loss of rights for others. His article, "Archimedes," in Henry George's paper *The Standard*, July 27, 1889, describes how, if he owned the entire world, all the wealth of the world would be his and all the world's citizens would be his slaves.

While one's lack of full and equal rights is difficult to visualize when a person is accustomed to *exclusive* ownership to what nature provided free for all, it is easy to see if one uses a gift of nature, such as air, that has not yet been alienated from the commons. Air is one of nature's gifts and if a group could claim title to it (when windmills were invented, such efforts were made), each person would have to pay for the right to breathe just as now they have to pay for the right for a place to live.

One notes that water was still free long after land was fully claimed. As population density increased and water became scarce, it became profitable to claim *exclusive title* to water. Whenever those claims of ownership are encoded in law, water sources will develop high capitalized values and society will become accustomed to paying dearly for its drinking water. As one analyzes monopolies, it becomes apparent that *exclusive title* to gifts of nature creates unnecessary social costs while simultaneously creating massive wealth for monopolists. Instead of society paying non-producing monopolists, a proper share of nature's bounty should be distributed to all citizens through *conditional titles* to land, and equal rights to patents and a nation's financial, and communications systems. The secondary monopolies (insurance, health care, law, etc.) are social technologies with modest amounts of tangible, labor-created values. They are eliminated by replacing titles (licenses) with rights to those services.

Pride in Ownership must be maintained

Land is, unquestionably, social wealth. However, the right to one's space on this earth, the pride it returns to its owner, and the care normally given to one's personal property, are compelling reasons to keep land under a *conditional* form of private ownership. If equal rights for all to a share of the production of land are acknowledged through society collecting resource rents, private ownership is socially efficient and fully justifiable. What is unjust is the unrestricted subtle monopolization of what nature freely provides on, above, and under, land. It is necessary to keep private ownership of land and its benefits while eliminating subtle land monopolization and its unavoidable inequities.

The Feudal Origins of Land Titles

Societies have battled for title to land for millennia. One society's violent claim to land is another society's violent loss. Today's landowners are the descendants of the winners of the latest clashes of cultures. After the collapse of the Roman Empire at the hands of the Germanic tribes, the common people regained their rights to the land, and the use of nature's wealth in common again developed a powerful following.[4] Their belief in freedom and natural rights resembles our belief in these principles today.

However, this reversion to social wealth in public ownership came under attack by powerful clans. Petr Kropotkin, that unique historian, describes the repression of these rights as the origin of the modern state: "Only wholesale massacres by the thousand could put a stop to this widely spread popular movement, and it was by the sword, the fire, and the rack that the young states secured their first and decisive victory over the masses of the people."[5] Those people were struggling against imposition of a legal structure which protected *exclusive* title to land, and all the resources on and under the land, previously owned—and used—by all in common.

As described by Kropotkin, the medieval roots of our culture grimly parallel the massive slaughter in many countries of the developing world today. People in these countries are fighting to retain—or reclaim—their right to a fair share of the earth's wealth—resources now owned by the cultural descendants of earlier violent thefts of land. The resemblance here is not a coincidence; current struggles are a continuation of that medieval battle over who shall have rights to nature's wealth and—as we have stated and will be demonstrating further—today's land titles still have remnants of feudal *exclusive* property rights in them. However unjust, if a legal title to land or any other gift of nature can be established, those with unrestricted title can lay claim to the wealth produced by others.

In the 14th century, the sharing of social wealth in common was still practiced by local communities. But, tragically, that century saw the beginning of a 300-year-effort by the aristocracy of Europe to erase all trace of communal rights. Kropotkin explains:

> The village communities were bereft of their folkmotes [community meetings], their courts and independent administration; their lands were confiscated. The guilds were spoilated of their possessions and liberties, and placed under the control, the fancy, and the bribery of the State's official. The cities were divested of their sovereignty, and the very springs of their inner life—the folkmote, the elected justices and administration, the sovereign parish and the sovereign guild—were annihilated; the State's functionary took possession of every link of what formerly was an organic whole. Under that fatal policy and the wars it engendered, whole regions, once populous and wealthy, were laid bare; rich cities became insignificant boroughs; the very roads which connected them with other cities became impracticable. Industry, art, and knowledge fell into decay.[6]

The efforts to alienate the individual from common use of the natural wealth of the land are documented in Britain by the nearly 4,000 enclosure acts passed between 1760 and 1844 that effectively gave legal sanction to this theft.[7] Those enclosure acts were the continued privatizations which, in turn, are the continuations of rent seeking appropriating wealth produced by others.

For the powerful to protect their title further, it was necessary to erase from social memory all traces of the earlier custom of social ownership of social wealth. Kropotkin points out that, "It was taught in the universities and from the pulpit that the institutions in which men formerly used to embody their needs of mutual support could not be tolerated in a properly organized State."[8] Classics for the past 400 years justified that injustice and we hear those justifications yet today: "This is the most efficient and proper social structure."

The classic descriptions of the evolution of capitalism explain how trade and industrial capital usurped the preeminent position of nobility with their historical title to all land. Yet in parts of Europe an elite social class still owns large tracts of land. As late as 1961, the Duke of Bedford, the Duke of Westminster, and the British Crown owned the most valuable sections of London, and large estates still abound throughout the countryside. In fact, at the turn of the 20th century,

> the English upper class consisted ... of around ten thousand people drawn almost entirely from a core of 1,500 families.... The aristocracy owned great estates and houses and works of art—but, above all, they owned land. Well over ninety percent of the acreage of Britain was theirs.[9]

Today's neoliberal philosophies are ongoing efforts to prevent a rekindling of mutual support beliefs and social wealth held in common. Today we are taught—by those who parrot the original disinformation—that an efficient economy requires all property being privately owned with each individual a "free" bargaining agent. To avoid repetition, I suggest returning to the Introduction and read again that analysis on the evolution of *exclusive* titles to nature's wealth being the beating heart of today's monopolies and how their elimination is the answer to most of today's economic problems.

Henry George's and our disagreement with the current *rule of law* is that title to land, or any other gift of nature (mechanical and social technologies), should—since no person built land and all are entitled to their share of nature's wealth—be *conditional. Exclusive title* as opposed to *conditional title* is that remnant of feudal law which is the primary cause of today's inefficient economies creating a wealthy few and an impoverished many.

Private Ownership of Social Wealth moves to America

Parts of America's land ownership were originally structured under the same *rule of law* as in Europe. The "manorial lords of the Hudson Valley" owned huge estates "where the barons controlled completely the lives of their tenants." One such estate in Virginia covered over five million acres and embraced 21 counties.[10] Such excessive greed contributed to the widespread dissatisfactions that fueled the American Revolution.

> Under Governor Benjamin Fletcher, three-quarters of the land in New York was granted to about thirty people. He gave a friend a half million acres for a token annual payment of 30 shillings. Under Lord Cornbury in the early 1700s one grant to a group of speculators was for two million acres.... In 1689, many of the grievances of the poor were mixed up in the farmers' revolt of Jacob Leisler and his group. Leisler was hanged, and the parceling out of huge estates continued.[11] [B]y 1698, New York had given thousands of acres to the Philipses, Van Cortlands, Van Rensselaers, Schuylers, Livingstons and Bayards; by 1754, Virginia had given almost three million acres to the Carters, Beverleys, and Pages—an early example of government "aid" to business men.[12]

Despite the egalitarian rhetoric of the American Revolution and an attempt to place a proclamation in the Declaration of Independence for a "common right of the whole nation to the whole of the land," the powerful looked out for their own interests by changing the wording of Locke's insightful phrase: "All men are entitled to life, liberty and land." This powerful statement that all could understand coming from a highly respected philosopher was a threat to those who subtly monopolized the land, so they restructured those words to "life, liberty and [the meaningless phrase] pursuit of happiness." The substitution in America's Declaration of Independence of phrases which would protect every person's rights to nature's wealth for words that protect only the monopoly rights of a few should alert one to check the meaning and purpose of all laws of all societies carefully. Only portions of the huge estates described below were confiscated, and "speculation in western lands was one of the leading activities of capitalists in those days:"[13]

> Companies were formed in Europe and America to deal in Virginia lands, which were bought up in large tracts at the trifling cost of two cents per acre. This wholesale engrossment soon consumed practically all the most desirable lands and forced the home seeker to purchase from speculators or to settle as a squatter. [Moreover, observes Beard], as the settler sought to escape the speculator by moving westward, the frontier line of speculation advanced.[14]

Some of America's famous leaders were deeply involved:

> In the Ohio Valley a number of rich Virginia planter families, amongst whom were counted both the Lees and the Washingtons, had formed a land company and this, the Ohio Company, founded in 1748, was given a crown grant of half a million acres.[15] [And with] every member of the Georgia legislature but one [having] acquired a personal interest in the speculation schemes, [they sold thirty-five] "million acres to three ... land speculating companies for a total payment of less than $210,000.[16] [That is six-tenths of a cent per acre. Thus,] as the frontier was pushed back during the first half of the nineteenth century, land speculators working with banks [and corrupt legislators] stayed just ahead of new immigrants, buying up land cheap and then reselling it at high profits.[17]

Those who participated in these later land grabs knew well that the route to wealth lay in claiming *exclusive title* to land so that those who followed would have to buy it from them. Whether rented, or sold at high capitalized values, a share of the wealth produced would be siphoned to the owners without expenditure of their labor.

Individuals, such as the butcher's son John Jacob Astor who had title to much of Manhattan Island, became immensely wealthy. Matthew Josephson, in *Robber Barons*, and Peter Lyon, in *To Hell in a Day Coach*, document the greatest land grab in history when the railroads, through control of state and federal governments, obtained unrestricted title to 183 million acres of land (9.3% of the land in the United States). By the turn of the century this included "more than one-third of Florida, one-fourth of North Dakota, Minnesota, and Washington and substantial chunks of 25 other states."[18]

> The state of Texas was the most generous of all: at one point they had actually given away about eight million more acres than they had in their power to bestow; as it finally turned out, they forked over to twelve railroad companies more than thirty-two million acres, which is more real estate than can be fitted inside the boundaries of the state of New York.[19]

Those to whom this land was parceled out had taken care to buy Congress and codify their *exclusive title* in legal statutes (inequality structured into the *rule of law*). The arrival of the railroads provided easy access to these lands and—as Henry George taught us—made them valuable. Instead of immigrants being allowed to choose land on a first-come first-served basis and using its rental value to develop social infrastructure, the land-hungry poor were forced to buy from these profiteers. Land sales by speculators were contracts that siphoned a part of the future labor of those who bought the land to the speculator.

America's celebrated Homestead Act of 1862 came after most of the choice land had already been claimed by speculators. Some 600,000 pioneers received 80 million acres under this act, but this was less than half that allotted to the railroad barons, who were only the latest in a long line of profiteers. These new lords of the land thoroughly understood the legal mechanics of siphoning wealth produced by others to themselves. They knew that all the surplus land had to be owned before their land could have significant value, thus the Homestead Act was vital to their plans of attaining great wealth.

Saleable Land Titles permitted the Mobilization of Capital

Once land had been confiscated from the masses in the Middle Ages, it belonged permanently to the lord of that land and could only be lost through war. When English law changed to permit the sale of land, this created the foundation for modern capitalism. When an entrepreneur wished to speculate by building a factory or ship, land could be mortgaged for that venture. This provided a broader base of wealth to loan against than loaning against potential profits from monopoly trade rights issued to favored friends by royalty.

The privatization of land and resultant mobilization of capital was a key stage in the development of capitalism that expanded rights to more people. However, those *exclusive titles* to nature's wealth still maintained the *structure of law* which permitted nonproducers to claim what is properly social wealth.

An efficient economy will have neither those appropriated values nor the huge blocs of capital currently buying and selling them. Starting from a clean slate, money had to be created to buy those first capitalized values and, when those *exclusive titles* are restructured to *conditional titles* (a return to that clean slate) that amount of money (roughly 60% of all finance capital) must disappear right along with the capitalized values of all monopolies that finance capital had been buying and selling.

Slave labor was also a method to accumulate capital and pockets of slavery remain today. Export platforms in the developing world that avoid taxes and pollution laws and pay dimes per hour for workers to produce items for sale in the developed world—where workers with the same qualifications are paid $6 to $24 an hour—is a simple capital accumulation scheme akin to slavery.

The forced acceptance of opium sales to China a century ago and the turn-a-round sales of drugs to the developed world today accumulates capital.

Charging Japan's well-paid citizens triple the price for Japanese manufactures or food as the same item would cost in Europe or America was also a capital accumulation scheme.

The "Robber Barons" of the late 19th and early 20th centuries accumulated capital at an unnecessarily great cost to all others in America. That cost is not acknowledged because—even with massive destruction of natural wealth (timber, topsoil—etc.), the remaining vast resources could still provide a good living for the relatively small population. (The timber burned to clear the land could have provided a fine set of hardwood furniture for every family on earth and topsoil could have been preserved to feed people for millenniums.)

Through hard work, frugality and/or good fortune, a family owns a valuable piece of land. When the breadwinner's buying power decreases or ceases due to death, tracts of land are sold off piecemeal to maintain the accustomed standard of living. All money from land sales deposited within the banking system as savings become part of the nation's finance capital. Eventually all the tracts of land are sold, some of the money becomes accumulated capital, and the part spent to maintain the family—that also could have been accumulated capital if that person had worked for his or her living—becomes consumed capital.

John Jacob Astor's *exclusive title* to a large share of, and piecemeal sale of, Manhattan Island is probably America's leading example of wealth accumulation through land monopolization. As tracts of land became smaller and smaller, their *use values*—and thus their *capitalized monopoly values*—rose higher and higher. The values (potential capital) unrealized, the capital wasted through high living of heirs and the enormous monopolized values restricting others' rights to land tells us there are better ways to accumulate capital.

A simple adjustment in the law—society collecting resource rents—attains those rights. The "mother of all monopolies" (the private taxation of land) will have been eliminated. Each will have rights to land and their share of the wealth produced.

Profound Thinkers Who Believed in Society Collecting Resource rent

The French Physiocrats were the originators of laissez faire—the philosophy of little government interference. They held as a cornerstone of their beliefs (appropriated from the work of John Locke, William Penn, Baruch Spinoza, and Richard Cantillon 50 to 100 years earlier) that society should collect resource rents. One of their most respected members, Mirabeau the Elder, held that this would increase social efficiency equal to the inventions of writing or money.

David Ricardo formulated the law of rent, which supports the logic of Mirabeau's statement. Put in simple terms, Ricardo's law of rent means that all income above that necessary to sustain labor will be claimed by the owners of the land without the expenditure of their labor. A subtle land monopolist retains ownership of land until some innovative entrepreneur sees its potential for more productive use. The high price demanded effectively siphons a part of the wealth produced by that entrepreneur and society's labor to the previous owner, now the holder of that mortgage and sales contract.

It was Henry George who most clearly understood how Ricardo's law of rent siphoned society's surplus wealth to the owners of land and how that monopoly maintained itself through the ever-rising price of land. He outlined how wealth came directly from land and accrued to the owner; how all wealth above the survival needs of the hard working people flowed to those with title to the land without expenditure of their labor; how these profits capitalized land values ever higher, perpetuating the flow of newly produced wealth to titleholders; how commercial successes were dependent on location and those profits too went largely to owners riding its value up to ever higher levels.

Adam Smith's statement that "every improvement in the circumstances of society raises rent" tells us he knew that title to land claims much of the wealth produced by the increased efficiencies of society.[20] The respected economist John Kenneth Galbraith—although questioning changing tax policy at this late date—accepted the justice of society collecting resource rents. In 1978, the conservative economist Milton Friedman stated, "In my opinion the least bad tax is the property tax on the unimproved value of land."[21]

Earlier philosophers who believed in the free enterprise philosophy of the Physiocrats—"society collecting the land rent"—include Thomas Paine, who is credited with proposing much of the Bill of Rights; William Penn, the founder of Pennsylvania; Herbert Spencer, the noted philosopher in his classic *Social Statics*; Thomas Sperry of the Newcastle Philosophical Society; and philosopher John Stuart Mill. These early economists were not radicals. They all "believed in the *sacredness* of private property, *particularly land*."[22]

The Robert Schalkenbach Foundation lists over 100 more famous thinkers —including Confucius, Moses, Thomas Jefferson, Mark Twain, Henry Ford, John Maynard Keynes, Albert Einstein, President Eisenhower, and several popes—who recognized the principle that the natural product of the land belongs to all citizens, and lists various places in the modern world where these policies have been, at least in part, implemented.[23] In the late 19th century and early 20th century, Henry George's concept of a more efficient *rule of law* had substantial influence and candidates for public office were being advised to take a stand for society collecting resource rents.[24]

But those who owed their fortunes to the structure of property rights and taxes were too well entrenched to be dislodged. Their fear of Henry George's *inclusive* philosophy motivated the funding of neoliberal economics professors and politicians to prevent governments from adopting those policies, silenced the democratic dialog begun by Henry George, and protected their vested monopoly interests.[25]

Just as corporations today fund professors and universities to produce studies that support their products or causes (the pay is good, both in money and identity, and one can find professors to produce studies to back up any cause), those who opposed Henry George's vision paid scholars to bend the truth and thus prevented people from insisting on their democratic rights.

Those corrupt scholars accomplished this feat by distorting economic language and later academics unwittingly continue to teach that elite-protective philosophy. Classical economics clearly points out that finance capital combines three elements of production—resources (land), labor, and industrial capital—to produce a nation's wealth. Biased neoliberal economists combined land with industrial capital leaving only industrial capital and labor as elements of production. Those redefined terms created an economic jargon, confused the public debate, and prevented the spreading of the concept of society collecting resource rents.[26]

Mason Gaffney's and Fred Harrison's analysis of the working papers of these professors leaves no doubt that they were specifically designing their philosophy to eliminate the threat of Henry George's *inclusive rule of law*. This is a replay of Kropotkin's statement, "It was taught in the universities and from the pulpit that the institutions in which men formerly used to embody their needs of mutual support could not be tolerated in a properly organized State."[27]

Commercial Land

Visualize a trade in a primitive society with someone standing by collecting tribute for trading on a particular piece of ground. The landowner does no productive labor—he only monopolizes that land. Of course, to avoid paying tribute, that early trader only needed to move to another piece of land. Today that nearby land would also be claimed.

As Henry George taught us, the closer one approaches the center of commerce, the higher the price of land. Every transit line from the suburbs to a commercial district will raise commercial land values a calculable amount. This high value represents the cheapness and the quantity of trades within any population center and that saving (efficiency of trades) is recognized by the price business is willing to pay for that land.

Because rent lays claim to a large share of the wealth produced by commerce, the land values are very high in large population centers. Land values gradually lower as the distance from the center of population becomes greater and the trades become less frequent and more expensive. In a matter of minutes on an acre in the middle of a city there would be millions of dollars' worth of trades in grain, diamonds, stocks, land, finance capital, or consumer products. A share of each trade is remitted to the landowner as rent: thus the high value of land within population centers.

It is not unusual for commercial land to be valued at three, four, or even 10 times the value of the buildings placed upon it.[28] Probably the highest priced acre in the world was in the center of Tokyo, valued—before prices dropped over 75%—at $1.5 billion. The space of one footprint in Tokyo was valued at $8,000. The land area of the 23 wards of Tokyo was equal in monetary value to the entire land area of the United States. The land upon which the emperor's palace sat was valued at the price of all the land in California. All the land in tiny Japan was worth four times as much as all the land in the America. "In fact, the real estate value of Tokyo [in 1989] at $7.7 trillion [was] so high that, once collateralized and borrowed against (at 80% of [the then] current value), it could buy all the land in the United States for $3.7 trillion, and all the companies on the New York Stock Exchange, NASDAQ and several other exchanges for $2.6 trillion."

Farm Land

The quality of farmland depends on rainfall, growing season, fertility, and accessibility to markets.) Once the quality has lowered to where one can earn only the wages expended in production or distribution (at the margins, the economic edge of profits), the land's value reaches zero.

By exporting food to countries that—if their lands, resources, and trade were not subtly monopolized—could just as well feed themselves, by farming the public Treasury agriculture in the United States has made handsome profits and evaded Ricardo's law of rent. Unearned income (rent) from the subtle monopoly created by those laws is capitalized into, and maintains the value of, land. Under Ricardo's law of rent, but without sales to countries able to feed themselves or government supports (in 2005 in America $28 billion, $350 billion in the richest 30 countries), the price of land would be almost zero while the *equally-shared use value* of the world's farmland would, because it would be feeding more people better, be greater than ever.

Home Sites

In smaller cities of America, a typical $240,000 house will be on a $60,000 lot. In major population centers, it is not uncommon for the same house to cost double, triple, or even 10 times that price. In Honolulu and parts of California a comparable home would be over $1 million and in Washington, DC it would be $1.6 million. As labor and material costs are relatively equal, the price differentials are the costs of land functioning under Ricardo's law of rent. The price of land accurately measures the resource rents paid by producers of wealth to the subtle-monopoly landowners who did no work.

The powerbrokers took from the Physiocrats' free enterprise philosophy only that which protected, and further extended, their wealth and power. As historically most members of legislative bodies were large landholders, naturally they did not accept that society should collect resource rents. If that were to happen, everyone would have immediate rights to their share of nature's wealth. The "divine rights" of private ownership of social wealth siphoning large amounts of wealth from those who produced to those who did not, those capitalized monopoly values bought and sold on the markets, would be converted to "*conditional* rights" where only those who produce are paid. The *use value* of land is then distributed to all through socially collected resource rents funding governments, education, roads, etc.

Take homes for an example: real estate taxes are currently levied mostly on the improvements and only a small part on the land. That tax structure is the key to subtle land monopolization. At 7% interest, the previously described $60,000 lot, if sold, would return $4,200 per year. The taxes on this typical home would be possibly $4,200 and the land possibly $500. Removing all taxes on the house and placing them on the land (for a total of $4,700) and collecting the same tax ($4,700) on all equally-valued unused lots and a lesser—but still substantial—tax on lots of lower *use value*, would convert current privately-collected land rent (a private tax) to socially-collected resource rent. Those lots would then produce no profit and the price of that land drops to zero.

There would be no increase in costs for homeowners. The amount once paid annually in interest on land purchases would now be paid to society as resource rent. Even though the monetized value of the land disappears, its *use value* actually increases. As value in land per se would be eliminated, the purchase price would be only the value of labor and material that built the house. The initial capital required to purchase a home would drop to the cost of building the house or the depreciated value of an older home. The annual cost of resource rent is offset by the even greater reduction in taxes.

Occasionally a city council person will become aware of the social efficiency of taxing unused land within their jurisdiction (if idle land is properly taxed it will quickly be put to use). But these alert local officials quickly find that—frightened by Henry George's exposure of their centuries-old land monopolization scheme—powerbrokers have inserted restrictions into state constitutions and passed laws on local communities' ability to tax land.

Land held in unrestricted private ownership creates high capitalized values. True free enterprise requires breaking that subtle monopoly through *exclusive* title—society should collect the rent. Distribution of land by capitalized value (price) would then be replaced by distribution of land by rental value paid to society. The net cost to the homeowner would be slightly lower (much lower if Mason Gaffney and Fred Harrison's estimation of 35% of national income being resource rent is correct) but there would be no interception of others' labor through private collection of rent on what nature provided.

Oil, copper, iron ore, and the like, while still in the ground, are land and can very properly be privately owned so long as society is paid resource rents. The world has adequate reserves of most of these minerals. It is only richer deposits and cheaper labor in the developing world that make their minerals more available. Under Adam Smith's unequal free market philosophy, *the developed world's more expensive deposits are not mined until the undeveloped world's cheap deposits are exhausted.*

Developing land—clearing, drainage projects, shaping the land, irrigation dams, canals, and so forth—all involving capital expenditures and labor, require special consideration. Those who invest in such improvements should be well paid. However, un*conditional title* to land development becomes *exclusive title* to the land. Currently the government pays a substantial share of development costs. Investors/developers can be fully reimbursed by deducting the remaining costs from resource rents.

The market measures the rent value of land. The resource rent collected by society would be slightly less than that now collected both publicly (taxes) and privately (interest). The price spread of resource rents between the choice sites and lower-valued sites should still be maintained. The current private resource tax (interest or rent) is converted to socially-collected land rent that would be slightly lower than the former combination of taxes and land payments.

If Society Collected Resource rents, other Taxes could be Eliminated

According to Gore Vidal:

> In 1986 the gross revenue of the government was $794 billion. Of that amount, $294 billion was Social Security contributions, which should be subtracted from the National Security State. This leaves $500 billion. Of the $500 billion $286 billion went to defense; $12 billion to foreign arms to our client states; $8 billion to $9 billion to energy, which means, largely, nuclear weapons; $27 billion to veterans' benefits, the sad and constant reminder of the ongoing empire's recklessness; and finally, $142 billion to loans that were spent, over the past forty years, to keep the National Security State at war, hot or cold. So, of 1986's $500 billion in revenue, $475 billion was spent on National Security business.... Other Federal spending, incidentally, came to $177 billion ... which is about the size of the deficit, since only $358 billion was collected in taxes.[29]

In 1929, federal government expenditures were 1% of GNP—at the peak of the Cold War, they were approximately 24%.[30] David Stockman, a member of President Reagan's cabinet, calculated that after deducting bureaucratic waste and payments to

> law firms and lobbyists and trade associations in rows of shining office buildings along K Street in Washington; the consulting firms and contractors; the constituencies of special interests, from schoolteachers to construction workers, to failing businesses and multinational giants, all of whom came to Washington for money and legal protection against the perils of free competition ... that leaves seventeen cents for everything else that Washington does. The FBI and national parks, the county agents and the Foreign Service and the Weather Bureau—all the traditional operations of government—consumed only nine cents of each dollar. The remaining eight cents provided all the grants to state and local governments, for aiding handicapped children or building highways.[31]

The American government no longer keeps track of total land valuations. Extrapolating from 1990 land values of $3.7 trillion,[32] we can safely say 2005 values of land were well over $10 trillion. Resource rents at 4% of value would be over $400 billion per year. That is over three times the percentage of GDP that ran the peaceful American government in 1929[a] and to that must be added the resource rents from oil and minerals. To those rental values we must add profits collected through *socially-owned* banks. Society will have adequate funds for all essential services and the only taxes necessary will be for Social Security and universal health care, which are really insurance premiums.

When necessary to regulate commerce, other taxes are proper but those funds should also be returned to society through social services. For example, ecological taxes can support pollution-free energy development and resource conservation. The proper level of sin taxes (alcohol, tobacco, etc.) will lower disease through lowering consumption and the funds collected would offset health care costs incurred from such habits.

All farmers and business people know that machinery and inventory are relatively easy to obtain; it is the price of land that restricts ownership of farms and businesses. While land prices would drop to zero, *use values* and private ownership rights would actually increase. Commerce would flourish as business people, farmers, and other entrepreneurs—all true producers—would be able to start businesses with only the capital necessary to buy buildings, machinery, and inventory. They do not have to purchase monopoly values that—in the form of *use values*—belong to everyone.

Resource rent being paid to society out of cash flow means only hard working and talented people would own farms and businesses. The mechanism whereby excessive rights of absentee or incompetent landowners intercept the labor of others through *exclusive titles* would be replaced by society receiving the earnings from that social wealth. Labor costs to industries and businesses would be reduced by whatever taxes (both upfront and hidden) labor previously paid. The elimination of sales taxes, income taxes, and a lowering of finance capital costs would make replacing all taxes with society collection of resource rents and loan profits a bargain for any business.

Although society would be enormously richer, land will not have monetized (capitalized) value. Society collecting resource rents would create a modern land commons in which the wealth produced would be distributed relatively equally while retaining the efficiencies of private ownership. Society, not the landowners, puts that value there by increased population, roads, water systems, sewers, electricity, communication systems, etc. The wealth collected through land rent, profits of *socially-owned* banks, and all other rental values collected from nature's wealth and technologies should be returned to the people through those same social services. Opportunities to appropriate unearned

---

[a] The 2007 budget is $2.77 trillion. But Social Security is a paid-for insurance, not rightly part of that budget. With costs hidden in other parts of the budget, the actual cost of the military is far above the $423 billion listed. We will be listing other areas where massive savings are possible (see Conclusion). Assuming Stockman's estimate that only 17 cents of each budget dollar will operate "all the traditional operations of government," those needs in this year's budget are $470 billion. A peaceful economy with full and equal rights, as we propose, will eliminate all other costs.

wealth will be almost nonexistent and all will be well cared for even as all the functions of government are well funded and citizens are well cared for. There will be no taxes beyond that for secure retirements and resource protection.

Michael Hudson and Baruch A. Levine (*Privatization in the Ancient Near East and Classical World*) trace the 5,000 year history of privatization of nature's wealth. Henry George's *rules of law,* restructuring those *exclusive titles* to *conditional titles* (as applied in this thesis), has—in one stroke—retained the claimed efficiencies of privatization (private property, individualism, competition) even as it restores (in modern form) the commons that was the original economic structure for every people on earth.

---

[1] All works of Henry George and many authors writing on him are available from the Robert Schalkenbach Foundation, 41 East 72nd St., NY, NY 10021 (212-988-1680).

[2] Mason Gaffney and Fred Harrison, *The Corruption of Economics,* (London: Shepheard-Walwyn, 1994), pp. 13, 193.

[3] Michael Parenti, *Power and the Powerless* (New York: St. Martin's Press 1978), pp. 184-85, quoting Jean Jacques Rousseau, "A Discourse on the Origins of Inequality," in The *Social Contract and Discourses* (New York: Dutton, 1950), pp. 234-85.

[4] Kropotkin, Petr , *Mutual Aid,* (Boston: Porter Sargent Publishing Co., no date) p. 225.

[5] Ibid.

[6] Ibid., p. 226.

[7] Ibid., pp. 234-35.

[8] Ibid., p. 226. Read also George Renard's *Guilds in the Middle Ages* (New York: Augustus M. Kelley, 1968), chapters 7-8.

[9] Lewis Mumford, *The City in History* (New York: Harcourt Brace Jovanovich, 1961), p. 264; Angela Lambert, *Unquiet Souls* (New York: Harper and Row, 1984), p. 6.

[10] Charles A. Beard, *Economic Interpretation of the Constitution* (New York: Macmillan, 1941), p. 28; Howard Zinn, *A People's History of the United States* (New York: Harper Colophon Books, 1980), p. 48.

[11] Zinn, *People's History,* p. 48. See also Howard Zinn, *The Politics of History* (Chicago: University of Chicago Press, 1990), pp. 61-68.

[12] Herbert Aptheker, *The Colonial Era* (New York: International Publishers, 1966), pp. 37-38.

[13] Zinn, *People's History,* p. 83; Herbert Aptheker, *The American Revolution* (New York: International Publishers, 1985), p. 264, quoted in Beard, *Economic Interpretation,* p. 23; Petr Kropotkin, *The Great French Revolution* (New York: Black Rose Books, 1989), p. 143.

[14] Beard, *Economic Interpretation,* pp. 23, 27-28, quoting C.H. Ambler.

[15] Olwen Hufton, *Europe: Privilege and Protest* (Ithaca, NY: Cornell University Press, 1980), p. 113.

[16] Herbert Aptheker, *Early Years of the Republic* (New York: International Publishers, 1976), p. 125; Abraham Bishop, *Georgia Speculation Unveiled* (Readex Microprint Corporation, 1966), in forward.

[17] James Wessel, Mort Hartman, *Trading the Future* (San Francisco: Institute for Food and Development Policy, 1983), p. 14.

[18] Quoted by Peter Lyon, *To Hell in a Day Coach* (New York: J.B. Lippincott, 1968), p. 6. See also Edward Winslow Martin, *History of the Grange Movement* (New York: Burt Franklin, 1967); Joe E. Feagin, *Urban Real Estate Game* (Engelwood Cliffs, NJ: Prentice-Hall, Inc., 1983), pp. 57-58; speech by U.S. Representative Byron Dorgan, North Dakota, the statistics researched by his staff and quoted in *The North Dakota REC* (May 1984).

[19] Lyon, *To Hell in a Day Coach,* p. 6.

[20] Adam Smith, *The Wealth of Nations* (New York: Modern Library Edition, Random House, 1965), pp. 247, 647, 773-98.

[21] *101 Famous Thinkers on Owning Earth* (New York: Robert Schalkenbach Foundation); Durand Echeverria, *The Maupeou Revolution* (Baton Rouge: Louisiana University Press, 1985), p. 182; Guy Routh, *The Origin of Economic Ideas* (Dobbs Ferry, NY: Sheridan House, 1989), p. 62; John Kenneth

Galbraith, *Economics in Perspective* (New York: Houghton Mifflin, 1987), chapter 5, especially pp. 55, 168; Mark Blaug, *Great American Economists Before Keynes* (Atlantic Highlands, NJ: Humanities Press International, 1986), p. 86.

[22] Herbert Spencer, *Social Statics* (New York: Robert Schalkenbach Foundation, 1995 unabridged edition); Dan Nadudere, *The Political Economy of Imperialism* (London: Zed Books, 1977), p. 186; Phil Grant, *The Wonderful Wealth Machine* (New York: Devon-Adair, 1953), pp. 416, 434-38; Hufton, *Privilege and Protest*, p. 113.

[23] 101 Famous Thinkers.

[24] Eugene M. Tobin, *Organize or Perish* (New York: Greenwood Press, 1986), pp. 14, 21, 56.

[25] Gaffney and Harrison, *Corruption of Economics.*

[26] Ibid.

[27] Kropotkin, *Mutual Aid*, p. 226. Read also George Renard's *Guilds in the Middle Ages* (New York: Augustus M. Kelley, 1968), chapters 7-8.

[28] Grant, *Wonderful Wealth Machine*, pp. 389-95.

[29] Gore Vidal, *"The National Security State: How To Take Back Our Country,"* The Nation, *June 4, 1988, p. 782.*

[30] E.K. Hunt, Howard J. Sherman, *Economics* (New York: Harper and Row, 1990), p. 511.

[31] William Greider, *The Education of David Stockman and Other Americans* (New York: New American Library, 1986), pp. 6, 17.

[32] Samuelson, " Great Global Debtor," p. 40.

3. Henry George's Rule of Law, A Modern Technology Commons

The original meaning of a patent was, "A grant made by a government that confers on an individual fee-simple title to public lands." A land patent as the original meaning of title to land affirms our analysis that all later monopolies were patterned after aristocratic exclusive titles to land. Copying the legal design of land monopolization, later monopolies were structured through exclusive titles to patents and to license holders.

Before the advent of title to social wealth through industrial capital and finance capital, all sustenance for life and all wealth were processed directly from land. Finance capital is the money symbol for industrial, distribution, and operating capital and these factories and distribution systems are only extremely efficient tools to process and distribute products from the land. So the subtle monopolization of finance capital and industrial capital are only extensions of the subtle monopolization of land. When wealth began to be produced by industrial capital as well as land, powerful people undertook to lay claim to (monopolize) those tools for the production of wealth just as historically they had laid claim to (monopolized) land.

If you claim that technology is produced by labor and is not a part of nature, put yourself in the position of the rest of the world when denied its use even if independently invented. Or consider technology that is thousands of years old, patented within monopoly capitalism's *rule of law*, and denied its free use to those who have used it for those millenniums.[a]

We addressed a money system as a social structure known for centuries so—unless it is monopolized to create a monetized value—there is nothing there to own. Patents too are a part of nature waiting to be discovered and

---

[a] Henry George points out that "we *must* treat the elements of nature as common property." *Protection or Free Trade*, p. 280. On pp. 306-08 he addresses many of the monopolies we cover as just forming.

thus honest ownership can only be under conditions that protect the rights of all.

Communication technologies are as much a part of nature as any other technology. Communication systems are a natural monopoly in the same sense as are sewers, water systems, electric systems, natural gas, roads, railroads, and garbage collections. It is well understood that their duplicated services and private ownership is highly wasteful economic nonsense.

To fully understand monopolization, it is important to remember that social technologies are also a part of nature and they too have been monopolized, primarily by license. We address secondary monopolies created by license within a monopoly system later.

Systems of government are also social technologies and any thought of monopolizing governments would be ridiculed. Yet most governments are monopolized through power—witness the firm control of Western governments throughout history by the very monopolies we are exposing.

For centuries—as modern economies developed—the hidden hands of the alert and powerful (those monopolizing governments) were busy structuring property rights to gain, or retain, title to wealth-producing sectors of the economy. Patent laws and stock markets were simultaneously being structured to subtly monopolize technology.

That stock markets are crucial to raising investment capital in a modern economy is a myth. Most stock traders have no contact with new issues of stock and those who do are primarily taking an already established private company public. Most corporate investment needs are financed from profits, liberal depreciation schedules, and borrowing. These are primarily investments in the monopoly structure of patents. They are not investments in production per se.

Expanding markets means increased profits capitalized into the value of a company's stock and, with the potential for profits thoroughly analyzed by the market; those capitalized values are claimed before those profits are banked. "Behind the abstraction known as 'the markets' lurks a set of institutions designed to maximize the wealth and power of the most privileged group of people in the world, the *creditor-rentier* class of the first world and their junior partners in the third."[1] Restructuring *exclusive patent* laws to pay inventors well and place those patents in the public domain will erase those centuries of carefully crafted subtle-monopoly laws.

Under that simple legal change to *conditional patent titles*—the inventors are well paid and their patents placed in the pubic domain—the monopoly structure (offices and labor)—grinding up enormous wealth—disappears, the price of consumer products drop roughly by half and a large share of the capitalized values of stocks through which that unearned wealth was appropriated disappears. Combining those social savings with free trade between equally developed regions, with managed trade between unequally developed regions, and dropping protections in step with the harmonization of previously unequal economies, would protect both labor and capital worldwide.[2] The masochistic destruction of jobs and capital under current internal economies and world trade structure based on monopolization of technology and control of resources would be eliminated.

Capital Destroying Capital

Factories moving offshore for low-paid labor sharply lower buying power. The profits from lower cost production sold on the high-priced markets of the imperial centers go into corporate coffers to be distributed to owners of stock, corporate managers, and stock traders. Those increased profits create higher capitalized values which—so long as there is broad ownership of stocks and an increase in taking in each other's wash, cooking each other hamburgers, or giving each other heart transplants (service industries) so as to maintain the circulation of money—offsets labor's loss of buying power.[a]

By expanding productive capacity without expanding equal buying power, capital destroys capital. It is unrealistic to assume that this will be the first time in history those rising stock and real estate values that have been providing the consumer buying power will not go down and collapse the imperial center's buying power.

Japan's industrial capacity operated at 65.5% of capacity for 12 years and today, 2006, much of the industrialized world is producing at two-thirds capacity. Michael Moffit quotes Stanley J. Mihelick, executive vice-president for production at Goodyear:

> Until we get real wage levels down much closer to those of Brazil's and Korea's, we cannot pass along productivity gains to wages and still be competitive." With factory wages in Mexico and Korea averaging about $3 an hour, compared with U.S. wages of $14 or so, it looks as if we have a long way to go before U.S. wages will even be in the ball park with the competition. That the decline of U.S. industry is the natural and logical outcome of the evolution of the multinational corporate economy over the past twenty-five years has been a bitter pill to swallow and it will become increasingly distasteful as time goes on. *One consequence will be a nasty decline in the standard of living in the United States....* [W]e have the outlines of a true vicious circle: the world economy is dependent on growth in the U.S. economy but the U.S. domestic economy is [now] skewed more towards consumption than production and investment, and this consumption is in turn sustained by borrowing—at home and abroad.... The deal with surplus countries essentially has been as follows: you can run a big trade surplus with us provided that you put the money back into our capital markets.[3]

The excessive accumulation of capital by stateless corporate imperialists and the denial of capital to the world's powerless are two sides of the same coin. There is too little buying power among the dispossessed to purchase all the

---

[a] Forty years ago the United States economy was 30% services and 70% industrial. In 2005, it was 20% industrial and 80% services. We have yet to find out what happens to the world economy when its primary market, a service economy, collapses into a depression. As this is the first service economy, that will be a historical first.

production of industrial capital. When there is already an excess, capital building more industry without developing more consumer buying power will destroy other capital:

> So long as global productive capacity exceeds global demand by such extravagant margins, somebody somewhere in the world has to keep closing factories, old and new.... South Korea will be losing jobs to cheap labor in Thailand and even China may someday lose factories to Bangladesh.[4]

Ford motor's U.S. factories lost $1.6 billion in 2005 yet its credit department and overseas factories brought the year's profits to $2 billion. When China develops brand names and sells cars and other consumer products on the world market 40% below current prices, those overseas profits of Ford, other auto makers, and other consumer products will disappear. So will American and European jobs.

> The world's existing structure of manufacturing facilities, constantly being expanded on cheap labor and new technologies, can now turn out far more goods than the world's consumers can afford to buy.... The auto industry is an uncomplicated example: Auto factories worldwide have the capacity to produce 45 million cars annually for a market that, in the best years, will buy no more than 35 million cars.... Somebody has to close his auto factory and stop producing.[5]

Labor should employ Capital

That capital is properly owned and employed by labor is recognized by Adam Smith. His bible of capitalism, *Wealth of Nations*, states: "Produce is the natural wages of labor. Originally the whole belonged to the labourer. If this had continued all things would have become cheaper, though in appearance many things might have become dearer."[6] The "appearance of becoming dearer" is because each worker would have been fully paid. Things would have been cheaper because purchasing power of those fully-paid workers would have advanced in step with productive capacity and those who once made their living through claiming a share of others' labor would have to turn to productive labor. Those well-paid workers would have purchased more from other fully-paid workers and with that increased buying power others would produce more to take advantage of that market.

In short, purchasing power—which is so hard to generate under current subtle-monopoly rules—would have developed in step with the producing power of easily-built industrial technology. If monopolization could have been avoided, labor would have been fully paid and the world could have developed rapidly without destructive wars.[a]

---

[a] This cannot happen until democracy is established. Theoretically we have democracy today but, as said, that is only theoretical. Once those subtle monopolies are eliminated, a full democracy will emerge. Likewise if a crisis transposes our society

If labor owned the capital it produced, then labor would employ—rather than be employed by—capital. Once subtly monopolized by *exclusive title*, capital's use *can be denied* to labor at any time, *and it will be denied* if no profit is made. The natural order of labor employing tools (capital) is reversed. If land and capital (both industrial and financial) were not subtly monopolized, land, labor, and capital could freely combine to produce social wealth, workers would receive their full wages from what they produced, and the owners of industry would receive full value for use of their capital. Elimination of the subtle monopolization of technology under current stock market and patent structures would increase social efficiency equal to the invention of money.

As all people are stakeholders in their nation's—and the world's—economy, no sector should have excessive rights (monopolization) structured into the *rule of law*. Just as with land, we are accustomed to wealthy people claiming ownership of the nation's industrial capital. We are taught that this is the proper and most efficient social arrangement. Therefore we do not recognize the obvious, capital is social wealth. It is composed of all tools of production, it was produced by labor (capital is but stored labor), those technologies are only a part of nature that has been discovered, and all should be entitled to the opportunity of employing capital, or being employed by it, and receiving a fair share of what is produced.[a]

Capital, however, is often more productive under private ownership and, when this is so, private ownership is justified. In such cases, entrepreneurs—whose special talents lead to increased production—properly buy this capital from those who produced it. A substantial share of society's capital has been justly claimed in this manner. Capital that is obtained by means other than trading useful labor (physical, innovative, or special talent) is an unjust interception of wealth produced by others.

Capital which is more efficient under social ownership belongs to all society, with all citizens receiving the profits. For example, no profits are directly distributed from the increased wealth produced by highways, airports, harbors, or post offices. But the wealth that society is able to produce

---

into a full democracy, restructuring to Henry George's *inclusive rules of law* will eliminate those monopolies.

[a] This thesis is easily tested. Factories are only a series of tools. Without tools you must pay a shop to repair anything. Most homes have those simple tools and carry out simple repairs in a few minutes at no cost. Monopolize those tools in the same manner as industrial technology is monopolized and you have to pay someone else to do those repairs. Likewise, eliminate the monopolization of technology through the patent process and other communities and societies can produce their own consumer products. Two monopolizations have been eliminated, that preventing others' use of a technology and the superstructure—the stock markets—managing that monopoly. This first is proven by the rest of the world quickly industrializing and the second by the roughly 50% drop in price of consumer products that would occur.

and distribute through the *common use* of these natural monopolies is many times more than a normal interest charge on their construction cost. Just as each ones' share of the *use value* of land in a modern commons is realized by all through society collecting resource rent, the efficiency gains of technology are—under the *inclusive rules of law* we address—distributed to all silently and efficiently through cheaper production/distribution costs and no wealth will have been claimed by subtle monopolization.

Social capital,[a] "real" private capital, and "fictitious" capital are all currently lumped together and collectively treated as private capital. Ownership of capital is considered proof that it was justly earned and that the owner deserves compensation for its use. Below we distinguish between social, private, and fictitious capital. Once identified, the proper owners can claim their capital and the profits it produces. Fictitious capital, like that in banking and land monopolization described above and others described below, can be eliminated altogether.

Efficient Socially-Owned Capital

The basic difference between what is properly social capital and private capital is that everybody uses social capital. It forms a natural monopoly, while proper private capital is used only to produce products or services for specific needs of specific people. Capital that is required for society's basic infrastructure (which is by its nature a monopoly and used by all citizens) cannot justly be bought and sold as private property. It is properly part of a modern commons through a modern legal/social structure. This includes not only highways, airports, harbors, and post offices, but also railroads, electric power systems, community water systems, banking and WiFi (wireless fidelity) communications systems. Most will recognize that these natural monopoly infrastructures should be *socially owned.*

Although such facilities and services are publicly held in most Western nations, U.S. citizens are unaccustomed to railroads, electric power systems, banking, and communications being *socially owned.* These are nothing less than natural monopolies, and all claims of efficiency under private ownership are rhetorical covers to hide the siphoning of the fruits of others' labor to those who hold title to those economic crossroads.[7]

Almost 24% of the America is served by consumer-owned electric utilities (13.4% are publicly owned, 10.2% are rural cooperatives). Privately-owned companies charge 42.5% more for electricity than those that are publicly owned. Yet, since they serve population centers with the highest density of customers per mile, privately-owned electricity costs should be

---

[a] "Social capital," as used here, refers to the physical products of labor that benefits all (roads, schools, airports, harbors, etc). The term is also used by some scholars to refer to the unquantified—but real—value of social interconnections that aid the functioning of society, typically meaning a higher education level.

far lower. The difference in electricity costs between privately-owned and publicly-owned electric companies is even greater than these statistics show. Not only do they sell cheap electricity to private companies, the publicly-owned utilities provide enough profits for some of those communities to build swimming pools, stadiums, and parks.[8]

Matthew Josephson's classic *Robber Barons*, Peter Lyon's even more profound *To Hell in a Day Coach*, and Edward Winslow Martin's *History of the Grange Movement* cover how the American railroads were built at public expense. As much as half the funds collected for building them were pocketed and over 9% of the land in the United States was deeded to these railroads. The pocketing of those funds, claiming title to these natural monopolies, and being deeded that land were little more than thefts of public wealth. Martin describes the building of the Union Pacific Railroad as perhaps the most flagrant example but the pattern was typical:

> Who then was Crédit Mobilier? It was but another name for the Pacific Railroad ring. The members were in Congress; they were trustees for the bondholders; they were directors, they were stockholders, they were contractors; in Washington they voted subsidies, in New York they received them, upon the plains they expended them, and in the Crédit Mobilier they divided them. Ever-shifting characters, they were ubiquitous—now engineering a bill, and now a bridge—they received money into one hand as a corporation, and paid into the other as a contractor. As stockholders they owned the road, as mortgagees they had a lien upon it, as directors they contracted for its construction, and as members of Crédit Mobilier they built it.... Reduced to plain English, the story of the Crédit Mobilier is simply this: The men entrusted with the management of the Pacific road made a bargain with themselves to build the road for a sum equal to about twice its actual cost, and pocketed the profits, which have been estimated at about thirty millions of dollars—this immense sum coming out of the taxpayers of the United States.[9]

"By 1870 the states alone had given $228,500,000 in cash, while another $300,000,000 had been paid over by counties and municipalities." Of course those millions of 19th century dollars would be hundreds of billions in inflated 21st century dollars. In the process of building those railroads, promoters skimmed off possibly one-half of this public investment and stockholders' capital, while simultaneously claiming 9.3% of the nation's land through land grants. [10]

With enforced privatizations through imposition of Reaganism/Thatcherism (the first heavy promoters of this philosophy) on the collapsed former Soviet Union, social wealth was being placed under *exclusive* private ownership in the 1990s at a rate that makes America's robber barons of the late 19th and early 20th centuries look like country bumpkins. Those defeated nations were paid pennies on the dollar to give up title to their natural wealth, their banks, and their limited industrial capital. The citizenry, of course, have little to say. In many cases, if not most, one member of these less than honest groups (to put it mildly) would be signing as government agent and another was the buyer.

Obviously there is no savings to society from the private ownership of a natural monopoly such as railroads, electricity, post offices, power systems, sewers, water systems, communication systems, etc. And, as shown in the communications chapter (5), the true cost of low-frequency WiFi—when properly structured under a public authority and used in common—would be only pennies per dollar of current costs.

Basic infrastructure (roads, railroads, water, electricity, sewers, communications, etc.) is integral to a nation. *Society is a machine*; even though these basic facilities do not directly produce anything, a modern society cannot function without them. They are an integral part of production and are just as important to social efficiency as modern factories.

To demonstrate this, compare the labor costs of a society with an undeveloped infrastructure to those of a society that is developed. Vacation to any wilderness park, hike for a day, and calculate how efficient virtually any economic activity, such as sending and receiving mail, would be from that spot. In the 18th century, a letter traveling by U.S. mail from New York to Virginia (400 miles) took four to eight weeks and cost 60 cents a page.[11] Today it is 39 cents (possibly equal to less then a penny 200 years ago) for several pages anywhere in the nation and that letter normally arrives within 1 to 3 days. When China built a road into the almost inaccessible Tibet, the price of a box of matches dropped from one sheep to two pounds of wool.[12]

Efficient Privately-Owned Capital

Commercial activities producing for variable individual needs rather than everybody's needs are properly privately owned. As has been demonstrated in the former Soviet Union, the thousands of personal preferences (clothes, furniture, jewelry, hobbies, recreational activities, etc.) cannot be provided efficiently by a public authority. Such personal needs can only be assessed by perceptive and talented individuals close enough to recognize and fulfill those needs. The capital to provide such services is more productive under private ownership.

Most of the construction and production for basic social infrastructure operated under public authority is quite properly provided by tens of thousands of privately-owned industries. This free-enterprise, privately-owned capital can, under contract, accommodate the needs of public institutions. We see this every day in contracts to build that infrastructure.

Fictitious Capital

Few economists agree on exactly what constitutes capital. Most include all wealth that produces a profit (titles, stocks, bonds, etc.). But—although the wealth this paper represents has a firm claim on part of society's income—much of it was skimmed off and resurfaced in another investment. The skimmed off share of that first certificate of investment is properly defined as *fictitious capital.* Bonds used to construct harbors, deepen riverbeds, and build railroads represent true capital. But if 50% were pocketed and reinvested elsewhere, that leaves two dollars in claims against each dollar of value.

In the previous example of building the Union Pacific Railroad, half the money was used to build; the other half was pocketed and reinvested elsewhere. The share of those certificates that had a claim on social production yet had produced nothing, were fraudulent. This fictitious capital may represent wealth to the owners, but it is not, on balance, wealth to society. Those debt instruments that build only half the industrial capital as promised are 50% fictitious capital.

There are three physical foundations to production—land, labor, and capital. Land commands rent, labor is paid wages, and honest interest can only be for the productive use of true capital. Subtle patent monopolies capitalize stock values far above tangible values and those high values demand profits. Through those excess profits on unearned wealth, the production of others' labor is siphoned from those who produce to those who produced nothing. The share of capital that demands payment where no labor value has been expended is properly labeled "*fictitious capital.*"

We have covered the wealth appropriated through unearned profits of banking and *exclusive title* to land and patents. The same is true of the unearned wealth of monopolies we have yet to address. Though that money buys and sells monopoly values in today's monopolized economies, the property rights structure under which that wealth was appropriated was—and is—unequal. Restructure to a modern commons throughout the economy and those blocs of capital currently buying and selling those appropriated values are no longer necessary even as economic efficiency rapidly increases. As proven by the increase in economic efficiency when the capitalized values they were buying and selling were transposed to roughly *equally-shared use values*, it was fictitious capital all the time.

Yes a large share of that appropriated capital built industries, water systems, sewer systems, etc. But the problem is that it was unearned and we have thoroughly documented that—if there is a shortage of finance capital—a *socially-owned* banking system can create money for a nation's infrastructure and, when under crisis or when first developing a region, it can be created for any essential need. If maintaining investment integrity required a debt—as typically it will—there would still be no appropriation of wealth. Payments, plus interest, cycle back into bonds to build and maintain more infrastructures. To maintain a stable money supply, required reserves can be, within reasonable limits, increased or decreased.

Invention, a Social Process

> There is no isolated, self-sufficing individual. All production is, in fact, a production in and by the help of the community, and all wealth is such only in society. Within the human period of the race development, it is safe to say, no individual has fallen into industrial isolation, so as to produce any one useful article by his own independent effort alone. Even where there is no mechanical cooperation, men are always guided by the experience of others. —Thorstein Veblen

These words from one of America's eminent philosophers are well spoken. The long march of technology leading up to the present sophisticated level is based upon thousands of earlier discoveries—fire, smelting, the wheel, lathe, and screw—and untold millions of improvements on those basic innovations.[13] Many primitive, but revolutionary, technologies were discovered by Asian and Arab societies. Greek, Roman, and other cultures improved upon these methods, which were—in turn—used by later Western cultures. As a social process built upon the insights of others, Stuart Chase's list of inventions of 5000 years ago barely touches the subject:

> The generic Egyptian of 3,000 B.C., though unacquainted with iron, was an expert metallurgist in the less refractory metals. He could smelt them, draw them into wire, beat them into sheets, cast them into molds, emboss, chase, engrave, inlay, and enamel them. He had invented the lathe and the potter's wheel and could glaze and enamel earthenware. He was an expert woodworker, joiner and carver. He was an admirable sculptor, draftsman and painter. He was, and is, the world's mightiest architect in stone. He made sea-going ships. He had devised the loom, and knew how to weave cotton to such fineness that we can only distinguish it from silk by the microscope. His language was rich, and he engrossed it in the handsomest system of written characters ever produced. He made excellent paper, and upon it beautiful literature was written.... He had invented most of the hand tools now in existence.... He had worked out the rudiments of astronomy and mathematics.[14]

There were also wedges, drills, wheels, pulleys, and gears—all were necessary before modern machines were possible. There had to be countless earlier inventions, back to the control of fire, before the Egyptians could have reached even that level of technology.

Not only does every modern invention rest on millions of insights going back to antiquity, its development requires thousands of people with special talents. For example, a British scientist's accidental discovery of penicillin has benefited almost every person in modern civilization. More people worked to develop and produce this antibiotic for the wounded in WWII than worked on the atomic bomb, and they were all funded with public money. Yet the drug was patented by an American who recognized that, if he could obtain that patent, he would have a subtle monopoly with a capitalized value that would lay claim to vast wealth although he had neither created nor produced anything.[15]

Every innovation is a part of nature. Just like land, oil, coal, iron ore, or any of nature's wealth, if something is to be discovered it had to have been there all the time. As technology is a part of nature that has been discovered, everybody should share its fruits. Inventions not only use the insights of millions of people throughout history and prehistory, they require the support and skills of millions of present workers as well. Stuart Chase estimated that at least 5,000 people were involved in contributing data to the writing of his book and they depended on others for their knowledge.

These people provided tools, materials, and services: pencils, paper, graphite, rubber, lead, typewriters, telephones, cars, electricity, typing, printing presses, book distribution, banking, and so forth. The people directly involved in Chase's knowledge required educators, authors of textbooks, and their educators, ad infinitum. Every one of these consumer items required the labor and skills of thousands of people, some in distant parts of the world (such as producers of rubber or tin). Though the labor charge of some is infinitesimal, each is real and definite. Collectively they accumulate a substantial, though incalculable, value.[16]

While the contribution of any one person to the pool of social knowledge is truly small, the wealth diverted to those who own the patents to social knowledge can be substantial. It has been estimated that, if the developing world were capitalized to the level of the developed world, the royalty claims would be $1 trillion a year. These royalties would normally be going to people who "own" these efficient technologies but neither invented anything nor labored productively for this wealth. They are designed commercial chokepoints structured into the *rule of law* and the subtle monopolization of these tools of production (technology) permits huge overcharges that siphon wealth produced by others to owners of patents.

Consider how expensive consumer products would be if the use of wheels, levers, gears, fire, and thousands of other early inventions required the payment of royalties. By our calculations, half the costs of consumer products operate the offices and staff overseeing the patent monopoly system (the stock market) or go to patent holders. Those huge overcharges create excessive stock market values which become the blocs of unearned wealth owned by monopolists that—through restructuring *exclusive titles* to nature's wealth (patents in this case) to *conditional titles*—disappear as they are transformed into efficient, relatively *equally-shared, use values.*

Inventors rarely receive much reward for their discoveries and innovations. The few who are compensated receive but a small share of the tribute charged by those who own this social wealth. That a small number of powerful people subtly monopolize inventions—and ever afterwards siphon to themselves the wealth produced by others—defies both decency and justice. This was well known to prominent inventors and industrialists such as Thomas A. Edison and Henry Ford. Both "agreed that all patent laws should be repealed since they benefit the manufacturer and not the inventor."[17]

We disagree with patent laws being repealed. They should be redesigned to be a part of a modern commons within the *inclusive rules of law* of

Henry George in which any person can use that technology by paying those inventors well and placing those patents in the public domain (see below).

Capitalizing Actual and Fictitious Values

Inventions are a "more or less costless store of knowledge [that] is captured by monopoly capital and protected in order to make it secret and a 'rare and scarce commodity,' for sale at monopoly price[s]. So far as inventions are concerned a price is put on them *not because they are scarce* but *in order to make them scarce* to those who want to use them."[18]

The patent structure capitalizes value far above tangible values and, through those excess profits and without expenditure of their labor, intercepts wealth produced by others. Where inventions once went unchanged for decades or even centuries, many, if not most, patents are now obsolete before their 20 year life expires. By the time a key patent has run out, newer patents are able to boost efficiency yet more. As many of the earlier technologies are still essential to production, the owners of the latest patents control both the latest technologies and the expired patents of support technologies. Honda's *exclusive* ownership of patents on the stratified charge engine, even though the basic principles for this crucial technology were invented 100 years ago, makes all this quite evident.

Corporations are in such powerful bargaining positions that only occasionally will a new invention pose a threat to them. As corporate control of other critical patents limits the inventor's options, these patents are bought for a fraction of their true value, or they are patented around and the inventor receives nothing. Controlling markets is integral to controlling patents:

> Any move by the neo-colonial state to revoke the patent law as a defensive measure would have very limited results since the market belongs to the monopolies. This becomes quite clear when it is realized that the other markets to which such products would be exported would still have such legislation protecting the same patents, and the transnational corporation would be in a position to require compliance. The mere ownership without the actual know-how which is guarded by the monopoly at headquarters would be useless. This is the whole point about monopoly. The world imperialist monopoly market would not exist if such a system of market control were not in operation.[19]

We view the inventions of 400 to 1100 years ago as primitive, yet in their time these simple inventions could produce—with less labor—both more and better products. Someone powerful enough to control these new techniques could trade one day's work for two, three, five, ten or as many days' production of other people's labor as the efficiency of his invention and political power allowed.

For example, the invention of the windmill was extremely valuable. If it could be monopolized, its owners could siphon to themselves the production of large amounts of others' labor. This potential created a dispute between the nobles, priests, and emperor "as to which one the wind belonged."[20] A 17th century French patent granted such a right to selected owners of windmills."[21]

However hard they tried, claiming ownership of the wind was quite difficult. But it was not so with other technologies. The water mill, first used in Europe during the 10th century, permitted one worker to replace as many as 10 others. A stone planer eliminated seven workers out of eight. One worker with an Owens bottle machine could do the work of 18 hand blowers.[22] Modern technology has created even greater efficiency gains. Many credit the steam engine with the greatest single increase in productive efficiency, but Stuart Chase cites a study by C.M. Ripley of work costing $230 done by hand labor that would cost only $5 using electric power.[23] Modern electric furnaces and continuous casting have brought the direct labor expended in the steel industry down to only 1.8 hours per ton of steel produced.[24]

The owner of that first water mill was able to trade his single day's work, grinding grain, for seven days' labor of a woodworker or blacksmith. In effect he was paid for seven days while working one. The owner of a patented stone planer would likely gain five days' value for only one of his own. A owning a patented Owens bottle machine could probably have claimed 12 days' pay for each day's labor. If the manufacturer in Ripley's study had been able to patent that efficiency, he could have charged 20 to 30-times the labor value in his product. However—just like claiming ownership of the wind—it would be difficult to claim *exclusive title* to electricity and that accounts for the drop in costs in Ripley's study.

Whether a market is in land or corporate stock what is being bought and sold under current property rights are primarily values produced by nature—or an aspect of nature—properly belonging to all in relatively equal shares. That value has been confiscated by the cunning and powerful through *exclusive title* to the various aspects of nature's wealth and those unearned values then capitalized in the markets by a factor of 10 to 30 times.

Royalty conferring Monopoly Trading Rights is the Origin of Patent Royalties

That the owners of patents are entitled to *royalties* exposes the feudal origin of the term. Patent rights to land and inventions were conferred upon favorites by kings and queens, with the understanding that the person so favored would share the earnings—royalties. In short, the origin of patents is indistinguishable from paying bribes for the privilege of doing business. Such bribes were the precursors of today's patent royalties.[25] *Exclusive title* to patents, as opposed to *conditional title* (Henry George's concept though he may have rarely used that term), is the *remnant of feudal patent law* that must be restructured to attain full rights for all to the benefits of ever-more efficient technology.

The Ever-increasing Efficiencies of Technology

In a final analysis, the foundation of most law is power expressed through military strength. Long before governments protected patents, they were protected by violence. "The struggle against rural trading and against rural handicrafts lasted at least seven or eight hundred years.... All through the fourteenth century regular armed expeditions were sent out against all the villages in the neighborhood and looms or fulling vats were broken or carried away."[26] Those early claims to technology, enforced by violence, were the forerunners of today's industrial patents. Those who would control technology have just become more sophisticated. They encode these *exclusive* rights in legal titles. Today, being accustomed to it—and unaware of society's large losses—we accept this as normal.

The growing efficiency of textile machinery started the Industrial Revolution. Primitive looms were improved upon by inventions such as Kay's flying shuttle, Hargreave's spinning jenny, Crompton's "mule," and the power loom. Between 1773 and 1795, the labor time to process 100 pounds of cotton went from 50,000 hours to 300 hours, an efficiency gain of 16,666%.[27] That efficiency gain within a time span of only 22 years exposes how the owners of these technologies quickly dominated world trade. Quite simply, technology was not shared. It was subtly monopolized through restricting the rights of production to the owners of patents.

The widespread use of machine weaving came about only because the technology was copied and the patents ignored. That 16,666% gain in 22 years is dwarfed by 150 power looms in Formosa weaving 24 hours a day under the watchful eyes of only one agile female operator on roller skates.[28] This is a gain of hundreds of thousands, if not millions, of times in efficiency. The labor component in the price of a yard of cloth produced by modern industry is small. This includes the labor to smelt the ore and fabricate the machines which is stored in that capital.

The economically powerful will say they are not claiming the production of anyone else's labor as there is hardly any labor involved. But this is exactly how wealth is siphoned to those who subtly monopolize the tools of production. The price charged for those products is far above the cost of production and others are forced to trade large amounts of their labor for what was produced with that small amount of labor.

All society is denied the full benefit of cheap industrial goods when labor is charged more than they are paid to produce that product. If a product requires one hour's labor to produce and distribute, and then sells for three hours' labor value, it effectively siphons away the value produced by two hours of labor. (If that production is traded to a country where equally-productive labor is paid one-third as much to produce the product, it siphons away nine hours of labor.)[29] Standard economics and accounting do not measure this overcharge because it shows up in stock prices far beyond intrinsic value. If that cloth were priced relative to the price paid labor to produce it (including fair interest for the stored labor value represented by that machinery) then it would be priced within reach of the world's low-paid labor.

A bushel of wheat required three hours to produce in 1830 but only 10 minutes in 1900.[30] A call to Montana State University in Bozeman revealed that in 1986 it took only 3.2 minutes of labor to produce one bushel of dry-land Montana wheat. Other crops have similar efficiency gains.

Railroad labor costs per ton-mile in 2006 are roughly only 2% that required 70 years earlier, and that 500% efficiency gain is dwarfed by the five million percent gain in transportation efficiency over the horse and wagon only 180 years earlier.

The public did receive a large share of the labor savings in textiles, agriculture, transportation, and other technologies. With the common people's newly won rights (the U.S. Constitution and Bill of Rights), and with the enormously wealthy and sparsely inhabited lands of the Americas, the gains were just too great for the powerful to claim them all. However—due to the failure to increase the buying power of all labor in step with the productivity of capital—there is much more production forgone and wasted than that which society so gratefully receives.

Patent laws evolved specifically to claim title to the gains of technology. With multiple patents—occasionally with only one key patent controlling markets—the owners of technology siphon to themselves large amounts of the production of others' labor.

Ownership of a key technology, the telephone, was Bell Telephone's advantage when that subtle monopoly was established. (Inventions not controlled by Bell, such as the dial phone, were suppressed for many years.) The telegraph and telephone reduced communication costs by an amount comparable to the savings created by new technology in textiles and transportation. These efficiency gains of technology, protected by patents, produced the subtle monopoly profits that established Bell Telephone, a corporation larger than any in textiles or transportation. At 10 times the capacity for 10% the cost (1% the cost per unit of capacity), today's WiFi technology, assuming they are not denied those powerful low frequency spectrums, has the potential of increasing communications efficiency far more than those early gains. In fact, those efficiencies are still advancing rapidly and this has the potential for the entire world gaining their freedom.

Henry Ford's assembly line was a milestone in industrial technology that rapidly picked up the pace of the Industrial Revolution:

> The factory is not a new tool but an organization of production that eliminates the periods of idleness in the use of tools, machines, and human beings that are characteristic of agrarian and artisan production. In the artisan's shop the saw, chisel, file, and so forth are idle while the hammer is being used. In the factory all the tools are simultaneously in use in the hands of specialized workers; production is "in line" rather than "in series." But production in line requires a large scale of to-

> tal output before it becomes feasible. The division of labor is limited by the extent of the market, as Adam Smith told us. But transportation, urbanization, and international trade provided a market of sufficient scale.[31]

During 1913 alone, the time required to assemble an automobile dropped from 728 minutes to 93. Until that year, the wage rate averaged $2.50 for a 10-hour day. Ford doubled the daily wages of his workers and reduced their hours from ten to eight, all while lowering the price of his cars.[32] This was unheard of in those times and drew much criticism from business and the press.

What Ford knew, and others did not, was that the profits were so large that with that 800% efficiency gain the wages could have been increased to almost $20 per day. Ford was strongly opposed by his managers and other investors. But Emerson had reached Ford on the morality of not maximizing the profit potential of his monopoly.

Attempts were made to subtly monopolize the emerging auto industry. George Baldwin Seldon, a patent lawyer, understood that—as the law was structured—patents laid claim to wealth produced by others. In 1899,

> he set his mind to working out the precise legal definition and wording of a patent that would give him the sole right to license and charge royalties on future automobile development in America.... Seldon had gone into partnership with a group of Wall Street investors who saw their chance to cut themselves in on the profits of the growing American car industry.[33]

The near success of Seldon and his partners in patenting the automobile illustrates the basic injustice of the current patent structure. Neither Seldon nor these investors had anything to do with the invention of automobiles. The first ones had been built in Europe 14 years earlier and virtually hundreds of auto companies were already in existence. Yet, if anyone had succeeded in patenting the process of building automobiles, every purchaser of an automobile would have had a part of the production of his or her labor siphoned to the owners of that patent who had invented nothing and had done no work.

Seldon's attempt at patenting the principle of the automobile is being successfully accomplished today in the patenting of processes. Corporations are being formed to patent embryo transfers, gene splicing, other advanced medical procedures—even title to human genes and genes of plants domesticated by primitive societies thousands of years ago. Any doctor who wishes to use these new procedures and any farmer who grows a patented plant has to obtain a license and pay a royalty.[34]

The current race to patent human genes clearly outlines the subtle-monopoly cost of patent laws. There are thousands of human genes that directly affect human health. As patent laws now stand, some corporation is going to have a patent on (own) each gene. Let us say that there are 300 genes to be studied in a standard gene test and the royalty to be paid to each patent holder only $1 per gene. If a couple wishes to test themselves for defective genes before conception or their unborn child shortly after conception, the cost would be $300 (60 minutes, July 29, 2001, suggested the possibility of $1,000 royalties).

This added tax—though common to medical equipment and drugs—has not previously been added to the cost of an operation or food crops. If ownership of procedures and food plants had been established years ago, every bill for an operation and the cost for every plate of food would have had royalties added. Only those licensed by the patent holder could perform operations or raise crops and the added charges would siphon wealth to whoever owned the patent rights. Every future improvement in patented surgical procedures or improved crop strains would also be patented and, as technological improvement is ongoing, the patent's subtle monopoly would never run out. Thus Microsoft's tens of billions of dollars of software overcharges—all built from purchasing the DOS computer operating system for $3,000 and patenting it—led to later patents eventually valuing Microsoft at hundreds of billions of dollars. The cost to society can be imagined if each producer or service provider had to pay a patent holder for the use of fire, wheels, wedges, levers, and gears. Inversely, the savings are evident in their free use because they are not patented.

About 7,000 patents worldwide are based upon indigenous knowledge of India. After spending millions to get one plagiarized patent invalidated, India is creating a 30-million-page Traditional Knowledge Data Library (TKDL) to be available to every patent office in the world.[35]

There is one recent and remarkable exception to this rule. In parts of Africa, "as many as sixty percent of the people over age fifty-five were partly or completely blind" from becoming infected with a parasitic worm. Possibly 18 million people were affected. The pharmaceutical corporation Merck and Company owned the patent on a drug (*Ivermectin*) used to kill worms in animals. In October 1987, Merck announced they would provide this drug free of charge for Africans afflicted with this parasite. The company chairman, Dr. P. Roy Vagelos, noted, "It became apparent that people in need were unable to purchase it."[36] Here the loss to society from *exclusive title* was so obvious and devastating that these corporate executives made a moral decision to save the sight of millions of people. The cost to them was negligible; the gain to society was beyond measure.

Cuba's plan to restore vision to 4.5 million treatable blind Latin Americans (100,000 already treated) over the next 10 years and Cuban doctors at work in many impoverished areas of the world, Cuban education equaling the best in the world, and Venezuela and Bolivia in the early stages of copying Cuban successes are further examples of how cooperation can quickly alleviate poverty while monopolizations only entrench it deeper.

An intense battle was fought over life saving drugs for AIDS victims. These drugs can be produced for a tiny fraction of the monopoly prices currently asked. Even at that fractional price few in the impoverished world can afford those essential drugs and at the monopolized price almost no one can afford them. Drug companies have reneged on agreements to lower prices for Aids victims in Africa and that struggle is still on-going (2006).

There is a loss to society from *exclusive* control of any technology, but it is usually not as obvious as in these dramatic examples, where the patent rules of exclusive use were abandoned. These examples demonstrate the original morality of the medical community when "*to patent an essential medicine was considered morally indefensible.*"[37] It is also morally indefensible for other inventions crucial to society. The Gaviotas community—regenerating the primeval Amazon forest of Colombia's barren Los Llanos plains while building a model community using modern production methods to live off the land—does not believe in patenting technology. Its inventions—such as a cheap, 100-pound, wind-mill driven water pump and cost-free, maintenance free air conditioning—are spreading throughout Latin America.[38]

Innovation and technology thus create large reductions in labor costs in all segments of the economy. Most are more modest than the previous examples, but reductions of 90% are common and "from 1945 to 1970, the average increase in efficiency output per hour was 34-40% per decade."[39] Such savings do not exert the immediate shock to the economy that these numbers suggest. It takes time to retool industries and these corporations are in no hurry to destroy the value of their old production and distribution complexes.

This subchapter alerts us that—if technology had been shared instead of monopolized—the entire world could have industrialized in step with the increased efficiencies of technology. Throughout those centuries—assuming equal rights to the fruits of nature had been taught as opposed to the teachings of Adam Smith—there would have been little poverty and few wars. With each enjoying full and equal *use rights*, the world would have been—at all times—many times richer in the form of *use values* than they were under monopolized values.

Most wars and poverty throughout the world today have their origins in the millions of laws the past 700 plus years through which the powerful monopolized technology. The two most obvious were: (1) Kaiser Wilhelm buying technology wholesale from his grandmother, England's Queen Victoria and cousin, King George V.[40] That breach of monopolist's absolute rule to never transfer technology to any other nation was the direct cause of WWI and WWII. (2) The massive suppression of the world's breaks for freedom the past 65 years. That this is conscious policy is again proven by providing technology to the defeated nations, Germany and Japan, and to Southeast Asia so as to halt fast expanding socialism with their opposing rule of law. That accident of history—technology allowed to develop outside the *imperial centers of capital*—again threatens to collapse the monopoly system.

The overcharges of the monopoly system cannot exist if labor is fully paid for their work. It only appears proper because people are accustomed to a subsistence wage for most labor, equally accustomed to all increased profits going to owners and management, and unaware of how rapidly that technology would spread around the world if capital were accumulated along the guidelines in this treatise (*conditional* patent titles, labor fully and equally paid, and productive jobs shared by all). Under those restructured rights, workers would have buying power, and technology would be regionally available to produce desired products, capital will have been accumulated to finance it all simply through the creation of money and the developing world being fully paid for their resources and labor.

A Nation's Wealth is Measured by, and Siphoned to Titleholders through, Capitalized Values

Shares in corporations are sold with the price based on how profitable they are expected to be—their capitalized value. This idea proved to be a real bonanza. Where conservative business people typically estimated the capitalized value of the company at 10 times the yearly profit, the stock markets—anticipating future increases in profits—capitalized these values far higher, frequently 20 to 30 times annual profits and occasionally even more. It is not uncommon for the price of stock going public (called IPOs, initial price offerings) to jump 500% the first week. This capital accumulation bonanza initially claims a share of a nation's loans and, when success is sustained, becomes a value backing its share of the money supply.

All in one stroke, an individual or group could lay claim to the efficiency of a technology through capitalizing its value and selling shares to investors. This siphoning of the production of others' labor—through the mechanism of capitalizing values of technology—concentrated wealth produced by the many into the hands of a few, was christened accumulated capital, and gave capitalism its name.

Through carefully structured laws laying claim to the wealth produced by nature and through technology, which is a part of nature utilized to increase the efficiencies of labor, the hidden hand of the wealthy and powerful kept claiming an ever-larger share of the wealth produced.

Labor, just as naturally, tried to retain or reclaim what they produced. The rights gained in the American Revolution and enshrined in its Constitution—and the natural justice of those rights—eventually increased the power and income of labor. This and the expansion of unnecessary labor as summarized in the next chapter led to more people retaining a greater share of society's wealth.[a] With these savings more broadly distributed, there

[a] A large share of the massive wealth distributed had been appropriated from the periphery of empire by imposed inequalities in trade and outright theft. That world

evolved the present diversified markets to sell shares in industry and concentrate money capital.

Most of the wealth measured by capitalized values is claimed by the various monopolies we are exposing. If these excessive rights of property were replaced by the rights of society to collect resource rents (a modern land commons), and the right for any person to use any technology through paying inventors well and placing inventions in the public domain (a modern technology commons), if all had full and equal rights to created money and finance capital, if productive jobs were shared, and if productive labor were fully paid, all society would be wealthier even though monetized (capitalized) wealth would be far lower.

By removing these subtle monopolizations, sharing the resultant fully-productive jobs, and paying labor fully for what it produces, measured values (the price of consumer products) would equal the rental value of resources, the labor, and the capital (stored labor) that produced that wealth.

The Financial Structure to Harvest the Profits of Subtly-Monopolized Patents

As that is where the profits from *exclusive title*s to patents are collected, the battle for corporate ownership is centered in the stock market. Millions of hours are spent by speculators (they call themselves investors) trying to figure out which company is going to increase its capitalized value. The game is calculating profits that will translate into capitalized value. It is viewed as a simple method of keeping score. But claiming the production of others' labor—through profits from shares in the nation's industry as technology continually replaces labor—is the underlying theme. Values properly shared by all through lower prices are claimed by the shareowners of the new industrial technology. Value claimed by monopolists is capitalized, sold or borrowed against, and that multiple of annual wealth appropriation becomes finance capital. Through restructuring *exclusive titles* to patents to *conditional titles*, creating a modern technology commons, those monopolized values and huge blocs of finance capital are—in the form of lower prices—transposed into relatively *equally-shared use values.*

Lester Thurow explains that the impoverishment of many while wealth is accumulated by a lucky few is due to "the process of capitalizing disequilibrium" (distortions of trade, either internal or external, and thus distortions of values) and that "patient savings and reinvestment has little or nothing" to do with generating large fortunes.[41]

> at any moment in time, the highly skewed distribution of wealth is the product of two approximately equal factors—instant fortunes and inherited wealth. Inherited

---

trade story is told in the simultaneously published *Economic Democracy: A Grand Strategy for World Peace and Prosperity* by this author.

> fortunes, however, were themselves created in a process of instant wealth in an earlier generation. *These instant fortunes occur because new long-term disequilibriums (sic) in the real capital market are capitalized in the financial markets....* Those who are lucky and end up owning the stocks that are capitalized at high multiples win large fortunes in the random walk. Once fortunes are created, they are husbanded, augmented, and passed on, not because of "homo economicus" [economic man] desires to store up future consumption but because of desires for power within the family, economy, or society.[42]

Of course, the small fortunes accumulated by the upper middle class are from these same disequilibria in the value of land and capital. Except by violence or trickery (those *exclusive titles* to the wealth of nature), how else can wealth beyond what one produces be accumulated? The income demanded by those appropriated values is a private tax upon the rest of society, and quite accurately labeled *air*. "By reducing air to vendability, scarcity could be capitalized. Business would be richer—and every man, woman and child in the country would be poorer."[43]

A study of the market over a full boom and bust cycle will find these fictitious values developing in most stocks. The reasons given may be many but the underlying cause is clear: the steady rise in the nation's efficiency is captured by—and mirrored in—stock and land values created through appropriating wealth which should have been—and under a modern commons would have been—relatively equally distributed to all.

Every speculator dreams of becoming wealthy by owning some of these stocks or land. The powerful and cunning—with better than even odds—buy and sell in rhythm with the inflation and deflation of stock and land prices to lay claim to much of this new wealth.

Those who win the gamble on who will own the world's land and industrial and distributive technology are freed from the necessity of laboring for their living. This is not a contradiction. Their speculative efforts are certainly labor, however—when unnecessary—that labor is fictitious and such earnings are first appropriations of wealth properly distributed to all and later they are the winnings of bets as some win and some lose in the gambling casinos called stock markets. .

Capitalizing values is necessary to decide the sale price of a business. However, not only should everyone involved receive proper compensation for his or her labor, innovations, and risk; society should receive its share. Society not only provided tens of thousands of necessary preceding innovations; it also provided the schools, skills, tools, labor, markets, and infrastructure. Nature provided the resources, including the inventions that were waiting to be discovered. Thus the *conditional title* to patents is an extension of Henry George's concept of *conditional title* to land.

There is a necessity for a stock market. However, that the stock market's primary purpose is financing the nation's business is pure fiction; trades in the stock market have little to do with capital investment:

> Buying a stock from a broker does not add one red cent to the corporate treasury and provides no investment capital except if the stock is newly issued. But new issues by major corporations are fairly rare because issuing new stock dilutes equity and depresses stock prices. As a result, the bulk of shares now traded on the stock markets were issued twenty or fifty years ago. Since then the shares have passed through many hands, and their prices have fluctuated over a wide range. Yet all these transactions have been strictly between the buyers and sellers of stocks, aided and abetted by stockbrokers trying to eke out a modest living.... [S]peculators are not really interested in the company whose stock they temporarily own. They want to take their profits and get out. They are not investing in the proper sense of the word; they are simply gambling. Ownership of corporations has become largely a game of chance in which the individual players try to guess what the other players will do.[44]

Market Bubbles and Crashes

Speculators are unaware that their gains are unearned. If the market wipes them out, they feel they have lost earnings when actually it was just the odds of the gamble and their turn to lose. Like the casinos they are, the stock markets are primarily a mechanism for the redistribution of wealth, not its production. It is a gambling game in which the rest of society's members are spectators—spectators who continually have their share of the nation's increased wealth thrown on the table of a game of chance they are not playing. The danger of gambling with the nation's wealth was addressed by *Business Week's* 1987 cover story, "Playing with Fire":

> By stoking a persuasive desire to beat the game, innovation and deregulation have tilted the axis of the financial system away from investment toward speculation. The U.S. has evolved into what Lord Keynes might have called a "casino society"—a nation obsessively devoted to high-stakes financial maneuvering as a shortcut to wealth.... "Speculators may do no harm as bubbles on a steady stream of enterprise. But the position is serious when enterprise becomes the bubble on a whirlpool of speculation. When the capital development of a country becomes a byproduct of the activities of a casino, the job is likely to be ill-done."[45]

What is normally spoken of as a market "bubble" is only the claiming of wealth produced by others through *exclusive titles* to nature's wealth which has gotten out of hand. History is replete with examples. Charles Mackay, in *Extraordinary Popular Delusions and the Madness of Crowds*, describes the tulip craze that broke out in Europe in the 17th century. Before that particular insanity dissipated, one particular tulip bulb cost "two lasts of wheat, four lasts of rye, four fat oxen, eight fat swine, twelve fat sheep, two hogsheads of wine, four tuns of butter, one thousand lbs. of cheese, a complete bed, a suit of clothes and a silver drinking cup."[46]

One wonders at the variety of commodities traded for that one flower bulb, but their total value of 2,500 florins serves as a guideline to the money value paid for other bulbs. During this period, prices ranged from 2,000 florins for an inferior bulb to 5,500 florins for the choicest varieties. "Many persons were known to invest a fortune of 100,000 florins in the purchase of 40 roots."[47] Although tulips are not stocks, the principle is the same.

At the turn of the 18th century, John Law implemented a plan to sell stock in enterprises in the Mississippi wilderness to pay off the huge debt of the French government. Though this scheme was seriously flawed, Law's banking reforms were quite sound and the French economy prospered. The plan went awry when the money rolled in. Those selling paper were so busy getting rich they neglected to invest in production anywhere; they merely reinvested in more paper. In a speculative frenzy, fortunes changed hands as people sold, and then bought back, nothing but paper.

The stock in this Mississippi scheme had no value because there was no investment and thus no production. Law's scheme was borrowed from the cunning financiers in England who a few years earlier sold stock in a South Seas venture, known today as the "South Sea Bubble." Although Spain controlled most of South America, and the English had limited trade rights within it, stock companies were set up to trade within this territory. Visions of wealth stirred up a speculative fever, companies were formed for very unlikely endeavors, and the money rolled in as speculators dreamed of getting rich. Soon, so many joined the game that it got out of hand and the government had to call a halt to new issues. The intention of most of these promoters can be summed up by one audacious proposal. This promoter touted "a company for carrying on an undertaking of great advantage, but nobody to know what it is."[48]

Since the organizers of these companies had no intention of producing anything, their capital was 100% fictitious. Proof that this capital was not real was when the speculative bubble collapsed. There were no tangible assets, production, or services to back the value of the stock; there was only the transferring of wealth from the naive to the cunning or lucky.

When wild speculation breaks loose, there is no relationship between value and price. Even when the stock market behaves normally, there are always stocks whose prices defy logic. This activity can only be attributed to crowd psychology, as described by Mackay, although sly promoters pull strings at every opportunity.[a]

---

[a] Before the Great Depression of the 1930s, the price earnings ratio reached 19 to 1. The world is watching to see if price earnings ratio of 30 to 1 will lead to the next crash. This time around the market dropped 40% the first three years of the market slide. The first two years of the collapse leading into the Great Depression the market dropped 25%. Creating an enormous bubble in the housing market provided enough buying power to carry the economy past that 40% slide and it has now partially recovered (January 2006).

Options, Futures, and other Derivatives are Gambling Chips in a Worldwide Casino

The markets for stocks, bonds, commodities, futures, options, currencies, mortgages, money markets—in fact virtually every exchange market anywhere in the world—are now one huge market. Options or futures are only the buyer betting the stock will go up and the seller that it will go down; neither has a stake in that stock beyond the gamble. Options and futures may appear to have a legitimate purpose in takeover schemes, but they are not even gambles. The psychology of the market almost guarantees that the stock price will rise when word gets out a takeover is in progress. This increase in valuation backs the money required for the takeover.

The historic speculations in options, futures, and other simple bets are dwarfed by the derivative markets of the late 20th to early 21st century which evolved both to reduce risk and bypass the market's margin limitations. Long-Term Capital Management's bankruptcy crisis in 1998 uncovered the unsettling reality that this small hedge fund with a capital base of only $2 billion had over $1 trillion in bets in the derivatives markets, betting primarily on the Russian Ruble. This was a margin of only 0.02% and many of the estimated 400 other hedge funds would have similar slim margins bet on similarly volatile currencies."[49] "Corporations have become chips in a casino game, played for high stakes by people who produce nothing, invent nothing, grow nothing and service nothing. The market is now a game in itself. "[50] Capitalized fictitious values are also like chips on a poker table; they finance the game. But, unlike chips, when the game is over those deflated stocks cannot be traded in for full value.

The markets are a high stakes, *low risk* (except at the peak of a bubble) gambling casino where these overcapitalized values are distributed. Everyone recognizes the high stakes. The unacknowledged low risk is due to the constantly increasing value of the nation's capital accruing to stockowners. This increase in value is due to the capitalized value of the production of labor claimed by the owners of increasingly efficient technology. Due to exposés of fraud in the commodities and futures markets, farmers became aware of this fact and some clamored for the closing down of the nonproductive futures markets.[51]

Just as selling short and other trading practices developed in the early established markets as a form of harvesting profits, sharp traders have leveraged world markets with stock and currency options, futures on options (meaning options on options), futures on interest rates, warrants (a form of option), and thousands of other similar subdivisions of value called "derivatives":

> Futures contracts on interest rates did not exist in 1971.... Today there are outstanding contracts for $3 trillion worth of them, a little more than half of the gross national product of the United States.... The market for tradable options has grown

> from essentially zero in 1973—the year the Chicago Board Options Exchange opened for the first time—to a market where more than $170 billion changes hands each day. One hundred and seventy billion is enough money to build 1.7 million average homes.... Eight hundred billion dollars ... is exchanged each day in the world's currency markets.... Every three days a sum of money passes through the fiber-optic network under the pitted streets of New York equal to the total output for one year of all of America's companies and its entire workforce. And every two weeks the annual product of the world passes through the network of New York.... Sums of similar magnitude pass through the streets of Tokyo, London, Frankfurt, Chicago, and Hong Kong.... [This] "financial economy" is somewhere between twenty and fifty times larger than the real economy. It is not the economy of trade but of speculation. Its commerce is in financial instruments [paper].[52]

Yearly currency exchanges were $888 trillion in 2003, over 82 times the U.S GDP. It has been estimated that a healthy economy requires $2-$3 speculated for every $1 that runs the real economy.[53] Allowing a multiple of the high figure, $3, means $30 trillion per year moving through the money markets will run the American economy leaving $850 trillion as needless speculation which puts the world at risk even as it transfers massive sums from producers to speculators.

Strip away the hype and derivatives are simply bets on the direction of a particular market. With personal computers able to track stocks, bonds, commodities, futures, options, etc, in virtually any of these markets worldwide, there are massive gyrations of values as speculators buy and sell these packaged paper symbols of wealth.[54] Just as the formation of the stock market and the manipulation of stock values became the primary mechanism through which robber barons appropriated the industrial wealth of America and laid the base for America's financial aristocracy, a new breed of robber barons are harvesting fortunes running the markets of the world up and down. A fresh crop of bright people have placed themselves between the world's savers and its producers and consumers to intercept the new wealth produced by the increased efficiencies of technology. As these speculators produced nothing and thus had nothing to trade of value, the wealth they accumulated can only have come from true producers.

While the world economy staggered and labor's share of wealth declined, the world market in paper symbols of wealth missed a few beats on: the U.S. stock market collapse of October 19, 1987 (from which it recovered), the savings and loan and banking crisis in the United States in 1990 (now recovered),[55] the collapse of the Tokyo stock and land markets (possibly now recovering), the 1997-2003 financial meltdown of 40% of the world, all on the periphery of *imperial centers of capital* (they appear to be recovering), and the 2000-2003 40% stock value collapse in the U.S. (now recovering,). Insecurity forced capital to flee back to its imperial centers, forcing those markets to new highs, then new lows, and they continue to rise and fall as speculators jockey for position or flee for safer havens.

We have yet to see if the enormous sums of accumulated capital in the *imperial centers of capital* will bid the limited available stocks to further atmospheric heights and then crash, whether it will be used to build even more industrial capacity to service a shrunken world consumer market and crash from that excess capacity, or whether a fascist financial and military fix will protect the current monopolizers of capital.

Bringing the World's Markets under Control

Buying and selling investments is the legitimate purpose of stock markets; any activity beyond that is gambling. Eliminating subtle monopolization through restructuring primary monopolies (money, land, technology, and communications) into a modern commons and eliminating secondary monopolies (next chapter) through full and equal rights for all would eliminate all need for derivatives and other wasteful speculations. Once full and equal rights have stabilized markets, rank speculation in commodities and markets would disappear. Those of speculative nature can still invest in the beating heart of capitalism, entrepreneurial speculation.

Restructuring Patent Laws

> I know of no original product invention, not even electric shavers or heating pads, made by any of the giant laboratories or corporations, with the possible exception of the household garbage grinder.... The record of the giants is one of moving in, buying out and absorbing the smaller creators. —T. K. Quinn, *Giant Business: Threat to Democracy*

That garbage disposal was also an appropriated idea.[56] The importance of societies retaining and furthering technical knowledge is demonstrated by China having the basic knowledge required for an Industrial Revolution at least 800 years before Europe invented and used these technologies. A millennium ago the Chinese were producing massive amounts of iron and steel. They had invented the compass and rudders for large ships. They had paper, movable type, and the printing press. They built suspension bridges. They had matches, wheelbarrows, wheeled metal plows, mechanical seeders, horse collars, rotary threshing machines and a drill to tap into natural gas. They knew the decimal system, negative numbers, and the concept of zero. And they once knew how to produce primary tools of world conquest, gunpowder, cannon, and large ships.[57] But that technological knowledge was forgotten because of disuse and the lack of a recording system.

Inventions and innovations are the cornerstones of prosperity. To establish them in social memory and reward the inventors and innovators, those technologies must be recorded, be used, and those inventors and innovators must be well paid.[58] It is necessary to reward both those who had the original innovative ideas and those who put those ideas to work.

The present policy of restricting access to technology should be changed to one of easy access with proper compensation for inventors, developers, and producers while returning the maximum savings to society.

The patent system could be far simpler and administration costs lowered to almost nothing by evaluating the value of a patent, paying inventors and developers its capitalized value, and placing their innovations in the public domain (a modern technology commons as per Henry George's *conditional titles* to nature's wealth). The inventor and/or developer would be well paid, all would be free to use the inventions, and there would be no cost for accounting or for disbursing royalties. The patent's value will be instantly capitalized with the inventor the gainer, instead of the current complex process of capitalization of wealth produced by others and appropriated by monopolists through *exclusive titles* to nature's technologies.

Most inventors would want their inventions to have maximum use and opt for instant cash and free use by all. Inventions not originally recognized as valuable, a frequent occurrence, would be proved by developers who would then file development patents, each would be paid a capitalized value, that patent would be released to the public domain, and both inventor and developer would be well paid.

Because producers can use the most efficient technology to remain competitive, businesses and communities would no longer have to shut down because their market was overwhelmed by a competitor with a patent monopoly (capital destroying capital). With feudal exclusive title to nature's wealth restructured to *conditional titles*, the world's communities would be quite secure as all gained maximum benefits from the newest technologies.

The expense and risk involved in product development and market penetration are normally greater than those associated with invention. Through a *development patent,* developers of technologies should be well paid for their risks.

Under this mutual support structure, new inventions would be available for all to use. The inventors, developers, and producers would be adequately paid for their ideas, capital, labor, and risk. And society would be paid through low-priced products and services.

Again we will point out: "Whether a market is in land or corporate stock what is being bought and sold under current property rights are primarily values produced by nature or a technology of nature, properly belonging to all in relatively equal shares, which have been claimed by monopolists through *exclusive titles* to nature's wealth and those appropriated values capitalized by a factor of 10 to 30 times."

By restructuring the current monopolized patent titles/stock markets to a modern technology commons (pay inventors well and all have equal rights to use any technology), those huge blocs of finance capital owned by monopolists, currently buying and selling monopoly values on the markets, are transposed into relatively *equally-shared use values.* Assuming all other monopolies and their huge accumulations of what is properly others' wealth were eliminated, economic efficiency would double.

Patent monopoly profits are collected through the stock market. With each having full and equal rights to the fruits of nature, the need for 80 to 85% of the offices and staff overseeing, and the businesses and labor servicing, the patent/stock market industry disappear.

Economic efficiency gains from these relatively small changes (but huge effects) in property rights establishing a modern technology commons would—assuming buying power is protected through sharing the remaining productive jobs—equal the invention of electricity.[59] Such massive economic efficiency gains require democratic, communitarian oversight to prevent stripping the earth's resources and to protect the environment.

Again it must be pointed out that the wealth appropriated from truly productive labor through *exclusive title* to nature's technologies is invested; through taxes or overpriced products and services that principal—plus interest—is paid for by those from whom it was first appropriated; it is again reinvested; and it is again paid for. That *impoverishing cycle* continues into perpetuity and is broken only by economic collapses as the wealth is concentrated into too few hands—leaving the majority without adequate buying power. The elimination of those huge blocs of appropriated wealth and resultant large increase in economic efficiency and elimination of poverty is the essence of Henry George's *inclusive rules of law.*

Before we address the 4th primary monopoly, communications—through which our rights can be reclaimed—we will address secondary monopolies.

---

1 Doug Henwood, *Wall Street* (New York: Verso, 1997), p. 7.

2 J.W. Smith, *Economic Democracy: A Grand Strategy for World Peace and Prosperity* (Radford, VA: The Institute for Economic Democracy, 2006), chapter 1.

3 Michael Moffitt, "Shocks, Deadlocks, and Scorched Earth," *World Policy Journal* (Fall, 1987), pp. 560-61, 572-73.

4 William Greider, *Who Will Tell the People?* (New York: Simon and Schuster, 1992), pp. 378-79, 399-400.

5 Greider, *Who Will Tell the People*, p. 399.

6 Adam Smith, *Wealth of Nations* (New York: Random House, 1965), p. 64.

7 John D. Donahue, *The Privatization Decision:* (New York: Basic Books, 1989).

8 *Public Power Directory and Statistics* for 1983 (Washington, DC: American Public Power Association, 1983); Jeanie Kilmer, "Public Power Costs Less." *Public Power Magazine*, May/June 1985, pp. 28-31; the late Montana Senator Lee Metcalf and Vic Reinemer, *Overcharge* (New York: David McKay, 1967).

9 Edward Winslow Martin, *History of the Grange Movement* (New York: Burt Franklin, 1967), pp. 62, 70.

10 Matthew Josephson, *Robber Barons* (New York: Harcourt Brace Jovanovich, 1962), p. 92; Joe E. Feagin, *The Urban RealEstate Game* (Englewood Cliffs, NJ: Prentice-Hall, 1983), pp. 57-8; Peter Lyon, *To Hell in a Day Coach* (New York: J.B. Lippincott, 1968), p. 6; see also Martin, *Grange Movement.*

11 Wilfred Owen, *Strategy for Mobility* (Westport, CT: Greenwood Press, 1978), p. 23.

12 John Prados, *The Presidents' Secret Wars* (New York: William Morrow, 1986), p. 152.

[13] Lewis Mumford, *Pentagon of Power* (New York: Harcourt Brace Jovanovich, 1964), pp. 134, 139; Stuart Chase, *Men and Machines* (New York: Macmillan, 1929), chapters 3-4.
[14] Chase, *Men and Machines*, pp. 42-43.
[15] PBS, *Nova* (September 2, 1986).
[16] Stuart Chase, *The Economy of Abundance* (New York: Macmillan, 1934), chapter 8.
[17] Phil Grant, *The Wonderful Wealth Machine* (New York: Devon-Adair Co., 1953), pp. 301-06.
[18] Dan Nadudere, *The Political Economy of Imperialism* (London: Zed Books, 1977), p. 251, quoting in part from E. Penrose, *The International Patent System*, 1951, p. 29.
[19] Ibid, pp. 186, 255.
[20] Karl Marx, *Capital* (New York: International Publishers, 1967), volume 1, p. 375, footnote 2.
[21] Nadudere, *Political Economy of Imperialism*, p. 38, quoting Leo Huberman, Man's Worldly Goods, pp. 128-29.
[22] Lewis Mumford, *Technics and Civilization* (New York: Harcourt Brace Jovanovich, 1963), pp. 227-28, 438. Read also Nadudere, *Political Economy of Imperialism*, pp. 51-55.
[23] Chase, *Economy of Abundance*, p. 166.
[24] Lester Thurow, *Head to Head: The Coming Economic Battle Among Japan, Europe, and America* (New York: William Morrow, 1992), p. 187.
[25] Grant, *Wonderful Wealth Machine*, pp. 301-306.
[26] Karl Polanyi, *The Great Transformation* (Boston: Beacon Press, 1957), p. 277, quoting from Pirenne, *Medieval Cities*, p. 211.
[27] Marx, *Capital*, volume 1, pp. 372-74, 428, 435, 562; Eric R. Wolf, *Europe and the People Without History* (Berkeley: University of California Press, 1982), pp. 273-74, 279.
[28] Richard Barnet, *The Lean Years* (New York: Simon and Schuster, 1980), p. 260.
[29] J.W. Smith, *Economic Democracy: A Grand Strategy for World Peace and Prosperity* (Radford, VA: The Institute for Economic Democracy, 2006), chapter 1.
[30] Howard Zinn, *A People's History of the United States* (New York: Harper Colophon Books, 1980), p. 277.
[31] Herman E. Daly, John B. Cobb, Jr., *For the Common Good* (Boston: Beacon Press, 1989), p. 11.
[32] Robert Lacey, *Ford* (New York: Ballantine Books, 1986), pp. 118-40; also Juliet Schor, *The Overworked American* (New York: Basic Books, 1991), p. 61.
[33] Lacey, Ford, pp. 105-06; Brian Tokar, *Redesigning Life? The Worldwide Challenge to Genetic Engineering* (London: Zed Books, 2001).
[34] Tokar, *Redesigning Life?;* Stanley Wohl, Medical-Industrial Complex (New York: Harmony Books, 1984), pp. 69-71; Ivan Illich, *Medical Nemesis* (New York: Bantam Books, 1979), p. 245.
[35] "India Protects its Heritage Against Privatization Theft," *COMER* (February 2006), p. 8. Taken from Globe and Mail (December 12, 2005)
[36] Stephen Budiansky, "An Act of Vision for the Developing World," *U.S. News and World Report* (November 2, 1987), p. 14.
[37] Jean-Pierre Berlan, "The Commodification of Life," *Monthly Review* (Dec. 1989), p. 24.
[38] Alan Weisman, "Columbia's Modern City," *In Context*, No. 42, 1995, pp. 6-8; *Los Angeles Times Sunday Magazine,* September 25, 1994.
[39] E.K. Hunt, Howard Sherman, *Economics* (New York: Harper and Row, 1990), p. 166.
[40] Kurt Rudolph Mirow, Harry Maurer, *Webs of Power* (Boston: Houghton Mifflin Co., 1982), p. 16.
[41] Thurow, *Generating Inequality*, p. 149.
[42] Ibid, p. 154, (emphasis added).
[43] Chase, *Economy of Abundance*, p. 165.
[44] Rolf H. Wild, *Management by Compulsion* (Boston: Houghton Mifflin, 1978), pp. 92, 94-95.
[45] Anthony Banco, "Playing With Fire," *Business Week* (September 16, 1987), p. 78.
[46] Charles Mackay, Extraordinary *Delusions and Madness of Crowds* (New York: Farrar, Straus and Giroux, 1932), pp. 90-97.

[47] Ibid, pp. 1-45; Lester Thurow, *The Future of Capitalism: How Today's Economic Forces Shape Tomorrow's World* (England: Penguin Books, 1996), p. 221; John Train, *Famous Financial Fiascoes* (New York: Clarkson N. Potter, 1985), pp. 33-41, 108-89.

[48] Mackay, *Delusions*, pp. 46-88; see also Train, *Fiascoes*, pp. 88-95; Charles P. Kindleberger, *Manias, Panics, and Crashes* (New York: Basic Books, 1978), pp. 220-21.

[49] Ibid

[50] 1987 presidential hopeful Representative Richard A. Gephardt of Missouri, in a speech to the Securities Industry Institute of the Wharton School of Business, Haynes Johnson, " 'Teflon' 80s Bear Striking Resemblance to 'Giddy' 20s," *The Missoulian*, March 25, 1987, reprinted from *The Washington Post.*

[51] Paul Richter, "Commodity Marts Face Fraud Fallout," *Los Angeles Times*, July 4, 1989, p. A2.

[52] Kurtzman, *Death of Money*, pp. 12, 17, 77, 128; see also pp. 39, 65, 64-65, 236.

[53] Lester Thurow, *Building Wealth: The New Rules for Individuals, Companies and Nations in a knowledge Based Economy* (New York: HarperCollins, 2000), p. 67; William Tabb, *The Amoral Elephant: Globalization and the Struggle for Global Justice in the Twenty-First Century* (New York: Monthly Review Press, 2001), p.83. Richard C. Longworth, *Global Squeeze: The Coming Crisis of First-World Nations* (Chicago: Contemporary Books, 1999), pp. 7, 256; Gowan, *The Global Gamble.*

[54] What Joel Kurtzman, economist and business editor for the *New York Times*, calls "images of labor, wisdom, and wealth" (Kurtzman, *Death of Money*, p. 161).

[55] Kurtzman, *Death of Money*, pp. 73, 96, 99, 113, 117, 120-21, 196, 228.

[56] Paul A. Baran, Paul M. Sweezy, *Monopoly Capital* (New York: Monthly Review Press, 1968), p. 49, quoted from T. K. Quinn, *Giant Business*: (New York: Exposition Press, 1954), p. 117.

[57] Lester Thurow, *The Future of Capitalism: How Today's Economic Forces Shape Tomorrow's World* (England: Penguin Books, 1996, p. 15; Lester Thurow, *Building Wealth: The New Rules for Individuals, Companies, and Nations in a knowledge-Based Economy* (New York: HarperCollins, 2000), pp. 85, 102.

[58] Michael Goldhaber, *Reinventing Technology* (New York: Routledge & Kegan Paul, 1986), p. 185.

[59] For another study see Vandana Shiva's *Protect or Plunder: Understanding Intellectual Property Rights.*

4. Secondary Monopolies Disappear under Henry George's Rule of Law

The American insurance system, legal system, health care system, welfare system, taxi medallions, etc., are exclusive marketing rights (subtle monopolies) which built up ad hoc due to lack of those services as a human right. Prisons, law enforcement, and other protective industries are not monopolies per se but they grew to the huge proportion of the economy that they are due to the inequalities and lack of rights in the monopolized sectors of the economy.

All social structures (governments, banking systems, Social Security, other insurances, a legal system, universal health care, welfare systems, etc.) are social technologies that have been discovered over the centuries and put in place. (Being quite natural and humankind being a part of nature, those are social technologies.) This is instinctively understood. The threat of ballot box revolutions due to periodic economic collapses led to Social Security, unemployment insurance, and—in many countries—universal health care becoming a right.

That these rights were given only during economic crises, and the fact that such rights are typically partially withdrawn during good times, proves the power structure is—for the purpose of increasing and protecting their wealth and power—denying full and equal rights to the citizenry. Even the novice can't help noticing that it would be much easier to fund those economic changes during prosperous times than during an economic crisis.

In the early to middle stages of the designing of democratic societies as Western society slowly evolved from Feudalism, the wealthy were so few and those producing their daily subsistence needs within their family unit—primarily from the land—were so many that not even the most alert could conceive of rights for all to retirement income (Social Security), health insurance, home insurance, unemployment insurance, support for the incidentally or accidentally impoverished, etc., all social technologies of the future.

As Western industrialized society slowly formed, ad hoc, labor intensive, capital intensive, monopolized, and expensive social structures arose to fill the needs of the citizenry as they were slowly brought into the flow of money within a capitalist system. The powerful, within the flow of money from the start were—at every later point—protecting and expanding their excessive rights. This is the process addressed two paragraphs above which prevented expansion of rights during good times.[a]

Do not confuse expansion of rights with increase in income. That increase in wealth within powerful nations is primarily appropriations of wealth of both weak nations[1] and the politically weak within nations.

Before universal education and modern technology, those without power who obtained their subsistence from the land were not given full rights in step with potential gains in social structures or the actual gains of technology. Even though we all have more rights now, a lack of full and equal rights is still the process which produces a wealthy few and impoverished many in most cultures today.

The masses, historically within a subsistence economy, could have quickly been brought within a money economy—and a wealthy society with full and equal rights for all established—if a banking, land, and technology commons, following the *inclusive rules of law* of Henry George, had been instituted. But the powerful would quickly calculate that every gain in rights to an equal share of nature's riches would deny them a part of their massive accumulations of wealth and full and equal rights would eliminate it all.

Not only were Western property rights designed to maintain wealth and power within national economies they were designed to claim the wealth of the peripheries of empires. This alerts us to the reason for the covert destabilizations of emerging countries worldwide as they attempted to break out of the strait jacket of imposed Western property rights so as to provide for their people. If they were permitted their freedom, others would notice their rapid rise in living standards and would quickly opt out of the monopoly system.

Excessive rights for a few and lack of rights for the many structured into the *rule of law* being the very heart of Western monopoly systems will stand exposed as we lay out further the simplicity of transposing monopoly rights and massive blocs of wealth owned by a few monopolists into *use rights* equally shared and utilized by all.

Insurance: Whatever is a necessity should be a right. Security is a necessity and—in most developed nations—some form of Social Security, a retirement insurance, is now a right. As it is recognized as a right, the powerful—

---

[a] Expansion of excessive rights is a regular occurrence within legislatures. Economic philosophers spotted the same appropriations of wealth we are addressing in special-favor laws and termed it rent seeking. Starting out as a service, the secondary monopolies we address here expanded into rent seeking. Henry George philosophers did make the Henry George/rent seeking connection to taxi medallions but seem not to have made the connection to the field of study of rent seeking or to the monopolies we address. Those who wish to dig deeper into the phenomenon of mini-monopolies as a further expansion of Henry George's thesis on rent should do a web search for "rent seeking." As secondary monopolies, most should be eliminated though a few, such as taxi medallions, should pay the rent value to society.

though they continually try—find it difficult to reduce life-sustaining guarantees for those final years. [2]

But health insurance, car insurance, and home insurance are equally as necessary as Social Security insurance and none of these are yet a right in America. Not having those rights, ad hoc insurance industries sprang up to take care of those needs. Instead of a right to insurance—similar to Social Security—being established by society, a "market" for insurance evolved and stock markets simultaneously expanded to buy and sell the capitalized values created by insurance companies' appropriations of wealth produced by others.

The annual sum of that appropriated wealth is capitalized 10 to 30 times (the monetization process). As these are newly created values, the Federal Reserve must create the money with which that new wealth can be bought and sold. So which comes first, the money or the wealth?

In this case, the wealth came first which means that capitalization of monopoly values create money. A truly productive society with full and equal rights creates money to create wealth while current capitalist economics monopolize wealth to create money. Roughly 60% of America's huge blocs of capital are just such values capitalized. That process produced the mirror image of those appropriated values, money, which made those values transportable and transferable. In short, in every monopoly, a part of the values rightfully belonging securely to each and all are appropriated, capitalized, sold, and banked, thus denying the citizenry their full share

Having rights or lacking rights is the crucial difference between a highly efficient sector of an economy and a highly labor-intensive, monopolized, wasteful sector, claiming wealth produced by others, capitalizing the profits, and buying and selling those appropriated values on the markets.

Up to this point—in banking, land (resources), and technology—we have eliminated wasteful monopolization by apportioning values produced by nature and labor directly to the citizenry. The monopolized sectors of the economy addressed in this chapter are unique in that the maximum efficiency is gained by totally replacing the marketing structure with a social right.

Rights can be given any time a power structure decides. But, not understanding the enormous power of a modern economy to take care of everyone's needs and—with heavily-funded think tanks pouring out *belief systems* (spin) protecting the powerful's excess rights—rights for all are viewed (or at least it is preached) as a loss of rights for both the masses and the powerful. Thus rights to Social Security that is accepted today as the norm were typically only given when a market economy broke down, people were starving, a revolution was imminent, and the leaders (those who had been continually blocking such key expansions of rights) stood to lose both wealth and power. True to our thesis, with 60 years of good times those powerful are working hard to roll back Social Security and other rights within today's *rule of law*.

When—under the threat of a ballot box revolution—the citizenry were given Social Security insurance as a right, annual management costs (deducted from earnings) turned out to be less than 1% of premiums collected through payroll deductions. In contrast sales, management, and profits of insurances in the market economy typically cost 50% of premiums paid. Meanwhile, insurances negotiated by unions and given as a social right to those select few, typically cost only 6% of premiums paid (by the company or, in part, by the insured) to manage.

Social Security is much larger than any several insurance companies put together. Few people have ever seen their efficient regional Social Security office. Restructure health, auto, and home insurances to a right and those insurance offices you see on almost every street, along with the office furnishings and those wastefully employed, disappear to be replaced by a regional office that—like Social Security—you will seldom see.

Your home insurance premiums will be paid when you pay your home loan, just as they are now, but will cost half as much. No fault auto insurance, paid as a percent of the price of gas, will greatly lower costs even as each pay equally relative to miles driven. Universal health care can be handled under payroll deductions at half today's cost. If one's insurance needs fall outside those parameters, simply sign up, pay the premium, and pocket the savings. That is, if the powerful will ever permit such rights to be allotted to the citizenry. The labor and capital once operating the highly inefficient insurance sectors of the economy are now available for truly productive uses.

Law: In a society with full and equal rights, both crime and the need for legal resolutions will drop to a very small fraction of today's epidemics of lawlessness and battles over divisions of wealth. As I write this (2006), a radio show host in Boston—incensed at the murders each week by drug dealers—blurted out, "Give me a call. I will find you a job." Within a week 10 of those battling for turf on the drug scene were enrolled in a cooking school. That violent life was not what they wanted; they simply did not have rights to a job.

With each having full and equal rights to their share of nature's wealth, rights to a productive job through a radical reduction in working days, being paid equally for equally-productive work, and—considering a total restructuring of society (see conclusion)—the daily struggle for survival will be replaced by an efficient, calm, *inclusive* economy with each having security and a quality life.

Assuming *inclusive* full and equal rights were sincerely put in place—which means each having the opportunity for a respectable identity and a secure life—the 2.1 million American prisoners now increasing 47,000 per year, will shrink to infinitesimal levels. Those building and guarding prisons, the police, private guards, the personnel operating the justice system, and its brick and mortar infrastructure will shrink accordingly.

But the savings go far beyond the criminal justice system into the civil courts. We quote from Fred Rodell's classic, *Woe Unto You Lawyers:*

> It is the lawyers who run our civilization for us—our governments, our business, our private lives....We cannot buy a home or rent an apartment, we cannot get married or try to get divorced, we cannot die and leave our property to our children without calling on the lawyers to guide us. To guide us, incidentally, through a maze of confusing gestures and formalities that lawyers have created....The legal trade, in short, is nothing but a high-class racket.[3]

Rodell goes further:

> The lawyers—or at least 99 44/100 per cent of them—are not even aware that they are indulging in a racket, and would be shocked at the very mention of the idea. Once bitten by the legal bug, they lose all sense of perspective about what they are doing and how they are doing it. Like the medicine men of tribal times and the priests of the Middle Ages they actually believe in their own nonsense.[4]

What Fred Rodell knew was that expensive divorces were replaceable by each party agreeing to how property is to be divided, each fill out and file a prescribed form, the judge question each party to ascertain each were fully aware, that the settlement was fair, and grant the divorce.

Some states have enacted such laws and the savings in both emotional distress and money were everything Rodell predicted. Special care is taken when children are involved but typically they too are rescued from the trauma of a messy, expensive, divorce. Note that most the trauma and expense before those legal changes were because citizens were denied a right—in this case the right to a simple, agreed-upon divorce.

Probating wills were—and many still are—subject to lawyers milking estates of the deceased. Norman F. Dacey produced a workbook with the instructions and forms to create and file an inter-vivos trust which can be changed as easily as you change your will. The filer is trustee of his or her own estate already deeded to his or her heirs but, since it can be changed at any time, it only takes effect upon his or her death when changes are no longer possible. There is almost no cost. As soon as papers of the trustee's death are filed, the heirs have full control of his or her share of the estate. Though lawyers are trying mightily to do away with this threat to their unearned income, no inter vivos trust has ever been successfully challenged.[5]

Legal forms are really a checklist of items that have to be addressed by all who wish to enter into a contract with each other or themselves. Most legal transactions are procedures requiring only the filling out of these ready-made forms. How else could it be? If most dealings between people were not based on custom, there would be chaos. This simplicity is blocked by the present legal system, which makes simple transactions complicated and tedious, thus *expanding labor and time* to justify large compensations.

Rosemary Furman, legal secretary and court reporter, estimated that, if the public were given access to standardized forms, about 70% of the legal work could be eliminated. With this access—and guidance from the clerks of court—literate adults could easily handle uncontested divorces, name changes, debt collections, tax matters, bankruptcies, real estate transactions, adoptions, patents, wills, trusts, and many other legal matters. Furman charged twenty-five to fifty dollars for these services while lawyers received three hundred to five hundred dollars. But whenever citizens use a prepared form and handle their own transactions there are no costs beyond filing fees. "Everything I do," said Furman, "is the responsibility of the clerk of court."[6]

Over half the compensations for accidents, product liability, and malpractice are claimed by lawyers. In New Zealand, the "Accident Compensation Corporation oversees the claims process. Injured people file claims whether their injury happened at home, at work or at play, and compensation is provided fully and fairly."[7] This process is equally applicable to product liability and malpractice suits. Divorce, accidents, and liability constitute at least 80% of all civil suits and in each it is possible to almost totally eliminate lawyers.

Early lawyers were paid by the word. This led to the current unnecessary legalese that few can understand:

> It has been the custom in modern Europe to regulate, on most occasions, the payment of the attorneys and clerks of court, according to the number of pages which they had occasion to write; the court, however, requiring that each page should contain so many lines, and each line so many words. To increase their payment, the attorneys and clerks have contrived to multiply words beyond all necessity, to the corruption of law language of, I believe, every court of justice in Europe. A like temptation might perhaps occasion a like corruption in the form of law proceedings.[8]

Lawyers intercept their share of social production by keeping secret the simplicity of everyday common agreements. Once language is simplified and the public has access to legal forms, the practice of law via obscurantism and hocus-pocus will disappear.

And we can go on and on: Conflict Resolution Law, corporate mini-trials, etc, are all examples of how to eliminate the current unnecessary expense of the legal system. But all this has been addressed and cited in depth in *The World's Wasted Wealth 2* by this author.

Though most the wealth consumed in the legal industry is wasted labor, wasted office space, wasted protective forces, wasted courtroom space, etc., huge profits are still made and, at times those appropriated values (private prisons, law firms listed on stock markets, incorporated but unlisted law firms, etc) are bought and sold.

Health Care: April 18, 2006, the American Medical Association released their study that, by U.S. Department of Justice guidelines, health insurers were effectively monopolies. Among the 50 most developed nations, only the United States and South Africa do not have universal health care. U.S. citizens spend 38% more than the Canadians, 39% more than the French, 42% more than the Swedish, 53% more than Germans, 62% more than Italians, 78% more than Australians, 90% more than the Japanese, 100% more than the British, and 466% more than the Cubans.[9] Universal health care of each of these countries equal or, when one considers that all their citizens receive medical care, exceeds that in the United States.

Markets for health care are far from efficient. The more products sold, whether needed or not or even if they may be harmful, the more profits that can be made. Such wasted labor and resources of secondary monopolies are not the result of intent. As a distribution mechanism, these unnecessary territories expand relentlessly in all the service segments of the economy. Businesses must operate at their maximum to maximize profits and people must maximize their labor time to earn a good living.

In their book, *Frogs into Princes,* psychiatrists Richard Bandler and John Grinder explained the process. One of their fellow psychiatrists treated patients in a state clinic and averaged six visits per client. "In his private practice he is apt to see a client twelve or fifteen times...and it never dawned on him what caused that....The more effective you are the less money you make because your clients get what they want and leave and don't pay you anymore."[10] The health industry, and much other labor expended in the United States, mirrors this psychiatrist's practice.

An episode of the *Sally Jesse Raphael Show* featured young women who, at fourteen years of age, were unjustly institutionalized.[11] With remarkable insight, these young women figured out the fraud and outwitted the system. A patient advocate who was a member of the Minnesota Mental Health Association was instrumental in freeing many of these young ladies. He pointed out that when hospital occupancy declined they expanded into child care and "hospitals and psychiatrists were preying upon parents and children." Seventy-five hundred children per year were institutionalized in that state and "typically only those who had insurance were hospitalized and the cures and discharges came miraculously when the insurance ran out."

In this author's *The World's Wasted Wealth 2* many examples are given but these summaries will suffice: The Children's Defense Fund suggests that at least 40 percent of these juvenile admissions are inappropriate, while a Family Therapy Network youth expert put that figure at 75 percent.[12] Few experiences could be more damaging to the self image of a youth than institutionalization during those crucial formative years. On balance—in the search for profits—the psychiatric industry can only have been doing far more harm than good.

A study by Rand Corporation found that 40% of hospital admissions were inappropriate because they involved simple procedures that could have been handled just as well in a doctor's office. Thirty percent of operations have been deemed unnecessary. Localities with fewer doctors had lower mortality rates and during hospital strikes in the United States, Canada, Great Britain, and Israel, the death rates went down. (In the Israeli and New York strikes, the hospitalization rate dropped 85%.) "It was as if the population was in better health when medical care was limited to emergencies."[13]

Canada is listed among those countries with lowered mortality rates when doctors were on strike. Yet "Canadians get bypass surgery half as often as

Americans."[14] When exposed, the installation of pacemakers under promotions reminiscent of staying in style was a disgrace.[15] This author listened on the evening news to Dr. David Graham, who blew the whistle on Vioxx, pointing out that, "The patients Vioxx was killing equaled the death rate of 2 to 4 airliner crashes a week and there were five more drugs he knew of that were highly suspect." Running an Internet search for "drugs, whistleblower" or "trans-fats, Denmark" will alert one that the problem goes far beyond those six drugs.

We could go much further but that is enough. This message emailed to me was sincerely appreciated: "I am a doctor and everything you said is true." David Himmelstein and Steffie Woolhandler are doctors at Harvard Medical School. In 2001, along with Dr. Ida Hellander, wrote *Bleeding the Patient: The Consequences of corporate Health Care.*[16] Here one will read 238 pages of unsettling facts on the American health care system paralleling that just described. Payroll deductions for universal health care as a right, with doctors paid well yet all incentives for unnecessary treatments eliminated, would quickly drop health care costs by half. A serious food and nutrition study and citizenry education not dominated by food and drug corporations would drop those costs another 50% (up to the last three years of life) while increasing life spans substantially

Welfare: In an *inclusive* society with full and equal rights the only welfare necessary would be for those severely mentally or physically incapacitated.

By right, the first jobs for which they are qualified should go to the functionally impaired (answering services for the blind, accounting and secretarial work for those in wheelchairs, janitorial and assembly work for the learning disabled, etc.). Surely there are jobs for most of these 14 million disadvantaged people, whose self-esteem would be greatly improved if only they could achieve self-sufficiency.[a]

The Americans with Disabilities Act (ADA) makes it illegal to discriminate against the physically or mentally disadvantaged in jobs they can handle. The severely impaired should have the opportunity but—since any evaluation would be arbitrary—not the obligation to work. It is those who have been faced with dependency who can best appreciate the need for the pride, equality, independence, and self respect achievable through productive labor.

When handicaps result in a lack of productivity, employers being compensated by society as they maintain their employment (a right already in law) would eliminate the welfare bureaucracy. Those once working in the welfare industry can now move to productive jobs.

Others would have the right to a job much as they do now—through talent, education, tests, interviews, contacts, seniority, etc. The major change would be a dramatic cut in the workweek by law which would—considering a total restructuring of society (see conclusion)—open up space for realization of

---

[a] Mary Lord, ("Away With Barriers," *U.S. News & World Report* [July 20, 1992]: p. 60) says 43 million. Fourteen million is the lowest figure I have heard. This law is a good start towards the disadvantaged obtaining their full rights.

that right. Who would object to a 50% reduction in employed hours with no loss of living standards?

With rights to land, rights to the fruits of technology, honest insurance, the elimination of legal hocus-pocus, a public taught responsibility for its own health, universal health care for those who still get ill, rights to a productive job which pays equally for equally-productive labor, and social safety nets for retirement and disastrous events that deny a person the ability to care for their family is the foundation of a truly democratic, *all-inclusive*, peaceful, productive society with almost no need for welfare.

Where the foundations for primary monopolies are various forms of titles to nature's wealth, secondary monopolies evolved primarily filling a need that citizens were entitled to (a right) but which powerbrokers neglected (refused) to establish in law. Doing so would eliminate their monopolies.

Waste within those monopoly structures was, as addressed above, further expanded through the sale of unnecessary services. Eliminating monopolization through legislating those necessary services into a right typically reduces service costs by half even as citizens are better served. Unnecessary infrastructure (insurance structures, prisons, law offices, courtrooms, etc.) and wasted labors can now be turned to productive use.

Agriculture: **O**n July 4, 2005, *Der Speigal* pointed out:

> When there's a drought in a region of Kenya, our corrupt politicians reflexively cry out for more help. This call then reaches the United Nations World Food Program -- which is a massive agency of apparatchiks who are in the absurd situation of, on the one hand, being dedicated to the fight against hunger while, on the other hand, being faced with unemployment were hunger actually eliminated. It's only natural that they willingly accept the plea for more help. And it's not uncommon that they demand a little more money than the respective African government originally requested. They then forward that request to their headquarters, and before long, several thousands tons of corn are shipped to Africa ... Corn that predominantly comes from highly-subsidized European and American farmers ... and at some point, this corn ends up in the harbor of Mombassa. A portion of the corn often goes directly into the hands of unscrupulous politicians who then pass it on to their own tribe to boost their next election campaign. Another portion of the shipment ends up on the black market where the corn is dumped at extremely low prices. Local farmers may as well put down their hoes right away; no one can compete with the UN's World Food Program. And because the farmers go under in the face of this pressure, Kenya would have no reserves to draw on if there actually were a famine next year. It's a simple but fatal cycle.

Zambia had 40 small industries producing clothes for Zambians. A flood of used clothes from America undersold those producers, those industries closed down, the economic multiplier went into reverse, and the number of impoverished Zambians rose rapidly.

The wealthy world feasts on chicken breasts while boatloads of imported chicken wings and drumsticks—supported by the high price the wealthy will pay for chicken breasts—undersell and devastate the economies of weak nations. Not only are poor countries unable to compete against subsidized imported food and consumer products within their own countries, they are unable to export to the wealthy world due to both high supports and tariffs.

This is what happens: The wealthy world sells items for roughly half the cost of production. But the money spent producing that item circulates within the exporting economy lets say four times (the economic multiplier). Each million dollars worth of exports sold at half the cost of production, in this case $500,000, still generates $2 million of economic activity in the wealthy country.

Now we look at the country to which we are so generously giving food. The wealthy world sells $1 million worth of highly-subsidized chicken wings and drumsticks for $500,000. The entire $1 million chicken business in the importing country disappears plus another million dollars worth of business where those chicken farmers and butchers spent their money. The multiplier factor going into reverse destroyed possibly $2 million worth of local business.

Let's reverse this process: If American farmers were undersold by subsidized agricultural surpluses from another society or that imported food was given to American consumers, U.S. farmers could not sell their crops. They would go broke, the tractor and machinery companies would be bankrupt, the millions of people depending on these jobs would be without work, resources and production of remaining industries would have to be sold to other societies to pay the import bill, and America would quickly become impoverished.

In a country not yet industrialized, the natural resources must be sold to pay for subsidized food and consumer products from the industrialized world and debt traps are put in place to maintain that *dependency*.[17] This process is currently at work in Mexico. As their food imports rose to 60% of their needs, wages fell drastically, industrial production shrunk substantially, and debts increased dramatically.

Throughout these subsidiary monopolies the pattern remains: Through licenses to provide services within a monopoly structure, the citizenry are denied full and equal rights and their costs double even as services are reduced. Give citizens full and equal rights (including insurance, health care, the law, etc. as a human right.) and those monopolies disappear even as the quality of services rises rapidly. Values equal to the massive blocs of capital that once bought and sold those monopolized service industries vanish and reappear as relatively *equally-shared use values*.

Again we must point out that the wealth appropriated is capitalized, sold, and becomes a bloc of capital which is loaned or invested. That money is continually reinvested as it is paid back. The citizenry from which that wealth was appropriated, through taxes or consumer purchases, repay that principal plus interest over and over again in perpetuity, and that *impoverishing cycle* continues, interrupted only by economic collapses caused by too much capital in the hands of too few and too little buying power in the hands of the many. The elimination of those huge blocs of appropriated wealth and resultant large increase in economic efficiency and elimination of poverty is the essence of Henry George's *inclusive rules of law.*[a]

We now turn to a modern information commons through which these rights can be realized.

---

[1] J.W. Smith, *Economic Democracy: A Grand Strategy for World Peace and Prosperity* (Radford, VA: The Institute for Economic Democracy, 2006).

[2] Greider, *Secrets of the Temple*, p. 630; Christian Miller, "Wall Street's Fondest Dream: The Insanity of Privatizing Social Security," *Dollars and Sense*, November/December 1998, pp. 30-35; Edward S. Herman, "The Assault on Social Security," *Z Magazine*, November 1995, pp. 30-35; Bernstein, Merton C., Joan Brodshaug Bernstein, Social Security: The System that Works (New York: Basic Books, 1988).

[3] Fred Rodell, *Woe Unto You Lawyers* (Littleton, CO: Fred B. Rothman & Co., 1987).

[4] Rodell, *Woe Unto You Lawyers*, pp. 16-17.

[5] Norman F. Dacey, *How to Avoid Probate*, updated (New York: Crown Publishers, Inc., 1980).

[6] Katherine J. Lee, "Justice Has Broken Down," *Americans For Legal Reform* 4/2 (1985), p. 5; and other issues of *ALR*.

[7] George Milko, "It's Hassle-Free Down Under," *Americans for Legal Reform* 6/3 (1986): p. 3.

[8] Adam Smith, *The Wealth of Nations*, Modern Library ed. (New York: Random House), p. 680.

[9] Rasell, "A Bad Bargain," p. 6; Robert Weil, "Somalia in Perspective: When the Saints Go Marching In," *Monthly Review* (Mar. 1993): p. 10. Others have somewhat different statistics: Tom Shealy, "The United States vs. the World: How We Score in Health," *Prevention* (May 1986): pp. 69-71; Ernest Conine, "U.S. Should Take a Tip from Canada," *Missoulian* (Apr. 2, 1990): p. A4; John K. Iglehart, "Health Policy Report: Germany's Health Care System," *The New England Journal of Medicine* (Feb. 14, 1991): pp. 503-08 and *The New England Journal of Medicine* (June 13, 1991): pp. 1750-56; Victor R. Fuchs, PhD., and James S. Hahn, A.B., "How Does Canada Do It?" *The New England Journal of Medicine* (Sept. 27, 1990): pp. 884-90.

[10] Richard Bandler and John Grinder, *Frogs Into Princes* (Moab, UT: Real People Press, 1979), p. 102.

[11] *Sally Jesse Raphael Show* (May 30, 1988). Patient advocates Bill Johnson and Tom Wilson.

[12] "Kids in the Cuckoo's Nest," *Utne Reader* (Mar./Apr. 1992): p. 38.

[13] Sale, *Human Scale*, pp. 267-68; André Gorz, *Ecology as Politics* (Boston: South End Press, 1980), p. 161.

[14] Hurwit, "A Canadian-Style Cure," p. 12.

[15] Donald Robinson, "The Great Pacemaker Scandal," *Reader's Digest* (Oct. 1983): p. 107.

[16] Himmelstein, David, Steffie Woolhandler, Ida Hellander, *Bleeding the Patient: The Consequences of corporate Health Care* (Common Courage Press, 2001)

[17] See Bhagirath Lal Das, *WTO: The Doha Agenda: The New Negotiations on World Trade* (London: Zed Books, 2003) and his many other books. See also: Vandana Shiva's *Stolen Harvest: The Hijacking of the Global Food Supply* (Cambridge: South End Press, 2000).

---

[a] Monopolies are all *structured in law.* Any time a law *entitles* one person or group to an advantage over another person or group that is a monopoly patterned after exclusive titles to nature's wealth and technologies. An Internet search for "rent seeking" will turn up many examples.

5. Henry George's Rule of Law: a Modern Information Commons

Restructuring the developed world is prevented because information is monopolized by the financial power of the four primary monopolies—land, technology, finance capital, and communications—and the major secondary monopolies—insurance, law, health care, etc.

Control of information controls people (albeit without their realization), which in turn protects these subtle monopolies. This process ensures that the distribution of wealth will remain in the same channels going to approximately the same people. *Use values*, produced by the wealth and technologies of nature, confiscated from productive labor through *exclusive titles* to nature's wealth and technologies, and monetized in the markets through capitalizing yearly profits by 10 to 30 times, will circulate among a predetermined group as they each jockey for position to maximize their interception of social production.

Belief Systems (*spin, framework of orientation*) are kept firmly in place through subtle monopolization of the communications industry and it requires no conspiracy. Each one does just what you or I would do: they fiercely protect the source of their livelihood and their opportunities to—under the legal structure of *exclusive titles* to nature's wealth and technologies—lay claim to unearned wealth.

Thus the citizenry know little about past battles through which the limited rights they have today were wrenched from those laying claim to the major share of the wealth produced by nature and technology. Professor Herbert Schiller explains how America's view of the world has been distorted through labor having been "sealed off" from much of their history:

> How many movies did [corporate America] make about the labor movement? After all, America is made up of people who work. Where is the history of those people?

> Where's the day-in day-out history of the African American population? Where's the day-in and day-out history of women? Not just one program. Where's the whole history of the people? Where's the history of protest movements in America? Can you imagine the kind of material that could come from American protest movements? The entertainment people are always saying that they don't have enough dramatic material. Who are they kidding? [1]

Just like the windmill, steam engine, and electricity becoming so cheap that the powerful lost monopoly control, low-frequency WiFi has the potential of being so cheap that—within both the wealthy nations and developing nations—African Americans, Latin Americans, environmentalists, the peace movement, lower-paid labor, and all other politically weak segments of society will be able to reach the citizenry with the histories of their dispossessions and battles. The wealth being confiscated from productive labor can then be reclaimed.

Make no mistake about it. Powerbrokers will use all the deceits and power at their disposal to prevent or delay the economic efficiencies that are possible and, just as they have been successful in the past, they may succeed again. Witness these four primary monopolies and many secondary monopolies which are firmly in place, yet we are told they do not exist. Those powerbrokers are, as we speak (September 2005), planning on auctioning off *exclusive titles* to the extremely efficient lower frequency communication spectrums and forever forcing the citizenry to pay those monopoly prices:

> Imagine … that you're relaxing on the white sand, with a slight breeze in the air, just steps from clear blue water. The beach is open to the public, but it's never too crowded. It's a great place to surf. But then one day you show up and there's a huge brick wall blocking your path to the shore. Without telling anyone, the government sold off this seaside spot to a private developer. … If you still want to dip your toes in the water, the new management expects you to pay through the nose. You'd be pretty angry. Right? Well that's exactly what is happening right now in Congress. Only the valuable public resource being auctioned off isn't the beach—it's a prime slice of the public airwaves. …
>
> The airwaves being taken over by the broadcasters are the Malibu of the radio spectrum—fine beachfront property. Signals at these lower frequencies travel farther at lower powers and can go through obstacles like walls, trees and mountains. That means lower infrastructure costs for broadband providers, encouraging the development of local wireless networks and lowering prices. With more unlicensed spectrum, the "Community Internet" networks being setup across the country would be faster and even more reliable. Super-high-speed broadband connections for just $10 a month could be a reality. … We're headed for a world in which all communications—television, telephone, radio and the Web will be delivered over the Internet. … We can sell off our public resources … or we can invest in the future, bringing the benefits of broadband to all Americans. But first our lawmakers need to pull their heads out of the sand.[2]

As this book goes to print, legislator's heads are still in the sand. This example of establishing *exclusive title* to nature's wealth and forever claiming wealth produced by others without providing equal value in return is a beautiful example of how *exclusive title*-monopolies have been structured into the *rule of law* for centuries. Each of those *exclusive titles* or licenses permits massive overcharges to the public for use of what is properly their share of nature's wealth or their right.

These public properties must be managed but, as we have shown throughout our research, *conditional titles* to nature's wealth are many times more efficient. Those *exclusive titles* were designed centuries ago specifically to monopolize the production of nature and forever force others to pay for what is already rightfully theirs. As we go to press, the monopolists are holding the line. However we are optimists and will assume that either the American Congress will wake up or the monopoly system will collapse and society will restructure. We will be addressing the enormous possibilities if the centuries-old monopoly system is swept into the dustbin of history.

Not only can community installed low-frequency WiFi bring you broadband connection for under $30 a month (assuming they are not denied those powerful low frequency spectrums), phone calls, television, radio, music, and pay-to-view movies can all be beamed over community owned and operated WiFi. That $10 to $30 a month cost, or free, compares to the well over $100 a month it would cost to obtain all those services over cable today.

Even if those extremely efficient lower frequency communication spectrums are auctioned off to corporations, we do not think they will succeed in maintaining their monopolies. In June 2005, Boulder Colorado finished installing solar panel WiFi in a six-block area at what would cost roughly $200 per home. They are getting calls from all over the world on exactly how a workable solar panel WiFi system is installed. And San Francisco is searching for ways to install WiFi for the same free use as their highways and city streets.

An Internet search (WiFi, San Francisco) will bring up a microcosm of the current struggle to monopolize that technology. It ranges from monthly charges of $20 a month (remembering that this would be a natural monopoly and that charge would soon increase), to free access paid through popup ads, to it being a public utility paid for through taxes. WiFi in Oregon covering hundreds of square miles is free to the public with police and other first responder's contracts covering those costs. Cleveland Ohio is studying on free WiFi for all its citizens. By the time you read this book there will be many free WiFi cities around the world. Other communities will have a hard time justifying monopoly charges for what their neighbors get for free (an Internet search for "WiFi, public, free" will keep one up with those developments).

With only 2% of those valuable low frequency bands crucial for WiFi technology now in use and many communities putting WiFi services in place for free, surely those monopolies will fall. But they are not planning on it. They are getting laws passed to restrict WiFi installation, are buying up spectrums, and, at a charge of roughly $70 a month, are bringing out their own WiFi broadband connections.

Efficient, cheap, Communications may Eliminate Monopolization

Communication is considered cheap. Yet a fully WiFi wired nation, region, or world will have 10 times the communication capacity for 10% the cost as when wired only with fiber-optics. Assuming the world breaks out from under the many forms of monopolization being continually structured into the *rule of law*, this means a 99% reduction in cost per unit of communication capacity is possible and technology is still rapidly advancing.

With satellite and/or WiFi reaching each home, it is possible to educate a population for as little as 5-15% of what is considered normal today. Here the developing world has the opportunity to make an end run around wealthy nations. Massachusetts Institute of Technology, NASA, and Google—combining their expertise and money—expect to have an indestructible laptop computer ready for sale this year (2006, Internet search, $100 laptop). This WiFi equipped, $100 computer (flash memory instead of hard drive) is designed for every child in the developing world to have their own computer. Governments are expected to distribute them to each child as their own to keep at home and take to school. This tool, utilizing satellite and/or WiFi, will permit education at home at very little cost. Rumor has it that Google is buying "dark cable" (already installed fiber-optic cable which is currently in surplus). Idealists speculate they are hoping to short circuit monopolization of the Internet so as to avoid monopoly overcharges. As this book goes to press, corporations are still pushing monopolization legislation through the American Congress.

Assuming monopolization can be avoided, it is possible for a nation, or the world, to establish a communications system where everyone can talk to anyone anywhere in the world for the penny per minute calculated 30 years ago. With operational costs for individual service now cheaper than accounting, those costs can be borne by society. By a community providing the communications system—just as they now provide roads, sewers, and water systems—those efficiencies can be attained. Already Skype users use VoIP (Voice over Internet Protocol) to speak to each other world wide for free.

Phone calls worldwide can ride along for free as TV and radio stations stream their programs into WiFi. TV and radio stations having access to every viewer and listener through WiFi eliminates the need for satellite stations. Consumer choices will expand dramatically as overseas TV and radio feeds and the then unemployed stand-alone stations designing and producing new programming join the list of choices.

The shakeout within TV and radio stations will be at the same pace as WiFi is installed. Every radio station—each with varied program content—will have equal footing with Clear Channel Radio which now monopolizes America's airways now relaying the same non-varied programming to their captive audience. With primary TV stations streaming over WiFi, the only way for the then-unemployed satellite stations to capture and keep viewers would be to provide more interesting programming. Take Oprah Winfrey for example: Her Chicago station would stream into WiFi and no longer need other stations to reach their loyal viewers. It is not likely that any of those now-unemployed stations can create a program to pull an audience from her or any other already-popular program.

Outside those loyal listeners, the market for programming without advertising will trump the advertising stations and the now-out-of-work TV and radio stations unable to gain an audience—which will be most of them—will have to produce programming for a narrow audience.

The five major news networks in America, currently habituated to parroting the same very incomplete news, will suddenly face the full brunt of competition as alternative news from around the world becomes available to all. Democracy Now, Link TV, Mosaic, BBC, AlJazeera, INN Report, Indymedia, documentaries, and news from all countries in all languages would present a view of the world that many citizens within the information-insulated wealthy world are totally unaware of and those major news networks will have to address those various views of reality or become irrelevant. Twenty-four hour news channels—currently presenting over and over little more than that presented in the 22 minutes on the evening news—will have time to present all the news and, to compete, they will do so. The ability to propagandize populations will be severely constrained and control of the citizenry through control of how they view the world will be severely restricted.

As few people can handle such an overload of viewing choices, sports will gravitate to one bloc of stations, music and sitcoms will each gravitate to their blocs, and the viewers will further subdivide into regional and other subdivisions such as a bloc of channels with pay-to-play movies.

No longer able to charge monopoly prices and unable to compete in a highly saturated market, stations forced to close will be picked up by NGOs and political groups for pennies on the dollar. Formerly forced to the margins, dedicated progressives (environmentalists, sustainable living researchers, permaculturists, the peace movement, minority rights, labor rights, women's rights, children's rights, antipoverty, and a thousand more causes) will be able to reach the citizenry with their views of the world.

Politicians then must address questions brought up that were previously kept off the table. Alert viewers will have hard questions; those answers will be available, will be voiced, and will be understood. Propagandists will no longer be able to create justifications for war and full and equal rights with peace and prosperity for all will be possible.

Communication Eliminates Intermediaries and Reduces Trading Costs

The difference between manufacturing cost and the consumer price measures the major cost of most products—distribution. Typically, manufacturing costs are under 20% of the final selling price.[3] With mail-order shipping charges from 2-5% of retail price, no one would pay intermediaries 3 to 5-times the production cost when it is feasible, in this WiFi age, to study the products on an Internet database, contact the producer, buy the item, and have it shipped directly at 30-50% today's cost.

A large share of American and European consumer products is imported. But, if full and equal rights were attained worldwide, production would be primarily regional, not international. Shipping half way around the world what could be produced next door is economic insanity. Once the common sense principle of equal pay for equal work worldwide is accepted and put in place, it will be much cheaper to produce and distribute regionally and those shiploads of consumer products from half way around the world currently consuming enormous finance capital, industrial capital, and energy will be history.

Besides doing office work over the Internet, with that same WiFi wired computer one can search for—and order—one's share of larger and more expensive consumer durables. Shopping requires information and middlemen are primarily in the information business. On the Internet, it would be possible for producers and consumers to trade directly and cheaply again, just as face-to-face trades for thousands of years. The subtle monopolization of distribution with its army of intermediaries would disappear.

Trades over the Internet are surging 22% a year (2005). As those marketing channels become operational, prices for middle-priced to expensive items should drop 50% or more within 25 years.

Currently America has 10 square feet of retail floor space for each shopper and—with four stores opening for each one closing—they are headed towards 12 square feet. In comparison, Britain has only two square feet per shopper. That surplus retail space can only mean higher costs as Internet shopping rapidly lowers costs to a fraction of current levels. A great shakeout of the retail industry is inevitable. The buildings and support infrastructure for at least 30% and possibly 60% of what the developed world today considers necessary for distribution will be available for productive uses.

Bill Gates—who accumulated $60 billion because he understood communications technology better than most—said, "The information highway isn't quite right. A metaphor that comes closer to describing a lot of the activities that will take place is the ultimate market,"[4] the market we are describing.

Big-ticket, Infrequently-Purchased Items

Autos, appliances, furniture, farm equipment, industrial equipment, and major tools are all big-ticket, infrequently-purchased items whose buying requires accurate information but not the promotional/persuasive advertising that hammers at us incessantly. We trust and get information from experience and we make the most important decisions by observing products in daily use. In a communications commons, customers would make purchase decisions by dialing a database containing all manufacturers and models of a product.

That database would have information required to make an informed decision—energy efficiency, noise level, hours of useful life, price, and other features. With tests by independent researchers—such as Consumer Reports—note the pressure this would put on manufacturers to make the most efficient products and stand out in this all-important master index. Buyers would, at their leisure, study engineering specifications, styling, and actual use of the product on their television or computer. Once a decision was made, they would only need to punch in the code for the desired order—such as model, color, and accessories—and a databank computer would instantly note the closest distribution point where that item was available. Or buyers could choose delivery from the factory.

The bank account number, thumbprint, eye-scan, thermogram and signature of an Internet shopper would be verified by a master computer and that account instantly debited. If a credit line had been established at the local credit union or bank and recorded in an integrated computer, credit needs would be handled simultaneously. The process, not involving advertising, sales, or banking labor, would greatly reduce transportation, storage, and sales costs.

Product guarantees, maintenance, and repairs would be taken care of by local private enterprise under standardized guarantees. Direct trades between manufacturer and consumer (elimination of distribution intermediaries) will be guaranteeing high-quality products at the lowest possible price.

Both seller and buyer would save time and labor, as verbal explanations and mailing of information will be largely eliminated. The current time-consuming exchange of information would take split seconds and studied at the consumer's leisure. This would conserve millions of acres of trees and eliminate huge amounts of financial and industrial capital as well as tens of thousands of jobs currently manufacturing paper, producing brochures and distributing that information—including salespersons and a large percent of the labor servicing and maintaining retail establishments as well as the retail establishments themselves.

Every qualified producer would enjoy the right to place his or her product or service in the databank and pay a very small percent of gross sales out of cash flow. In place of millions of dollars up front to advertise through the present openly-monopolized media, there would be only a small charge for entering the product information in a database. To eliminate clogging the databanks with useless information of producers no longer in business, regular minimum payments would be required to retain the privilege of selling through this integrated communications network.

This would break the subtle monopolization of production and distribution by huge corporations. Starting up a truly productive industry would become quite simple. A new company's advertising would have full billing alongside major entrenched producers. With consumers having easy access to all choices, a few wealthy corporations would no longer decide, through promotional/persuasive advertising, what the public wants.

In the United States, once direct contact is established between producer and consumer via product databases, it would only require roughly 100,000 railroaders, possibly 1 million truckers (down from 1991's 1.3 million), and a system of organized freight terminals to distribute the nation's production. It would be a freight postal system just as with Christmas packages today. The item would be delivered or consumers would receive notice—by phone—of the arrival of their purchases and pick them up at the local freight terminal.

There are normally several trucking companies in any moderate-size city, each complete with loading docks, storage capacity, dispatching equipment, and staff. The following shipping pattern is already operational:

(1) Shippers punch into a common-use database loads to be shipped;

(2) truckers with WiFi computers punch in their location, freight preferences, and where he or she would like to deliver the next load;

(3) the computer instantly shows where the loads are, the type of freight, the required pickup and delivery times, the rate per mile, etc.;

(4) the trucker chooses a load, informs the computer, and records his or her identification number;

(5) and the computer records the acceptance, removes that load from the databank, provides a contract number to the trucker, and informs the shipper.

There will be no need for duplicated dispatching services, loading docks, storage facilities, equipment, and personnel. Competitive monopolies created by the minimum capital requirements for trucking companies are eliminated, placing independent truckers on an equal footing with corporate truckers. The nation's freight will quickly settle into flow patterns and be moved as regularly as mail by the cheapest combination of rail, truck, ship, and plane.

It might take a consumer from three days (small items) to 10 days (large items) to receive a purchase, but, at one-half the price or less, they are well paid. Actual transit time between producer and consumer would be a fraction of that currently through jobbers, wholesalers and retailers.

Manufacturers' on-time delivery of parts to the factory that greatly reduces storage and finance capital costs will have been expanded to on-time shipping to consumers. Those within the retail system who formerly bought, stored, and sold these products are available to engage in productive labor. Society will eventually attain an undreamed-of efficiency. Over 50% of these intermediaries between producer and consumer will eventually be eliminated and—assuming society was alert and restructured labor's working hours and other crucial adjustments—all would be free to share the remaining productive work with employment outside the home of only 2 to 3 days per week.

Once those productive jobs are shared, the average workweek reduced, and labor fully paid, the small amount of time necessary to labor for one's share of the nation's wealth would be the proper measure of the price of products and services. Our continued research still concludes that an efficient economy using modern technology of production and distribution could reduce employed working hours by at least 50%. That potential reduction in costs through elimination of unnecessary labor and productive labor being fully paid is the meaning of Adam Smith's little-noticed insightful statement, "If produce had remained the natural wages of labor, all things would have become cheaper, though in appearance many things might have become dearer."

Inexpensive, Small, Frequently-Traded Items

The markup on perishable groceries is about 100% while the markup on small consumer durables is several hundred percent. There is a competitive sales monopoly at work in the latter. Taking full advantage of modern communications would remove all purchases above an intermediate price range out of the wasteful, duplicated retail outlets. Simultaneously, the consumers' choices would be increased by access to these products through databanks.

Groceries, household supplies, cosmetics, knickknacks and most small, inexpensive consumer items would be most efficiently distributed through the present retail outlets. The breakeven point would be in the lower range of the intermediate-priced occasionally-purchased items.

Wholesalers of small-ticket consumer items would keep the quality and price of all products posted in a databank. Once trust had been established, retailers would check those bulletin boards for the best buys. This would eliminate the need for many jobbers and other salespeople.

Shopping as a Social Event entails a Cost

Shopping is recreation for many people and a status symbol for others. Those status shoppers would have no trouble finding merchants to accommodate them. To compensate for the additional labor, showrooms, and storage, the products would cost more which is properly accounted for under socializing and recreation (Tupperware or Avon), or social status (Tiffanys). The majority would surely choose the most direct and least labor-intensive (cheapest) method of completing a trade. As direct trades would be only for intermediate to big-ticket items, this would in no way impinge on local coffeehouse-type trades where socializing is the primary activity.

Reserving TV Time for New Products

While innovations on a familiar product would be readily presented to the public through a databank, totally new products would require special access to the public. To complement other methods of familiarization, some TV channels should be specifically reserved to promote such innovations. Novelty buffs comprise a large segment of the population, and there are few who do not have some interest. A program demonstrating these creations would be quite popular.

Once a production/distribution infrastructure is in place with society energized to produce and accustomed to that standard of living, promotional/ persuasive advertising becomes wasteful. Rather than titillate the consumer with thousands of toys to be played with and discarded, it would be much more socially efficient to abandon promotional/persuasive advertising and permit people to advance to a higher intellectual, social, and cultural level.

The maximum average living standard within the capabilities of the earth's resources and ecosystem can be calculated. Society could—and should—use those proven promotional/persuasive methods to educate people about the waste of the current production/distribution systems. Just as many in the developed world have already abandoned the "conspicuous consumption" lifestyle, a rational lifestyle would be made popular.

If people are so dull that a society with a respectable living standard cannot function without promotional/persuasive advertising (which we do not believe), society could analyze advertising for essential and nonessential products for the desired standard of living. Many items (cigarettes, alcohol, and chemical-laden processed foods) lower the quality of life, spending social funds on their promotion is economic insanity. Even when spent by private industry, the public pays for the debasement of their lives through the purchase price.

Driving a $60,000 luxury automobile while others are driving $20,000 cars may draw admiration today, but if society were taught that this was at the expense of humankind's survival it would incur broad disapproval. The resources saved and pollution prevented by that refocused social mindset would be substantial, and essential to the survival of thousands of species, to humankind's quality of life, and most probably to our survival.

Music, Sports, Movies, and Game Shows

Music, sports, movies, and game shows draw large audiences. Fifteen to 20 WiFi channels should be reserved for each of these interests. Only pennies per viewer, paid painlessly through consumer purchases as per the product databases addressed above, would bring in millions per broadcast to the investors, stars, directors, managers, and support labor.

With communication channels no longer monopolized through high-priced promotion there would be many more people investing, designing, producing, and starring in many more shows. Along with more time to enjoy TV, viewer choices would rise and the truly talented artists would be well paid for their efforts. All would have a reasonable opportunity to prove their abilities. A formula of gradually reduced pay per million viewing hours as a show increased in popularity would compensate performers relative to their popularity, little different than now. With access to the public for new performers, monopoly control of entertainment industries disappears.

Investment and Job Opportunities

Several WiFi channels should be reserved for direct communication between those offering investment opportunities and investors looking for them. As everyone with savings would have access to investment information stored in databanks, money monopolists would be totally bypassed. Individual investors would put their risk capital in innovations that went unrecognized by regular loan institutions. If the investment were truly productive, investors would receive much higher than average returns. However, if their claims to insight were not valid, they would not be able to hide behind the protective shield of subtle monopolization.

An entrepreneur who had obtained community approval and initial investment capital from the bank (they need both now) would deposit a prospectus in a databank. Investors would study the various investment plans, buy shares in the most promising, and have their accounts automatically debited, all without intermediaries.

Talented workers would look over prospectuses, which would include labor needs and incentives, and—if they saw where their talents would be used productively and profitably (and assuming they had fulfilled their contract to train a replacement)—they could transfer to that new job. Labor would be mobile and free (not dispossessed as in a reserve labor force), with rights to their share of the efficiency gains of technology. (In a modern industrial society, each worker would work only 2 to 3 days per week. See the work of Charles Fourier 180 years ago and Thorstein Veblen, Bertrand Russell, Lewis Mumford, Stuart Chase, Upton Sinclair, and Ralph Borsodi in the first half of the 20th century. Late 20th century writers describing the same phenomenon are Juliet Schor, Seymour Melman—Samuel Bowles, David Gordon, and Thomas Weiskopf—Jeremy Rifkin, Andre Gorz, Hans-Peter Martin and Harold Schumann, and numerous European authors).

If a replacement were not immediately available, other workers at the factory could double their pay by working five days a week. Strict rules of later time off to compensate would have to be followed. Permitting doubling up on established jobs would appropriate the labor rights of others and subvert the economy through again creating a superior class with superior rights. The underemployed would be denied their share of social production while those working excessive hours would have more than their share.

For their risk, the original innovators and investors would receive the initial higher profits plus the increased values of a successful company. Through sharing in the profits, workers and management who bought stock through deductions of 10-20% of their wages would be well compensated. The profit potential would increase their desire to maximize efficiency and provide incentive to look for new industries to develop."[5]

Others would quickly analyze and duplicate the innovative production or distribution process; prices would fall to just that required to compensate the innovators, labor, and capital. Through low priced products, equal pay for equally-productive labor, and rights to a productive job, each member of society would be receiving their proper share of wealth provided by nature and the efficiency gains of technologies which are gifts of nature nurtured by inventors' labors and talents.

If a communications commons functioning under the *inclusive rules of law* of Henry George reduced production and distribution costs 60% and adequate compensation to the innovators was 10%—measured in hours of labor required to purchase a product—the public would quickly benefit by a 50% reduction in the price of consumer products. Through the reduced income of a shorter workweek matching the reduction in living costs there would be no loss in living standards. Societies which decided to forego a throwaway society and opt for hydrogen, fuel cell, hybrid car, bicycle economy and other efficient transportation systems would provide a quality lifestyle with even less labor.

Education

Children want the approval of their parents and other members of society. They love to excel and desire equality with their peers. They are curious and, if not discouraged, love to learn. Today's educational system creates too many barriers; "half of all gifted children float through school with average or worse grades, never realizing their potential ... almost 20 percent will drop out."[6]

There are many reasons: a child may be timid and terrified of school, an inferiority complex may prevent a student from functioning or excessive pressure to do well may be daunting. The school district may have obsolete books and teaching aids and students may not get the individual attention they need. Local peer groups (gangs) may replace parents and teachers as role models. Parents may not be involved enough in their child's learning. Or the curriculum may be so slow it is boring. With elimination of these and other barriers, many with low grades will blossom right along with their peers.

Schools are a commons but they need to be restructured to a modern commons. With 40 to 60 WiFi channels reserved for education, every subject now taught at elementary, secondary, college, and university level would reach every home free of charge. Each subject would have several recorded lecturers and be broadcast at various hours of the day. The competition would be intense for the teaching positions on such programs and these best educators in the nation would be well paid. Each recorded course would be edited for maximum clarity, simplicity, and comprehension. Everything in a book can be summarized in a recorded lecture. Reasoning is quite natural and nothing can beat a good educator whose recorded lectures anticipate, and are carefully structured to answer, most questions. With all society having access, the fictions and omissions of history (especially omissions) would be challenged, researched, and corrected.

With their lessons recorded, these high-quality educators would be spending less time teaching than any one of the tens of thousands they replaced. They would concentrate on studying their own and others' lectures for ways to improve. Modeling is the most potent teacher of all and these great teachers would be great role models.

The equipment required for each student would be a TV set or computer, while the local education system would provide workbooks to match the TV lessons. As these lessons would be in a databank accessible through the integrated communications system, downloading to a hard drive would record for later study. They could replay the lessons as many times as necessary for maximum comprehension.

So long as a student maintained an adequate grade average, a share of the money society saved on maintaining the present school system could be paid to each child's family. Allowing for each child's ability, it would be logical to pay this incentive for each subject and on an average of all subjects. This would be high motivation for families to restructure their time for home education. With spending money earned for each subject, motivated students would zip through many subjects. Developing nations do not have to deconstruct an entrenched, expensive educational system and their citizens' motivation for education is high so there would be no need for incentive pay. But they would have high incentive to utilize their current classrooms as administrative and testing stations and educate their populations—children and adults—through WiFi television.

With the 2 to 3 day workweek possible in a developed economy, there would be adequate time for parents to monitor their children's learning. With rapport between parent and child, the brightest would cover a current year's education in as little as four months, some in two months. The most intelligent and motivated would have the knowledge of PhDs at an age when they would normally be entering universities—which, incidentally, would eliminate another monopoly.

Actually those students would have a much broader education than most PhDs. Current doctoral studies are very narrow in focus. Without breadth of education, the answers to the world's problems will not be found. Conversely, if universities emphasized graduate degrees that covered a broad spectrum of disciplines instead of narrow fields, answers would be found relatively quickly. Through free TV studies, students would have that broad education. This is proven by over 1 million American children already being successfully home schooled, doing well in universities, and their numbers are growing 15% a year, all without government support.[7]

Students would not be pressured to follow the teaching of any one professor. Others might have a different view and students could listen to all views. Judgments would be made while still young and idealistic. All this would be gained while enjoying the irreplaceable quality time between parent and child.

Some talented students who do not have parental support would find a surrogate family by immersing themselves in education.

Private or public education centers would be operated for the few who could not function under home self-education. Those who were intellectually capable but failing would be required to attend specially structured classes. Upon doing satisfactory work, they would still receive incentive funds.

The compensations and identity received by siblings and friends for successful home schooling would be noticed by younger children and provide motivation to avoid the formal school setting.

Any child would be proud to go shopping with their own earnings and it is hard to visualize many children being irresponsible toward their education if it meant losing both their freedom of choice and their spending money. They would quickly learn responsibility when it meant both financial and emotional rewards. Society would quickly become accustomed to such a system and the need for brick and mortar schools would be very minimal.

Children can be just as easily culturally trained to quality as they can to trash. So it would be logical to eliminate the senseless violence in today's children's programs. At the least, quality programming could be assigned a bloc of channels so conscientious parents could maximize their children's intellectual and moral growth.

Incentive funds—as a right—would in no way impinge on others' rights. Those rights could only be exercised by obtaining a set grade average. Home education would save society far more than the incentive costs. In fact, those funds cost nothing; they go right back to the people from whom they came. Over time, such incentives would be looked upon as normal as wages.

Older students would soon learn to structure their flexible education time around their job. There need not be a sharp cutoff between school years and entering the workforce. The options for pursuing education for a career and earning one's living would be increased. Instead of a division between students and workers, the two would overlap until the young adults opted for a career.

Motivated children, youths, young adults, and adults would obtain most of their education at home and at their own pace. Children with a desire to learn, which is most of them, would find the field wide open. Left to their own devices, they would quickly learn that it was their time and labor that were being conserved by dedication and attention to the subjects being taught. The alert would be developing university level leaning skills while in grade school

Many talented children's potential—now lost through boredom and diversion to socially undesirable activities—would be salvaged. The brightest would attain a 12th grade education in less than eight years, the middle level in 10, and even the slower group—which currently sets the pace of a classroom—would learn more quickly. There would be adequate resources and time to give special support to the few who are unable to cope for various reasons. This would not only conserve society's labor, it would economize students' energy and time.

This potential was shown by an experiment with interactive videos reducing learning time while increasing comprehension by 30%.

Having watched great videos on Free Speech TV, Link TV, The Learning Channel, The History Channel, The Arts and Entertainment Channel, The Discovery Channel, and public broadcasting channels, we conclude that the statement, "A picture is worth a thousand words," should be changed to; "One documentary is worth a million words." The best of those documentaries combines the wisdom of many researchers developed by many lifetimes of study. All viewers will absorb that knowledge at some level. Avid reading will seldom bring one close to the understanding gained from a well-researched documentary. The gain for the slower and less avid readers would be of much greater dimension. As opposed to being bored and discouraged, students will enjoy their education.

A central testing facility would be maintained that would issue scholastic level certificates and incentive funds. These achievement tests would be designed to educate children to compete with the best in the world. This would quickly equip all nations to be competitive.[8] Since credentials are crucial for obtaining good jobs, all would have access to their scores, the right to analyze their answers, and the right to retake tests.

Classes requiring hands-on learning would be held in a classroom setting along with supporting recorded programs. Millions who dreamed of additional education would find it freely available in what was previously their idle time.

As no one's knowledge is complete, every curriculum would be subject to review and correction. The Great Saint-Mihiel battle of WWI that never happened and other examples of fraudulent history addressed throughout this author's books are not exceptions.[9] Severely distorted history is the norm and such failures to tell the full truth seriously retards democratic development while correct and full knowledge is critical to planning one's future.

Every day we learn something new or reinforce what we already know. To waste huge amounts of resources while continually affirming nice-sounding slogans about efficiency, justice, and compassion while operating an inefficient economy and violent foreign policy seriously limits true knowledge. Redesigning society to produce and distribute efficiently and peacefully would give children a better cultural education.

It is not possible to get every student to enjoy learning for its own sake. If given a choice, most people would choose to do things that best support their need for identity and security, for many that is obtained in work, sports, and hobbies rather than intellectual pursuits. There will be those who—though unable to compete across the board scholastically—will take great interest and do well in a field of their choice.

Schools—as now structured—do perform a babysitting function. But, if that is the criterion, society should be aware that the potential of many children is lost and that child care is what they are paying for, not education. One must also be aware that early industrialists hoped that "the elementary school could be used to break the labouring classes into those habits of work discipline now necessary for factory production....Putting little children to work at school for very long hours at very dull subjects was seen as a positive virtue, for it made them 'habituated, not to say naturalized, to labour and fatigue."[10]

Inspired Teachers for Every Student

People feel insecure at any suggestion of fundamental change in their social institutions and most are closely attached to the institutions of education. But, in the current school structure, where is that all-important role model if the student has a poor, mediocre, or burned-out teacher? Under the system proposed here there would be many great teachers, each teaching his or her deepest beliefs, and their recorded lectures would be freely available for all.

By eliminating the current monopoly on education (in the soft sciences—economics, political science, finance, some social studies, and, especially, history), what passes for education is, unwittingly, really programming encasing society within a *belief system* protecting the monopoly system, those *exclusive titles* to nature's wealth we all grew up with.

Certainly, good hands-on teachers are wonderful, but how can they hold enthusiasm with 25 or 30 children to teach? Would not the best possible teacher—backed by professional graphics—be able to put on an enthusiastic performance, and that enthusiasm is there forever on DVD or videotape? Even a slow student could learn more than in a crowded and socially isolated classroom. Would not that slow or timid student have a better chance of not developing an inferiority complex, and thus do better?

Parents Interacting closely with their Children's Education

With their increased free time, motivated parents would enjoy watching their children learn and answering their questions. Children would ask an interested parent many more questions than they would a teacher. A motivated parent will go into deeper detail than the teacher who has so little time to spare for individual attention. Students too timid to function freely in class would function confidently in a home setting. In the upper grades, motivated parents would share the experience and learn with their children.

Better Institutions for Socialization

Socialization is of high importance. But the elimination of this function within education would free students for concentration on their studies. Youth social clubs would spring up and children would sign up voluntarily as opposed to the requirement to attend school. When children join a social club by choice, they would be bound by the rules of social courtesy—not classroom discipline—and would mix, relate, and learn social graces at a faster pace than in a school setting. Parents would automatically seek such groups to replace the baby-sitting function of schools. With increased free time, the arts (music, dance, sculptors, singing, painting, and other skills) would expand rapidly.

Maintaining Curiosity, Creativity, and Love of Learning

Education freely available to all in their free time would bypass that greatest of all destroyers of curiosity and creativity, the straitjacketing of children into conformity. We cannot count on a great teacher in every classroom. We cannot count on even half being good. Witness Massachusetts—a state with much higher quality schools than the average—in 1998 over half the teachers failed state qualification tests. There are over 15,000 educational experiments yearly. Some show dramatic improvements in education scores. Yet the overall average of scores does not improve. Either these better teaching methods are not spreading to other schools or those schools do not have motivated teachers. Why not combine modern technology with the students' abilities and desires and trade the constraints of current classroom and university systems for the opportunity of an inexpensive, high quality, and enjoyable education?

Certainly one can point to great teachers and the gains for their lucky students. But there would be no loss to those children in this proposed educational structure. Instead, the number of children educated to their maximum potential would increase by a factor of two, three, or more. With easy access to classes in their spare time, many adults would broaden their education. Those who have a burning desire for another profession can gain credentials for their desired career even if finances are limited. Potentially great artists would have the opportunity to discover their talents—painters, poets, writers, singers, sculptors, ad infinitum?

There are undoubtedly many latent Einsteins currently spending their lives in drudgery who would educate themselves and have their genius suddenly blossom for all the world to see and enjoy in the form of a book, a song, a new theory, an invention. A large percentage of society educating itself to a much higher level would develop an even more efficient and productive society while protecting the environment and natural resources.

Once Borderline Teachable Graduating at the Top of Their Class

Inspirational teachers and programs have proven they can parent impoverished children with damaged psyches into becoming successful citizens. One such teacher is Ms. Marva Collins in Chicago. She worked among her students, rather than from her desk. Each time one did well she would put her hand under his or her chin, lift the child's eyes to hers, and say, "You are brilliant," or give some other sincere compliment. Minority children in her class deemed borderline teachable graduated from the university at the top of their class, and went on to become professors, lawyers, and other successful professionals. Failures were almost nonexistent.

Charles Murray, in his infamous book *The Bell Curve*, cited Ms. Collin's program, specifically, pointing out that such programs could not possibly improve academic achievement or cognitive functioning. Having documented Ms. Collins successes 20 years earlier, *Sixty Minutes* went back after Murray's book came out and checked on those 33 children. [11] Those students were the roaring successes described above and thoroughly proved Murray's thesis was racist nonsense supported by corporate hard-right think tank money as outlined in this author's primary research.

While restructuring to a just society, such programs would be used to salvage such at-risk children. Once all have equal access to a society's benefits and opportunities, most will be good parents and most children will be well educated.

Culture and Recreational Learning

Fine arts and recreational learning programs—such as are produced by public broadcasting stations—are enjoyable and add to one's knowledge. Fifteen to 20 WiFi channels should be reserved for these high-quality shows. The social benefits of learning while relaxing are self-evident and popular talk shows and good recreational/educational TV command a loyal audience.

One live commercial show can easily exceed one PBS station or alternative view station's yearly cost for all recorded shows. With their fair share of funds through restructuring funding as described below, the present financial struggles of those who broadcast quality programs would be eliminated which would lead to the production of many more great documentaries.

Among the cultural and educational programs would be one or more channels reserved for introducing and demonstrating innovations (including governing and banking concepts) and inventions. Alert, imaginative minds would relate their special expertise to other machines, production processes, distribution methods, and social policies. Along with alerting consumers to new products, society would be devising simpler methods of manufacturing, distributing, and governing.

Minority Cultures

Twenty to 30 channels would be reserved for ethnic minorities. Within the American culture they are inadequately represented and participate in national culture only to a limited extent. With these new rights, they would quickly develop outstanding media and political personalities to articulate essential issues and challenge the *belief systems* that protect power structures and keep others in bondage. With their own communication channels, equal access to land and jobs, and the right to retain what their labors produce, minorities would share the nation's work, its wealth, and participate in national decision-making. Every citizen might at last attain the full rights of equal citizenship.

Foreign Cultures

Though programs created by cultures of other nations will be streaming over WiFi, guaranteed representation of their views should apply also to foreign cultures. When the vulnerable are not present to defend themselves, *managers of state*—seeking followers for aggressive intent—portray them as enemies. With the world in all living rooms through WiFi wired communities with blocks of channels for each culture, it would be difficult for *managers of state* to hide their aggressive intentions as they create enemies to justify their wars.

By mutual agreement there should be reciprocal presentations of cultural programs between countries to provide cross-cultural information. Redrawn broadcast standards would limit propaganda. Beamed to every home, programs would show people throughout the world at work and at play. People would begin to appreciate and respect both what we have in common and what is distinctly different. Full rights globally will evolve if ever a federation of nations restructures their economies to full and equal rights for all.

Local Television

With all TV stations able to stream worldwide over WiFi, the meaning of a local station would totally change. Those with superior production teams could gain a national or even an international audience. As a source of community information and culture, citizens will share ideas and experiences. Local sports, concerts, plays, parades, and community information forums on a broad range of issues will be hosted. Meetings of governing bodies, normally open to the public by law, would be beamed over local TV.

Elections

With politicians having access to the public through reserved WiFi channels, there would be no need to spend private funds for elections. Politicians want to be just as honest as anyone else. With each of them having equal access to the voters, campaign funds could, and should, be made illegal. All understand they are bribes. With free access to the citizenry over WiFi assured by law, campaign contributions will be a liability and disappear into history.

Ten to 20 reserved TV channels would be needed for serious leaders to present their views. Serious—In this instance—means having a substantial segment of the population to represent—corporations, business people, farmers (all now over-represented), women (who have just gained representation), labor (represented but unwittingly supporting suppression of other labor worldwide [the purpose of the propaganda process]), minorities, the poor, conservationists, peace groups, and others.

Politicians must be in the spotlight. Those not attending in-depth background discussions would be relinquishing their claim to leadership. With authorities such as those cited throughout this book invited to these forums, it would be difficult to duck the issues. There would just be too many questions.

Only when all have the opportunity to present their views—making social-control rhetoric counterproductive—can there be true democracy. Those who presented a consistent and accurate view of reality and promoted a policy for the maximum good of the people would gather a loyal following. Interested people would make value judgments on the history leading to the present problems, study the different solutions that were presented, and analyze the intelligence and integrity of the leaders proposing these solutions. It is their opinions that guide the thinking of the nation.

These opinion makers (intellectuals, leaders, and the news media) would watch the information forums to inform themselves and—in turn—inform the public. To do less would leave one uninformed and lose one's followers. With elections structured for candidates to prove their mettle—like the famous Lincoln-Douglas debates—the now-informed citizens would be enabled to make responsible voting decisions.

It must be emphasized that monopolists will use every power at their command to prevent cheap communications between all people and all elements of society. However it will happen—either quickly or slowly—and when it does today's monopolies will—just like aristocracy—be history.

A Socially-Owned Banking System Paying for WiFi

We documented above the justifications for society collecting the profits from their banking system. There would be no shortage of funds for operating the economic infrastructure that would reduce both communication and education costs by 85% Access to the communications system would be as cheap as access to highways, sidewalks, and parks.

---

1 Herbert Schiller (Interview), "The Information Highway: Paving Over the Public," *Z Magazine*, March, 1994, pp. 46-50. See also Peggy Norton, "Independent Radio's Problems and Prospects," *Z Magazine*, March, 1990, pp. 51-57.

2 Craig Aaron, "Sun, Sand and Spectrum Policy," *In These Times*, September 19, 2005, p. 13.

3 Paul Zane Pilzer, *Unlimited Wealth* (New York: Crown, 1990), p. 44.

4 Steven Levy, "Bills New Vision," *Newsweek*, November 27, 1995, p. 68.

5 Steven Levy, "Bills New Vision," *Newsweek*, November 27, 1995, p. 68.

6 Anne Windishar, "Expert: 20% of Gifted Kids Drop Out," *Spokane Chronicle*, January 7, 1988, p. B7.

7 Rebecca Winters, "From Home to Harvard," *Time*, September 11, 2000, p. 55.

8 Thurow, *Head to Head*, pp. 273-79, especially p. 278.

9 George Seldes, *Even The Gods Can't Change History* (Secaucus, N.J: Lyle Stuart, 1976), p. 16.

10 Juliet Schor, *The Overworked American* (New York: Basic Books, 1991), p. 61.

11 *60 Minutes*, September 24, 1995; Herrnstein, Richard J., and Charles Murray. *The Bell Curve: Intelligence and Class Structure in American Life* (New York: Free Press, 1994), p. 399

6. Capitalism's Mighty Economic Engine: Henry George's far more Powerful Engine

To build a base to understand the forthcoming struggles we will summarize our primary research, *Economic Democracy: A Grand Strategy for World Peace and Prosperity*, the 1000 year history of *plunder by trade.* For roughly 800 years the City States of Europe fought to control the resources of the countryside. Processing those resources into consumer products was the source of both their living and their wealth. Those City States became nations. The resources required for wealth and power still lay outside their borders. This produced more wars. Reaching for more wealth and power, seven nations of Europe rushed across the world to—with minor exceptions—claim every square mile. Those early battles between City States and the countryside, and those between individual City States, were replayed by battles between empires.

The absolute rule to never transfer technical knowledge to other nations was broken when Kaiser Wilhelm of Germany bought technology wholesale from his grandmother, England's Queen Victoria, and cousin, King George V.[1] The result was German technology taking over the markets of British Industries leading to WWI and WWII. China taking over world markets in this century is recognized by many as a replay of that early 20th century crisis.

But 50% of the world industrialized, armed with nuclear weapons, and battling over access to resources and markets in the 21st century is different than 15% of the world industrialized, armed with conventional weapons, and battling over access to resources and markets in the early 20th century. There are too many nuclear weapons pointed at too many huge cities. Any nation which chooses nuclear war over sharing technology and resources may also be destroyed. Short of destruction by imperial nations (they committing national suicide in the process), China, India, most of East Asia, and possibly countries such as South Africa will successfully industrialize even under today's inefficient monopoly systems.

Developing and eliminating their poverty were the goals of periphery nations after WWII. Africa was planning on a United States of Africa.[2] Think of the threat Africa as one nation would have been to those depending upon those resources to rebuild from WWII. Knowing that is understanding the financial, economic, diplomatic, covert, and overt wars suppressing the colonial world's post WWII breaks for freedom that prevented the emergence of that super federation.

As all these wars were waged under the flags of peace, freedom, justice, rights, and majority rule, not even the countries being destabilized realized what was happening. They knew America had broken free, believed those slogans and looked up to them as saviors and supporters of their freedom.

But now they know that America has joined forces with their European cousins to deny emerging nations their rights and freedom. The alliances forming and the surges for equality and freedom today are identical to the hopes and dreams of the developing world 40 to 60 years ago and they now understand the tricks of the trade. As there are at least six *centers of capital,* with three being in Asia, competition for resources will be fierce. This is the undeveloped world's moment to demand freedom and equality and they know it. After all, industries are relatively cheap to build whereas resources—when priced at their true values—are expensive. Those costs will keep going up and one of the primary purposes of this book is to document that—once a regional labor force is trained and their own workers are used to process their resources and build and operate their industry—the currency cost of developing a region is not much more than the cost of printing money, all else is a region's internal processing of resources into infrastructure, industries, and consumer products.

The entire region surrounding the three Asian *centers of capital*, with over half the world's population, is rapidly industrializing. An alliance of the developed world in a war against the fast-developing world is recognized as likely destroying both. The quagmire in Iraq proves that covert destabilizations to install puppet governments are no longer options. That act of empire cost America the moral high ground and provided both the motivation and the opening for the world's poorest regions to start allying together. The massive resources inside the borders of those forming, alliances—combined with the world's six *centers of capital* competing for resources—should give those periphery regions equal negotiating power. Alliances between resource-wealthy developing regions and rising centers of capital increase the economic and political power of both.

Think back on the various monopolies that applying Henry George's *inclusive rules of law* exposed. Each are laying claim to massive amounts of unearned values; those annually appropriated values are capitalized by 10 to 30 times, those "earnings" (thefts) are invested in treasury, water, sewer, other bonds, etc.; those from which that wealth was appropriated now pay both the monopoly overcharges and payments on those bond; and this goes on and on, into perpetuity, until it gets so out of balance the economy collapses. Considering that fully 60% of America's huge blocs of accumulated capital is appropriated wealth, and that half those values are wasted in the process, the subtle-monopoly capitalist system is a *value harvesting machine*, not an efficient producer of wealth.

Each of the six times the American economy was poised to collapse over the past 25 years, due to too much wealth in the hands of a few and too little in the hands of the many, money was created and poured into the markets. So the finance monopolists have learned how to prevent a crash due to internal imbalances, just create money, pour it at those markets or ratchet up some part of the economy—the 2002-05 housing bubble for example—and those higher values prop up the markets which then rise to a higher imbalance.

Today this *value-harvesting machine* is sucking up the world's wealth. But suppressed and oppressed nations understand how the imperial nation's are swallowing up their wealth and distributing it amongst their own citizenry as their earned wealth. Those dispossessed can calculate that, like a Ponzi scheme producing nothing, in the end there is nothing left for them. Like all pyramid schemes, money is appropriated from the masses, great promises are made, but when it ends, as all do, the first few into the game have all the money.

Finance capital which powers capitalism's mighty engine depends on continuously appropriated from true producers. Continually invested profits from those invested funds are being paid for over and over by those from which it was first appropriated on into perpetuity, those huge profits reach out to buy up other societies wealth, and this expansion continues until so much wealth has piled up in so few hands and so little buying power is in the hands of the citizenry that monopoly capitalism goes into one of its periodic collapses.

Meantime, the super-efficient, much-smaller, economic engine of Henry George capitalism—money created within a *socially-owned* banking system funding the real economy—eliminates the waste of monopolization, maximizes the utilization of increasingly-efficient technologies, shares full and equal rights world-wide, eliminates war, expands across the earth with productive capacity and buying power in balance, has the power to eliminate poverty in 10 years and can provide a quality life for all world citizens in under 50 years.

That potential is not realized because the visible large increases in technological efficiencies are eulogized and the even greater potentials are unrealized. To restructure to such an efficient economy, within any country would be revolutionary. There is no middle ground, so we have chosen to address it within the framework of a velvet revolution. These final pages establish the framework and a theoretical time-line for those peaceful revolutionary changes.

---

[1] Kurt Rudolph Mirow, Harry Maurer, *Webs of Power* (Boston: Houghton Mifflin Co., 1982), p. 16.

[2] Crucial documentary on a U.S. of *Africa: Wind of Change*, order at Films for Humanity & Sciences 800.257.5126, item # BVL30750; Organizations formed to further African unity are: AU (African Union); NEPAD (New Partnership for Africa's Development) OAU (Organization of African Unity); OAAU (Organization for African American Unity (founded by Frantz Fanon); OCAM (Organization Commune Africaine et Malagache); OERS (Organization of States Bordering the Senegal River); UDEAC (Customs Union of Central African States); OERM (Economic Organization of North Africa); EACM (East African Community and Common Market); CEAO (West African Economic Community); CEDEAO (The Economic Community of West African States). Francois N. Muyumba, Esther Atcherson, *Pan-Africanism and Cross-Cultural Understanding: A Reader* (Needham Heights, MA: Ginn Press, 1993).

7. Summary

The odds are greatest that the world will continue battling over the world's resources rather than choose the path of peace and prosperity. But this short reality list demonstrates it can happen:

(1) Full fledged revolutions after both WWI and WWII that would have eliminated Western *rule of law* put in place the past 700 plus years were far closer than our history books acknowledge. In both cases all Europe was almost lost.[1] With the loss of its core, the monopoly system—the primary cause of most wars—would have disappeared worldwide, including in America.

(2) Along with supporting rationales, the first purpose of those two world wars was to prevent Germany from taking over England's markets. If that were to happen, Britain's empire would have quickly collapsed and that too would have either collapsed the monopoly system or placed Germany at the helm.

(3) A second purpose of WWII was to take out the Soviet Union whose economic successes also spelled doom for the monopoly system. The world could not be kept under control so long as that example was there for the world to see.

The Rudolf Hess saga assures us a secret agreement had been reached to take out that threat. Knowing that France and England would enter the fray and dictate the peace as they were defeating the Soviet Union, Germany—through conquering all nations between her and the Atlantic Ocean—took care of her back door first. Germany then flew their second in command, Rudolf Hess, to Britain to get the original agreement back on track, only this time it would be on their terms. She then attacked the Soviet Union.

There was no way Britain could shift the beliefs of their people from Germany as an enemy to an ally in so short a time, the struggle for control in Europe was on. America's embargo of Japan (oil and steel) was expected to shut that economy down in 60 days which led to Pearl Harbor. America joined the battle on both fronts and the rest is history. Now a part of that scenario is not what is recorded in history but lets be realistic, that is what happened. Hess finished his life out in Spandau prison permitted only to see his family under guard with instructions that only family matters could be discussed.

(4) Though few realize it, the 45 years of the Cold War was specifically to suppress the post WWII revolutions which were only continuations of the almost

successful post WWI revolutions addressed above in which the real reasons were conveniently left out of history books.[2]

(5) Oil producing nations quickly figured out that America's invasion of Iraq was only the first step in controlling oil throughout the Middle East and Central Asia, control the rest of the world through control of their oil supplies, and those weak oil-supplying nations are contracting (lightly allying) with Russia, China, and India to offset that threat. The undeveloped world has figured out that the slogans of peace, freedom, justice, rights, and majority rule were covers for suppressing their freedom and rights. The option of developing a few nations under the above slogans as allies against the remaining periphery nations is no longer viable. The option (cover story) being tried, bringing democracy to the world, is believed by almost no one. That imperialist democracies are really puppet governments while true democracies have been subverted and overthrown for the past 60 years is well understood. Imperialists are trapped as certified free elections replace those puppet governments with honest ones. Imperialist's control of puppet governments is now so well understood that even countries where external control of elections were once blatant—Venezuela, Haiti, Bolivia, and Chile for example—have thrown aside those puppets by the ballot. As the War on Terror worldwide is against them and they are fully aware of the above deceptions, the Muslim word interprets that war as being against their religion. Thus, for each Muslim killed in this "war on terror" several more take their place. As all this unfolds, enough citizenry within the imperial nations will understand that America and their allies are obviously operating an empire and more home support will be lost.

(6) Fully 60% of the industrial capacity of the world is now outside the borders of Europe and America. This is the same trade structure which led to WWI and WWII and this crisis for the imperial centers will be many times greater.

China has announced that she will soon be selling cars on the world market at 60% the price of other manufactures. Currently brand names are produced in China and marketed by Western traders at huge profit margins. China is busy developing brand names for all products. With an already hollowed out industrial economy, the profit structure within those wealthy nations will collapse as those brands, one by one, hit Western markets.[a]

As the huge profits currently earned by American traders are taken over by Chinese traders, China and other alert lower-paid nations where those products are produced will be banking the profits of capital, the wages of labor, and those huge trader profits. The current account deficits of the historic imperial nations will increase in step with foreign traders replacing domestic traders.

(7) Fast developing Southeast Asia may settle for equality but—whether America and Europe like it or not—they will not settle for second place.

---

[a] As all nations will be able to purchase those products at that low price, anti-dumping laws will not apply.

(8) As their enormous wealth and military might is based upon theft of the wealth of weak nations—and assuming America does not use its nuclear weapons to maintain its current fascist control of resources throughout the world—long before Southeast Asia reaches 50% equality the economies of America and Europe will collapse.
(9) All the world's major banking systems know the day of reckoning will come. Various countries are getting out of the dollar and into Euros. Girding to fight that battle, America's Federal Reserve quietly noted they would no longer release statistics on how much money they are printing. [3] The citizenry will not be alerted that massive money is being created and that the battle of the titans has begun. Seeing the writing on the wall, half the presidents of America's regional Federal Reserve banks have resigned.
(10) The rulers of the world are totally out of sync with its citizenry who are restive and demanding their reasonable share. A worldwide populist uprising is imminent, the communication systems are in place to sustain that revolt, and—sooner or later if the world's leaders do not wake up and run this world responsibly—that revolution will happen There is only one difference between aristocracy denying the common people rights for centuries leading to the French Revolution and financial aristocracy today denying the citizenry worldwide their reasonable share of the worlds wealth, modern communications will permit a large share of the world to revolt simultaneously.
(11) And, as there is plenty on this earth for all if it were shared equally instead of fought over, these battles over control of the *wealth producing process* are unnecessary.

So rational choices are only two:
(1) Powerful nations give up their selfish ways, operate responsibly, and share the wealth of the world relatively equally.
(2) Or this world is shattered and made largely uninhabitable by a 3rd World War using nuclear weapons.

Another two possibilities may avoid a world war but they are so morally repugnant and unlikely, we will not even consider them:
(3) The current fast developing nations will come to an agreement with the old imperial nations that together they will control the world and share the wealth. Africa, South America, Central Asia, and the Muslim world (targeted to be outside that circle of wealthy nations) will never accept that irresponsibility and laying down their tools, sabotaging resource extraction and infrastructure, roadside bombs, and suicide bombers will grind the world economy to a halt.
(4) Fascist control of periphery nations and their resources by the old imperial nations is how periphery nations have been controlled ever since WWII. That system is falling apart as we speak and—though habituated powerbrokers may try—we do not believe that approach is worth considering.

If the current alliance of America, Europe and Israel use nuclear weapons on Iran and other recalcitrant nations—as they are threatening to do as this book goes to press—that would be only a preview of WWIII. For that to succeed all other nations must agree to a far lower share of the wealth than that consumed by Europe and America and we do not believe that other nuclear armed nations will accept that. It would also mean Africa, South America, and the Muslim world will have to accept their resources providing a large share of that wealth and they receiving almost none. We do not believe that will be accepted either. The world's corrupt and selfish rulers must be replaced by others with vision and responsibility.

We feel that if we are in error it will only be one of timing. There is the possibility that fascist control of impoverished nations could go on for another generation. There is the possibility that battles over the world's resources will go on forever. We think that both those scenarios are highly unlikely. It will be either peace with sharing of the world's resources or it will be nuclear WWIII and we chose to assume the first of those possibilities—the world restructuring to peace with a quality life for all.

If peace does come to this world it will be because historic powerbrokers are faced by equal power, the current leaders are pushed aside by democratic forces, and new leaders agree to equitably share the wealth. Ever since WWII, only the alliance of developed nations, the ones imposing those unequal trades, has had that choice. The unallied impoverished world has no choice. If they are to ever rise out of poverty they must ally together and force the imperial nations and fast developing nations to include them in the *wealth producing process* and grant them their fair share. Once allied, their power will equal the nuclear armed world. No possible combination of military power can offset half the world laying down their tools and fighting back with industrial sabotage, suicide bombs, car bombs, and roadside bombs.

Having been appropriating the wealth of periphery nations under various cover stories (they have no souls, they are not capable) for centuries, the West refuses to bite the bullet and restructure to honest—truly productive—societies. But they may have to: Sprinkled throughout these concluding pages are other signs that a severe crisis for the wealthy world is brewing. All the ASEAN countries (Indonesia, Thailand, Malaysia, Singapore, Philippines, Brunei, Vietnam, Laos, Myanmar, Cambodia) plus Japan, China, India, South Korea, Australia, and New Zealand, representing half (three billion) of the world's people met in Malaysia, December 2005, for the inaugural of the East Asian Summit (EAS). That America was not invited is significant. Interest also quickened at the April 10, 2006 meeting of the South Asian Association for Regional Cooperation (SAARC).

With Evo Morales's election as president of Bolivia, 80% of the population of South America has a progressive government fully aware that American foreign policies are designed to maintain access to their resources below fair value, and that this is the cause of their poverty. On *Democracy Now TV*, John Perkins, author of *Confessions of an Economic Hit Man,* discusses an "EHM" (Economic Hit Man) walking into President Morales's office and failing to entrap Bolivia into their system of unpayable debts. An EHM has already struck a deal with

Paraguay but—if Brazil, Venezuela, and Bolivia make a better offer—that theft of Paraguayan wealth may fall apart.

President Hugo Chavez of Venezuela has just declared his country as fully literate and is forming trading alliances which promises to free many more countries in a shorter span of time than Simon Bolivar almost freed in his lifetime. His offer of cheaper oil to key members of South America's Mercosur alliance (Brazil, Argentina, Uruguay, Paraguay and Associate Members Chile, Ecuador, Columbia, and Peru) and his funding of Telesur—satellite TV, radio, and phone coverage for Latin America—plus the elections of more populist governments, is turning that long-standing free trade alliance into an affiliation for economic freedom comparable to the East Asian Summit.

Those alliances have the tools to thwart America's imperialist ambitions. Within weeks of its November 2005 startup, Telesur is being expanded. Named after Simon Bolivar and engineered by China, it has brought the Arabic station AlJazeera and others on board to expand to the entire world in various languages and that is planned to be operational by 2008.

That breathtaking advance towards full freedom is as catching as a cold. AlJazeera will not only be broadcasting on the Bolivar satellite, their satellites will be in place by mid 2006 to broadcast worldwide in English. Other nations will follow suit. The three billion people represented in that East Asian Summit, Central and Western Asia, and Africa will broadcast their views of current and past history to the world. Russia, currently limited to Europe and North America, will be speaking to the world. With the views of the world's dispossessed broadly disseminated, corporate media within the West must address the world more broadly and accurately or be irrelevant. Recordings of current events and history will then have a closer relationship to reality.

What can greater relevance to reality accomplish? President Chavez is so popular that the opposition—backed by America—dropped so low in the polls they withdrew from the 2005 elections and all South America (and beyond) is poised for a Bolivarian Revolution overthrowing unequal trade agreements. This gives insight into how fast a movement for freedom and rights can spread when unique world events provide that opening. The international havoc of America's disastrous foreign policies—an extension of European colonialism, totally discrediting the U.S. in the eyes of the world and costing the U.S the moral high ground—is just such an opening and the developing world has the communication facilities to inform their citizenry of their many methods of denying impoverished nations their share of the world's wealth. All people want to be free and an understanding of how it is imposed destroys imperial control.

Policies of imperial nations have been, and still are, to keep periphery nations individualized and marginalized. Only by they coming together in a firm alliance and educating their citizenry on the importance of coalition and cooperation, can freedom with full and equal rights be attained. Japan, China, India, and Russia already are signing mutually-lucrative mutually-protective trade deals with forming alliances across the undeveloped world. That—and the likelihood of an Asian and a South American trading currency (the early stages of federation)—has Western *managers of state* in a panic.

As they should be: President Chavez has moved Venezuela's reserves to Europe (traded dollars for Euros) and is suggesting just such a central bank for Latin America. Iran and Syria have moved their reserves to a safer haven and all Arab countries are considering that move. China announced it is diversifying its reserves (currently over $700 billion). With thousands of Chinese flooding into Africa to sign trade agreements with the East African Community (Kenya, Tanzania, and Uganda), CEDEAO (The Economic Community of West African States), and the African Union, that continent is stirring. With the examples of the European Union, the East Asia Summit, and South American alliances, they too will be forming trading alliances with regional currencies.

Those alliances, creating their own trading currencies and signing trade/development agreements with rising centers of capital, will effectively offset the IMF/World Bank/ GATT/ NAFTA/ WTO/ MAI/ GATS/FTAA/CAFTA/ military cartel designed by America to retain control of the world's resources and the *wealth producing process.*

Europe, North America, Australia, Japan, China, India, Russia, Taiwan, South Korea, Indonesia, Malaysia, and possibly Brazil and Argentina, over half the population on earth, will soon be modernized and the other half of the world—those with the resources necessary to keep the world's industries running—has plans for their own industrialization.

Let's face that reality: Under what strategy will a technologically developed China, India, Japan, or Russia be the most prosperous, with America and Europe as their primary trading partners or by sharing technology with Africa, South America, and Central Eurasia in trade for resources? Obviously—measured in consumer products and services provided their citizenry—they will be much wealthier under the second option than the first. Under that first option their massive accumulations of dollar reserves will become valueless in either an inflationary spiral or an economic crash. In that first scenario dollar values will fall daily while in the second America would quickly pass laws to prevent those reserves from buying up their properties. Those nations—plus Malaysia, Indonesia, and the substantial industry already in Brazil, Argentina, etc.—have enough technology to rapidly develop the remaining poor nations.

A nation can industrialize only with the support of an already developed country. Japan's success in the late 19th and early 20th centuries based on empire ended with their defeat by more powerful empires in WWII. The struggle between the British and German empires over control of world trade led to WWI and WWII. To prevent defeat and the shattering of the *rule of law* as designed, primarily by Britain over the past 700 plus years, required pulling America into both wars. Those holocausts taught Western empires that they had nothing to gain by fighting each other. NATO and the European Union evolved out of that realization.

The Soviet Union was not an empire, 15 individual nations quickly and peacefully federated after WWI. Openly declaring they would live off their own resources, they released title to all natural wealth outside their federation and took title to all within their borders.

Another legal structure not appropriating the wealth of either internal labor or that of other nations was a serious threat to empires whose *rule of law* was designed to appropriate the wealth of both their labor and the periphery of empire. The expenditure of 85% of Germany's firepower against the Soviets, and they still winning, was the primary reason for Cold War alliances after WWII. Not only was it crucial to contain the Soviet *rule of law*, the colonial world's break for freedom also had to be suppressed. Though the cost in lives and treasure—both within the imperial centers and on that periphery—were enormous, those suppressions were successful.

But that expensive success (it cost trillions of dollars, plus 12 to 15 million lives, and impoverished billions) was only temporary. As shown by periphery nations refusing for three years to sign the unequal trade agreements presented at the Doha round of the WTO, by the forming of trading alliances throughout the periphery as addressed above, by the old Soviet alliances partially reforming, and by the East Asian Summit—together representing fully 70% of the world's people—the periphery's break for freedom again threatens Western *rule of law.* As already addressed—unless Western powerbrokers are delusional—financial, economic, covert, and overt warfare are no longer options. Our analysis will proceed on the assumption that this reality will hold.

Utilizing financial and economic power (threat of sanctions), the Western world is trying to sign unequal trade contracts with the developing world with success in some places and failures in many. But, if challenged, those contracts signed under duress will not stand. Unequal contracts imposed by deceit or force are not recognized in any Western court. Those unequal agreements imposed by financial, economic, diplomatic, covert, and overt warfare can be quickly set aside and, as various countries of South America and around the world are renegotiating their resource extraction contracts, that process is already in motion.

Agreements of the latest WTO Doha round leaves the wealthy nations' subsidies —and the poorer nations' denial of the right to subsidize—in place. Recognizing that the 30 OECD (Organization for Economic Cooperation & Development) nations' $350 billion per year agriculture subsidies permitted imports to undersell India's farmers, before Trade Minister Kamal Nath left for the December 2005 WTO negotiations he said, "importing food is as good as importing unemployment" and he could sign a trade agreement on the terms offered only if the U.S. is "willing to provide a visa to every farmer displaced as a consequence of the import of cheaper and highly subsidized food." Minister Nath appears to have failed to keep that promise but the struggle continues.

When first developing, periphery nations need both money and industry. Assuming those alliances included one of, or all of, the three Asian *centers of capital*, they would have adequate capacity for rapidly developing the 50% of the world that has little industry. Normally it will take many years for a fully allied South America and another alliance of Africa to form. But these are not normal times. Those industrialized nations need the resources of the developing world just as badly as those poor nations need technology and an efficient economic infrastructure.

The flow of money is a super efficient accounting system and that flow is a mirror image of a modern economy. We just looked into that mirror and saw that well over 50% of the current flows of money were wasted efforts.

The heart of the monopoly system is *exclusive title* to nature's wealth and technologies and this includes social technologies. Proof that this is monopoly capitalism rather than honest capitalism is proven by economic efficiency doubling when those *exclusive titles* are restructured to *conditional titles*.

All are morally entitled to their share of nature's wealth and that can be attained only through eliminating those monopolies we are taught do not exist. Once eliminated, the costs of government (national, state, and local) are paid from resource rents and profits from a *socially-owned* banking system. Any necessary increase in the money supply is covered by building infrastructure with created money. Essential services (water, sewer, roads, WiFi communications) can be debt free. That requiring financial accountability or rationing (spacing out the use of) construction capacity can justifiably carry bonded debt but cycling those payments right back into necessary infrastructure makes those effectively debt free. The money created is determined by that needed for a stable and adequate money supply. Under those conditions—along with equal pay for equally-productive labor, rights to a productive job, and the elimination of most taxes—the wealth of nature is distributed relatively equally even as the labor necessary for a quality lifestyle drops to 2 to 3 days per week.

Monopolies claim a large share of the wealth produced; waste enormous amounts of resources, capital, and labor; restrict the efficiencies of an economy, claim unearned wealth, and all while lowering total production by roughly half. The social efficiency gains claimed, 50%, are so enormous that we will be challenged. But the truth is that—if technology had been shared rather than monopolized—the entire world would have developed in step with those efficiency gains. With all societies utilizing the latest technologies, the pace of inventions would have quickened. War and poverty would have been the exception rather than the rule the past 200 years.

Western societies evolved from aristocracy. Titles to nature's wealth and technologies today are copies of aristocratic property rights. Aristocracy fought for centuries to protect those exclusive rights and today's battles—both worldwide and within internal economies—are a continuation of those struggles. Full and equal rights for any great numbers have never been attained and we are outlining herein how—through utilizing the mighty economic and financial engines of Henry George's *inclusive rules of law*—they can be attained for all.

Add up the waste within America's internal economy as herein addressed, add in that wasted and destroyed worldwide,[4] add in the GDP for a respected living standard for roughly five billion impoverished people who could be enjoying a quality life today except for *subtle monopoly capitalism's* fifty years of covert and overt warfare—a struggle led by America for the purpose of controlling resources, controlling the *wealth producing process*, and imposing their system of property rights (*exclusive title* to nature's wealth and technologies) on the world which prevented their economies from developing—and you arrive at how much more wealth has been effectively destroyed or production forgone as opposed to how much wealth America produces. That honest look highlights America as a negative producer—consuming, wasting and destroying more wealth than she produces.

Henry George's concept of full and equal rights through restructuring *exclusive titles* to nature's wealth and technologies to *conditional titles* is applicable across the economic spectrum. That simple change in property rights eliminates both the unacknowledged primary monopolies (land, technology, money, and communication) and the secondary monopolies that are the essence of today's American economy. The appropriated values capitalized into huge blocs of capital disappear and reappear as relatively *equally-shared use values.*

All trained in classical and neoliberal economics will say, "Those appropriated blocs of capital owned by individuals were—and are—necessary to finance an economy." They will claim that "governments are inefficient allocators of financial and industrial capital." Both claims are unequivocally untrue. Financing is not needed to build land, nature built it. A large amount of financing is not needed to start up a bank. The only labor-created value there, beyond a small amount in brick and mortar, is a piece of paper, its license. Yes a private bank requires a minimum level of startup funds but a *socially-owned* banking system simply creates that money. That rule holds; an efficient banking system has no values to be owned beyond brick and mortar.

Values in technology are created by labor but currently the greatest share of those values are pieces of paper, monopoly patents. Communications need financing but there too finance capital is primarily buying and selling the enormous capitalized values of monopolized spectrums which is part of nature. Financing is needed for infrastructure (roads, railroads, water systems, sewer systems, post offices, electric systems, communications) but in the early to middle stages of regional development those can be built with created money. In the very early stages, even industry can be built with created money. In a crisis—as demonstrated below—created money can be pointed directly to any distressed sector of the economy, natural or manmade. For example: If America owned its banking system, created money could have been pointed towards the victims of hurricane Katrina, or any other natural disaster, and those whose lives were shattered could have quickly been made whole. The principles laid out in these concluding pages will prove that.

Current capitalism monopolizes all productive wealth and charges a rental value which must be paid by true producers. Those annual rents (improperly called earnings) are values which are then capitalized. Though most finance capital has been in existence for a long time, on balance money must be created to finance sales of newly-created monopoly values. Stage one of money creation under monopoly capitalism: (1) Capitalized values are created first then the money is printed to buy and sell those values (investing in monopolization instead of production). Stage two: (2) That created money circulates and—as savings in reserve deposits—is available to loan to create more wealth.

The reason finance capital is so hard to obtain under the errors of monopoly capitalism is that those monopoly values and the 60% of America's finance capital that funds those values reverses the proper order of money and wealth creation. Henry George's *inclusive rule of law* corrects that. In the early stages of development, stage one: (1) Money is created to fund infrastructure (debt free or bonded), and industry (bonded) and the circulation of that money operates industry and the economy. Stage two: (2) As development progresses, money is created to fund bonds for only infrastructure while savings within the circulation of money funds private industrial development along with housing and other consumer needs. The developed stage: (3) Money is created only when it is needed to expand the economy. That money and payments on previous bonds are used to fund later bonds to create and maintain infrastructure. Note: At no time were monopoly values bought and sold. Instead of financing monopoly created values, touchable and useable *use values* are financed, created, and bought and sold.

Private industries and services serving consumer needs are properly financed out of savings (reserve deposits). We are proposing a constitutional right to finance capital for regions of the world, countries, states, local communities and individuals. Individual financing is much simpler under full and equal rights than under the false values of equity-backed loans of monopoly capitalism. Needs can be calculated and allotted relatively easily and loans would be on merit.[a]

The exposed wasted labor, capital, and resources—and the roughly doubling of economic efficiency when those monopolies are eliminated—proves the wealth appropriated through collecting rental values is both unearned and unnecessary. The infrastructure operating monopoly systems are today's pyramids. They waste resources, capital, and labor and lower economic efficiency. The efficiency gains of technology are so enormous that—even though massive wealth is produced—under monopoly capitalism much is wasted and an equal amount that would have been produced under an efficient economic structure is not even realized. That this waste is unknown is due to the centu-

[a] As we addressed in the banking subchapter, "Accumulation of Capital under Henry George's inclusive *rule of law*" and the information subchapter "Investment and Job Opportunities."

ries of justifications by the classics that these systems of theft were efficient economies.

Walk into the heart of any city, look up at those huge skyscrapers, walk in, look at the plaques on the doors, and—when one understands monopolies intercepting, as opposed to producing, wealth—one realizes this is the superstructure of a wealth interception system and the entire building (and the next ones) are unnecessary, as are the companies which built them, those that built the furnishings, and those who service and clean them.

The offices and staff overseeing land, banking, technology, and other monopolies waste enormous amounts of wealth. Those monopolies disappear under the full and equal rights of a modern commons replacing *exclusive titles* to nature's wealth and technologies.

If citizens had equality and opportunity (full and equal rights through conditional title to nature's resources and technologies) instead of daily battles for survival feeding on the fringes of these massive subtle monopolies, family trauma would decline rapidly, fewer children would be abused and neglected, crime and prisons would shrink to almost non-existence, more than 70% of the insurance offices and staff would disappear even as society was better insured. Universal health care as a human right can shrink costs by half even as those needs are better cared for (proper eating [permaculture] and exercise, along with nurse practitioners can take care of 90% of all medical conditions). Eliminating patent monopolies eliminates 85% of the gambling casinos called stock markets, reduces product costs by 50%, and is crucial for eliminating poverty worldwide. Under full and equal rights provided by the *inclusive* principles of Henry George's *rule of law,* the police, legal, and penal systems would shrink to a very small fraction of their current size and expense.

Other nations would produce their own food and developed world corporate agriculture would shrink accordingly. Permaculture (a must) would become the norm creating a worldwide Garden of Eden and all the world's citizens will be more secure. Equities markets—and thus their wasted offices, labor, and other expenses of trading monopoly values—would shrink to a tiny fraction of today's trades even as entrepreneurs are more easily financed and—measured in labor time—the price of medium-to-high priced consumer products would drop by 50%. Thirty to 60% of the retail industry would disappear as moderate-to-high priced products are shipped from factories directly to consumers. The arms industry would be history and on and on. Utilizing the potential of low frequency WiFi, 85% of the structures and labor of the educational system would disappear even as the citizenry are better educated. The world is far richer than we realize; much of our wealth is wasted through the monopoly structures evolving directly from aristocratic *exclusive title* to nature's wealth and technologies that has been imposed upon the world.

The quality of life rises rapidly even as the hours of employed labor lowers to 2 to 3 days per week. The precipitous drop in GDP measures the previously wasted labor, capital, and resources of a subtly monopolized economy. The

GDP then rises as people utilize their new free time to develop their many artistic talents or to simply socialize with friends and family.

The fear during all crises is a ballot box revolution demanding those very rights. The powerbrokers, like the Czars of Russia in 1917, have nowhere to turn. In that crisis almost a century ago, the managers of the Russian state offered to change their government to the *inclusive* philosophies of Henry George—the *rules of law* we are pointing to as having the answers for most economic problems. That 1917 offer was rejected and the Bolsheviks took over.

For their philosophy to be chosen, Georgists will have to get their beliefs to the world. Staying only with social collection of resource rents will not cut it. Exposing the current waste of 50% of America's economic efforts and pointing out the possibility of a quality life working only 2 to 3 days per week utilizing Henry George's mighty economic and financial engines will catch the attention of everybody.

Under a modern commons within Henry George's philosophy, the just rights of private property are fully protected, individualism (through social support of the highly talented) and competition are strengthened and money no longer flows through subtle monopolies to the interceptors of wealth. Society's production is instead—through the *inclusive* principles of *conditional title* to nature's wealth and technologies—distributed relatively equally to all. Through equal sharing of productive jobs, each will have a just claim to their proper share and there will be no severe poverty. Under those rules of equality worldwide, the need for wasting wealth on immense military forces and their attendant massive slaughters disappears.

That each has full and equal rights within a monopolized system is a contradiction in terms. The Western system of capitalism (again properly titled *subtle monopoly capitalism*) is so skewered towards the rights of a powerful minority that it can be mathematically proven—and we prove—only a few will own substantial wealth while the overwhelming share of the citizenry will be poor.

Immediately we will be challenged that our large middle class is proof this statement is an error. But a substantial part of the high standard of living in the West is due to the immense wealth appropriated from the periphery of empire, sometimes through outright theft but primarily through inequalities in trade. That wealth is distributed among the citizenry of the imperial centers giving the appearance of an efficient, productive society.

Those owning and working within those subtle monopolies are the world's brightest and most talented, which is why they reached for and attained those positions. They will unanimously dispute their redundancy even as a few of them finance and guide the enormous propaganda process which protects their excess rights. The gains to society will be enormous when—under a system of full and equal rights with a sharing of productive jobs—those talented and brilliant people will be producing, instead of intercepting, wealth.

By analyzing the forthcoming struggle of those employed in the educational system to retain their current highly respected—but now obsolete—

positions and identities, one can understand why and how—as the efficiencies of technology advanced—full and equal rights were historically withheld from the masses. The efficiencies of technology will eliminate those jobs through which their identity, respect, power, wealth, and the needs for every day living had previously been distributed. Those in positions of respect and power destined for elimination quite naturally used their power and wealth to protect their power and wealth. With their living tied to those wasteful arteries of commerce, the citizenry unwittingly defend the system and thus support their own, and others, impoverishment.

Through maximizing the potential of WiFi, both the wealthy and developing worlds can educate their citizens for 5-15% the cost of brick and mortar schools. When discussing this thesis of the enormous wasted labor, capital, and resources with others, they easily understood the waste in all segments of the economy except theirs: "Oh no! Not my job! Our work is necessary." And a litany of reasons why would pour forth.

What takes place is the instinctive protection of territory within the economy from which one obtains respect, identity, and their living. I have watched teachers and professors bristle at the thought of their replacement by video lectures and documentaries presented by the world's best teachers to the entire country or even the world. Unless, and until, the current system totally collapses (which it will, monopolies always do)—and just as those whose identities and livings are tied to the arteries of commerce in other sectors of the economy destined for shrinkage to a fraction of current capital, labor, and resource needs—neither politicians nor the educational industry will make any serious effort to modernize that—or any other—economic sector.

But when that restructuring to an efficient education system does happen—and we have faith that it will—observe the many beautiful buildings which will be freed for fully productive use. Add those to the idle structures of the financial market, stock market (patents), insurance, prisons, and legal industries and one will be awed at the wasted labor, capital, and resources within an economy that is touted as the most efficient in the world.

We must emphasize that the appropriation of others wealth and the buying and selling of those unearned capitalized values were never necessary. Analyzing how massive wealth was created illuminates why and how this system of theft evolved. *Exclusive title* to nature's wealth and technologies gave the owner rights to collect rent (in economic language, rent seeking) or royalties (still rent seeking) for use of what were obviously necessities of life (land and technologies) nature offers free to all. Those unearned rents and royalties produce annual profits which are capitalized to a value of 10 to 30 times. Though there are honest capitalized values (*use values* created by productive labor), the capitalized values of non-productive monopolies are based upon values appropriated from true producers. There can be no other interpretation, either one has worked productively for one's wealth or one has appropriated it from others.

The secret of *subtle monopoly capitalism* turns out to be nothing more than monopolization structured into *exclusive* property titles. The values appropriated by those monopolies coalesced into huge blocs of capital which bought and sold those capitalized appropriated values and only gave the appearance of necessity and efficiency. That appearance of efficiency was protected by a culture pouring out rationalizations of efficiencies under the current legal/economic structure and by overwhelming any other culture attempting to break out of that *rule of law*. Economic efficiency doubling when those monopolies are eliminated proves these were just rationalizations and justifications. They were not reality.

Establish the most efficient banking system possible, leave other monopolies in place, and the banking system is no longer efficient. Capital, resources, and labor will still be wasted, the same share of labor's production will still be appropriated, the few will still be immensely wealthy, and the many will still be impoverished. Thus—before addressing how a fractional reserve banking system should operate—we had to address why no banking theory is complete that leaves those monopolies in place.

The expansion of competition along with sharing remaining productive jobs—the logical structure of Henry George's *rule of law*—brings all within the economic system on a relatively equal basis, eliminates the waste of monopolization, and creates an efficient, productive, peaceful society. With work time halved and free time doubled, the arts (music, sculptors, painting, singing, inventions, etc.) will expand rapidly.

The unnecessary 60% of the huge blocs of capital within the current monopolized economy represent the unearned wealth from both primary monopolies (*exclusive title* to nature's wealth and technologies) and secondary monopolies (licenses to provide essential services within a monopoly system).

The instant and costless transposing of those appropriated values bought and sold on the markets into relatively *equally-shared use values* through restructuring to *conditional title* to nature's wealth and technologies and providing full and equal rights to citizens (including insurance, universal health care, the legal system, etc. as a human right) proves that—although they were crucial for operating a monopoly system—the 60% of the blocs of capital currently buying and selling those values are the very heart of the inefficiency of subtle-monopoly capitalism.

When primary and secondary monopolies are eliminated, *use value* will determine market value. Under full and equal rights all are reasonably well paid, none receive compensation beyond the value of their labors, *use values* match market values, there will be no inflations or deflations, and thus there will be no economic collapses (see footnote, p. 23).

Under full and equal rights for all, each sum of money has real value—a true value produced by labor, not a false value created by monopolization or complex derivative values—behind it and that value can be realized at any time by its purchase with the now-sound money.

With no air pockets in the economy, thus full value attainable for all money spent—and assuming insurance protecting against individual or regional disasters (including occasional corruptions)—there are no risks of bank failures. With all deposits safe and secure, there is no need for reserves beyond that required to maintain balance within a fractional reserve banking system.

However, the need to maintain financial balance locally, regionally, nationally, and internationally will require the principle of fractional reserve banking. Through that now-honest banking system, money will be the efficient accounting of each person's production and consumption as it was designed to be when first invented using the clay accounting tablets of Sumer 5,000 years ago.

Under full and equal rights guaranteed by the *inclusive rules of law* of Henry George's philosophy and utilizing his mighty economic and financial engines, none would be in poverty; GNP and the average workweek would fall by half or more, even as average living standards rise. Those reductions in GNP will measure the current wasted labor, capital, and resources under *exclusive title* to nature's wealth and technologies. Eliminate those monopolies through restructuring to *conditional title* to nature's wealth and technologies and the money no longer flows through those low-productivity monopolies to provide a high living to those not producing.

An individualized society with half their waking hours free and each searching for identity will become chaos while a cooperative, communitarian society—providing camaraderie and a sense of belonging, yet retaining the efficiencies of money and competition—will thrive. Those who study gangs filling those emotional needs in an individualized society and those experienced in communitarian societies understand this well and we will leave that to be sorted out by these newly-free societies.

---

1 Edmond Taylor, *The Fall of the Dynasties: The Collapse of the Old Order, 1905-1922* (New York: Dorset Press, 1989), chapters 17-19.

2 Ibid

3 Robert McHugh, "Money Supply versus Interest Rate Policy," *Comer*, January 2006, pp 18-19.

4 J.W. Smith, *Economic Democracy: A Grand Strategy for World Peace and Prosperity* (Radford, VA: The Institute for Economic Democracy, 2006),

8. Conclusion: Henry George's Rule of Law Creating World Peace and Prosperity

Knowing imperial powers will do everything possible to prevent it and they may succeed, we will proceed on the assumption that fast moving events will bring developing world alliances together. Once allied—the early stages of a federation—each economic region should, and we assume will, establish a central bank, create their own currency, and sign contracts with the Asian *centers of capital* to trade resources for access to technology and training (industrial development). At that point, both East Asia's and the developing world's need for trade with Europe and America will be minor.

That potential for eliminating the West's 500 year control of the world's resources and the *wealth producing process* explains why America embarked on regime change in Iraq. Though oil was the primary resource being secured, a success there would assure worldwide control of other resources far into the future. If that colonial adventure successfully installs a puppet government or splits Iraq into three isolated political units with the oil regions controlled by America, if that control is expanded to the oil wealth of Central Asia, and if control is retained in Saudi Arabia, the old empires could offset the power of those forming alliances and retain access to resources worldwide on the same unequal terms. Other nations and alliances will have to abide by trade rules laid down by imperial nations or they would get no oil.

But the Iraq occupation is turning into a quagmire. The world understood America's plan, every abuse of power engenders a countervailing power and the opposing alliances described above quickly began to form.

The developing world understands well that the United Nations is not democratic. Given that title as a cover for dictates of a few powerful nations, it was specifically designed for superior rights for the already wealthy. Planned and established by the winners of WWII—with other nations essentially voiceless—that body as an extension of colonialism was a fait-accompli.

That intended "irreversible accomplishment" is centered in the Security Council. Each member has one vote and decisions are made by an affirmative vote of at least nine of the 15 members of that council (five permanent, the other 10 slots rotating every two years among the remaining 186 UN members). A 'yes vote' of all five permanent members (the United States, Britain, France, Russia, and China) is required before any action can be taken. A 'no vote' by any one of the five is a veto. Thus nothing of importance happens without the unanimous approval of those five permanent members.

The UN charter requires all members to accept and carry out the decisions of the Security Council. While other departments of the UN can make recommendations and many good things are proposed and accomplished, the Security Council alone has the power to make decisions on all matters of importance and that charter obligates all member nations to carry out those decisions. In short, on important issues, there is no United Nations; there is only a Security Council comprised of five of the seven most powerful nations in the world (the two other major powers, Germany and Japan, lost WWII).

As the UN—fronting as a quasi world government—has been used as cover for control of nations worldwide, most the 186 non-permanent members of the Security Council, and likely two of those permanent members—Russia and China—want a truly democratic institution. Though intended to be irreversible, in today's world it is possible for those new alliances to force a restructuring of the UN to a truly democratic format or totally replace it.

Of those five permanent UNSC members, only three—the U.S., Britain, and France—can be considered as allied.[a] Russia understands well how the former Soviet Union was destabilized and China knows just as well that there are movers and shakers within both American political parties who want to do the same to her.

Those same movers and shakers in the current administration have openly stated they are not going to tolerate any nation, or group of nations, to militarily challenge America. Translated that means maintaining worldwide control of resources and the *wealth producing process* through military force.

As addressed above, their first major move towards assured control of resources was the occupation of Iraq which has turned into a disaster. Not only does America have most Iraqi's against them, the entire Muslim world is aware that—with possibly 70% of the world's known reserves of easily-accessible oil within their borders—they are the primary target.

The world is aghast at the destruction, torture, and oppression of American foreign policy.[1] Once the moral high ground is lost, a nation's power is greatly diminished and this has America's mighty military essentially immobilized. Cover stories will be ignored, attempts at regime change anywhere in the world would be recognized for the imperialism it is, and, at some level, sanctions would be invoked.

---

[a] France would not go along with U.S. President George W Bush on attacking Iraq. But that was only because—with centuries of colonial experience—they knew better than to openly occupy a country to install a puppet government. The current (2003-06) quagmire in Iraq has proved them right. But—until another world order emerges—the entire European Union should be considered as American allies.

That Iraqi suppression alerted the former provinces of the old Soviet Union (Central Asia) to further protect themselves by trade and development agreements with Russia, China, and India. The immobilization of America's mighty military, due to loss of the moral high ground, is the opportune moment for the many forming alliances to restructure the UN to a fully democratic institution or replace it.

The keys are the immense resources within the yet undeveloped 50% of the world, the roughly 60% of the world's industrial capacity and trillions of dollars in reserves outside the imperial nation's borders, and the current immobilization of imperialism's mighty military due to America's loss of the moral high ground. Understanding those realities provides the opportunity for developing nations to respond to the ongoing assault upon control of their destiny by imperial nations.

The current imperial assaults are: U.S. Ambassador to the UN John Bolton's threat to defund the United Nations if they do not accept U.S. dictates on world trade, the Doha round ending with the wealthy nations' subsidies impoverishing the periphery of empire still in place, and forgiving debt to 18 countries on conditions of privatization and lowering the rights of labor to such an extent as to assure the uninterrupted appropriation of their wealth.

But the once powerless are getting stronger. Their many alliances will form a power that will be difficult to challenge and they can serve notice to the historic imperial nations that the UN be restructured into a democratic and moral forum or they will form their own world governing body.

That ultimatum will be rejected by the historic Western colonial powers. On the chance that the previous creators of history—those major Western powers—will change their minds, the new alliance should retain ambassadors and skeleton staff at the UN and reconvene under a new name in a major city within those alliances. The world will have moved closer to being openly and officially what it has been ever since the end of WWII, the wealthy and heavily armed developed world in open struggle with the undeveloped—previously unarmed—world over control of resources and the *wealth producing process.* All nations should be invited to that new world-governing body.

Many world federalist organizations have been working to have a constitution ready for that momentous day. The World Constitution and Parliament Association (WCPA)—as does others—has one ready for revision and acceptance by just such an alliance of nations. This alliance can choose the best features of each constitution, add what they feel is necessary, and accept it. The inequalities and injustices within the United Nations Charter compared against the equality and justice within the new world-governing body will highlight the efforts of current power structures to dictate and the new power structure to rule democratically.

With a name picked and a constitution for that governing body in place, the first order of business will be negotiations between the allied undeveloped nations and the *centers of capital* most amenable to their development, the fast-developing nations that must have access to those resources. Even though they will retain their staff at the UN—the developed and well armed Russia, China, India and Japan are the most likely candidates. Their presence in that new governing body will be counter-weights to those well-armed nations that historically denied freedom to the periphery of their empires. Being realists, Japan will likely join those negotiations.

Russia and China's veto power in the UN Security Council eliminates the option of military assault under cover of the United Nations. The loss of the moral high ground and the insanity of attacking the now-allied 70% of the world's population should keep the imperial nation's mighty military immobilized.

The first discussions between the fast developing nations and the undeveloped regions should be on access to resources for these rising *centers of capital* in trade for industrial technology and training. As they are busy signing such agreements as we write, we believe China, India, Japan, and Russia will see the greater security provided and quickly agree. The ironclad *rule of law* to never share technology except when allies were needed will have been replaced by equal access to technology and equal access to resources. An economy requires modern industrial capital, resources, skilled labor, finance capital, markets and—up to this point in history—a military to protect it all. Though nothing can protect against madmen, having all that gives this forming alliance substantial security. Those who do not join put their access to resources and markets at risk.

Financial monopolization will be lost. It has been calculated that using the euro as the primary currency in oil markets would collapse the value of the dollar (Internet search: "Petrodollar Warfare, Oil, Iraq, and the Future of the Dollar, William R. Clark"). Utilization of regional currencies or a world currency would deflate the value of all hard currencies except those within the new trading alliances whose economies would be expanding. That alliance of roughly 70% of the world's population, with possibly 60% the world's industrial capacity within their borders, will spread shock through the markets of the old industrialized world habituated to control of the world's resources and the *wealth producing process*.

That trap is much deeper than the collapse of markets within *imperial centers of capital*. *Rule of law*, as created by monopolists, has nothing to do with justice or rights. It only means that those laws—the very essence of the monopoly system—is the law and it applies to everyone.[a] Under current *rule of law*, those monopolists will flee the West's collapsing markets and invest in those most secure. The *managers of state* within those four *centers of capital* whom we assume will join this alliance understand the process well; they watched the flight of weaker nation's capital in 1997 which collapsed those nation's markets. Then a

[a] That is, unless monopolists find themselves trapped. Then they lobby the legislatures for relief.

small share sneaked back and bought up their productive industries for pennies on the dollar.

They understand just as well that massive capital fleeing to their markets will be gaining title to their wealth under the *rules of law* designed by monopolists over the centuries. They know that what appears to be a bonanza as their property values rise is only a chimera that can disappear with disastrous consequences and restrictions on cross-border money flows will be put in place. As such restrictions will also protect countries from which that capital is fleeing, agreements between the old centers of capital and the rising centers will happen. Dual currency systems, as addressed below, are the best protection against such threats to regional markets.

What we need to understand at this point is that the unequal aspects of the *rule of law* monopolists have created the past 700 plus years—and installed around the world—has to be replaced by honest *rule of law* providing full and equal rights to all. We will be addressing that using a theoretical restructuring of the American economy as an example. The same restructuring needs to be applied to monopoly laws throughout the world and the emerging world understands this. As addressed in our earlier work, America's financial, economic, and military might has suppressed every such attempt the past 65 years.

We are assuming that the certainty of an aggressor being destroyed along with those attacked eliminates nuclear war as an option and conventional war or covert actions will trigger embargos by rising resource powers. The enormous power of monopolized capital and their mighty military will be checkmated. At this historic moment, some of the levers of power will be in the hands of the undeveloped world and their allied *centers of capital.* We are assuming America's loss of the moral high ground will advance that natural flow of events by at least 20 years.

Capital fleeing to cheap labor de-industrialized the United States. Just as early America ignored Britain's patent laws and copied British industry, China is ignoring Western patent laws and is producing copies of almost every manufactured product in world trade. Those knock-offs and the education of 400,000 PhDs per year in the hard sciences is designed to bring Chinese technology abreast that of the wealthy world. At that point, a de-industrialized America would be in grave danger.

Key to those agreements between the fast developing world and the undeveloped world will be moving patents into the public domain. The first such steps have been taken. In the contract to launch satellites for emerging nations' worldwide TV, radio, and phone systems, China has agreed "there are to be no technological secrets kept from those South American nations." Establishing super-efficient low frequency WiFi throughout the alliance with no royalties to be paid will be a big move towards breaking patent monopolies.

The biggest hurdle, direct communication to keep all citizens abreast of plans to provide a quality life for all citizens will have been overcome. With many times the population of the wealthy world, with an equal per capita percent—but a far greater total—of geniuses, educating many times the engineers and scientists, and with those four *centers of capital* sharing their technological knowledge, within a generation the once-impoverished world will pour out inventions.

Even as technology was being denied to most of the world, we marveled at the fast industrial development of East Asia. Yes technology was shared with Japan, Taiwan, and South Korea and later with Malaysia, Indonesia and China. But that accident of history was only to stop fast expanding socialism.

Later, monopolists saw the opportunity for huge profits through moving their industries to low-cost labor countries. It is that lust for profits—through moving productive capacity to Asia—which created the trap monopoly capital finds itself in today and which opens an opportunity for world peace and prosperity.

As opposed to ad-hoc development of the world with major powers denying development to all except those deemed necessary for allies to stop fast expanding socialism, this new alliance will recognize the obvious: security for all means bringing the current impoverished world to a sustainable development level that provides a quality life for their citizens. As the resources are primarily within their borders, the half of the world that is without measurable economic infrastructure or industry can be quickly developed.

Full and equal rights for all and protection against those who would deny that should be the purpose of this alliance. All resources should be mapped and banks, roads, railroads, alternative energy power systems, industries, water and sewer systems, and all other infrastructure for an efficient, sustainable, regional economy should be planned. This takes care. Large industrial capacities (for tractors, construction equipment, etc.) are required to capitalize a region but, once a region is developed, only small production capacities are necessary to produce parts for that machinery.

Japan has more industry than necessary to produce for her 120 million citizens. That exports are necessary to pay for imports is valid under monopoly rules but only partially valid within a properly-planned sustainably-developed region. For examples, in a peaceful, federated world, Japan's defense needs disappear, permaculture and orchard farming on its own land can feed Japan,[a] and there is waste within the Japanese capitalist (cartel) economy just as we are documenting is in the American economy.

With efficient *centers of capital* ready to support them, an allied region—even entire continents—can be developed to a sustainable level and all poverty eliminated in a very short time. Compare that with the monopolized economies of America and Europe which have been industrialized for 150 years and they still have large impoverished populations. The problem is not whether it can be

[a] See Tikopia Island in Jared Diamond's *Collapse: How Societies Choose to Fail or Succeed*, 2005.

done or not. The problem of past history has been the suppressions of weak nations and appropriation of their wealth preventing their development.

The original designers of the *rule of law* for the monopoly system did not even consider the possibility that a large share of the citizenry could one day be well off. That this happened in Southeast Asia was an accident of history. Not only did monopolists need allies to maintain control of the world, they needed the allegiance of their own citizenry. That—and the enormous efficiency gains of technology—provided a quality life to many more people than ever anticipated. Those enormous gains were under *rules of law* designed to prevent sharing that wealth. *Establish laws and policies for equal sharing, of the efficiencies of technology and severe poverty will disappear in 10 years and a quality life for all can be attained in substantially less than 50 years.*[a]

The common thread that maintains impoverishment of resource-wealthy regions are the thousands of agreements and contracts based upon unequal and unjust *rules of law* (both in internal trade and world trade) designed by the Western world—primarily Britain—over a period of 700 plus years, locking others into their monopoly system. This is now understood and alliances are being formed to take control of their destiny. Venezuela and Bolivia are leading the way through renegotiating their unequal energy extraction contracts. Russia has renegotiated their contracts and oil companies now retain only six cents of every dollar above $27 a barrel.[2] Through modern communications (the Internet, the many national and international news programs on Free Speech TV, Link TV, the potential of WiFi, and the emerging TV networks controlled by the world's previously dispossessed spanning the world), the rest of the impoverished world will be watching these dramas unfold and strengthening their alliances to attain more negotiating power.

We will proceed under the assumption the imperial centers' mighty military and financial power has been checkmated and that disaster reflected in the collapse of their stock and financial markets. Since the alternative news and new world-wide communications systems will be telling that story, corporate owned

---

[a] Many see a fully developed world as destructive to the environment. With care in planning, the ecosystem can be well protected. Tiny Tikopia Island, addressed above, has successfully practiced three dimensional orchard farming for 3,000 years. That permaculture mixing of annual and perennial tubers, berries, vegetables, fruits and nuts is enormously productive and, due to that closely-planted mixture building its own defenses, essentially disease and insect free. Under such advanced permaculture, one's yard could produce a large share of a family's food needs and sharing between neighbors will provide variety. If the world replaced monoculture farming and shipping from hundreds or thousands of miles away with three dimensional orchard permacultures in back yards and surrounding communities, society could be living in a Garden of Eden continually improving soils as opposed to its rapid depletion under monoculture farming.

media within those imperial centers will have to address the reality that imperial foreign policies have turned into a disaster.

Due to the collapse of markets based on the theft of the wealth of once defenseless nations now protecting their resources and markets through powerful alliances, a realigned world government, and trade agreements between the rising centers of capital and resource-wealthy poor nations, the arteries of commerce and monopoly created values within the old imperial nations will crumble. After all, it is structured totally on the theft of wealth both within internal economies and world trade and those worldwide unequal trades are being checkmated.

Marvin Morris's review of Fred Harrison's book, *Boom Bust: House Prices, Banking and the Depression of 2010, GroundSwell*, Nov-Dec, 2005, agrees with our analysis that a financial and economic crash is coming. Leaders coming to the fore must face up to the reality that the cause of economic crises and wars is monopolization and the cure is abandoning that centuries-old system of plunder, war, oppression, and cyclical economic crisis.

Cultures within the above emerging alliances are not locked into the Western system of *exclusive titles* to nature's wealth and technologies—the essence of monopolization. Being the only way they were allowed within the world trade system, they have been forced into the Western system of property rights and they will throw it overboard as soon as reality dictates that those changes be made.

When that crisis arrives, their choices are only three: retain the Western system of *exclusive title* to nature's wealth and technologies, revert to some form of command economy (communal, socialist), or Henry George's mighty economic and financial engines with full and equal rights for all through *conditional title* to nature's bounty and tempered by communitarian principles.[a] Not being emotionally and culturally tied to the West's property rights system, some will choose elements of all three. Though either of the last two choices will keep their economies going, the *inclusive*, yet efficient, intensely competitive principles of Henry George's *rule of law* make it the best choice.

In every extreme crisis (aftermaths of WWI and WWII, the Great Depression of the 1930s) the Western system of property rights came close to being overthrown by ballot box revolutions.[3] It is not reasonable to think that the citizenry of America and Europe will patiently watch the developing *centers of capital* (China, India, and Russia) and Japan successfully ally with the emerging world while the West's economies become moribund and their children cold

---

[a] We tried to make this a synthesis of capitalist, socialist, communitarian, and Henry George *rule of law*. But the *inclusive* philosophy of Henry George blends the essential principles of the other three and adds one more, society should collect all resource rent. Expanding the principle of society collecting resource rents across the full economic spectrum to quickly provide a quality life for all tags this as an expanded Henry George thesis.

and hungry. As war against 70% of the world will be unacceptable to their own citizenry, new leaders must be voted in to restructure their economies.

The typical choice of government within the imperial centers during such a crisis—a fascist militarized command economy such as Europe turned to during the Great Depression of the 1930s—we have analyzed as no longer an option. After all, no *center of capital* or alliance of *centers of capital* can militarily conquer and control an awakened 70% of the world's people. Just like each of the various cover stories for the attack on Iraq quickly fell apart, every such cover story would be seen through and an awakened and informed citizenry within those imperial nations would also understand and not permit it.

The Western *rule of law* collapsing would leave America and Europe with the same choices of governing structures as the rest of the world—some form of a communal or socialist structure or Henry George's mighty economic and financial engines powered by the full and equal rights of honest capitalism. As their citizenry have been trained to distrust communal and socialist principles, Henry George's *inclusive rule of law* would be the likely choice. But, so few know about that philosophy, only a powerful president—such as Franklin Roosevelt in the Great Depression of the 1930s—could guide a nation to its own salvation.

In this crisis, like all others in history, families will be cold and hungry. Then is when an alert president can take the helm and guide the nation through the storm. Taking stock of the crisis, this president will calculate that much of the collapsed values which once measured the wealth of the citizenry will have been pledged to loan institutions. He or she will know that for centuries monopolists firmly enforced the rule that the final mortgage holder will—in the case of bankruptcies—own all property backing defaulted loans. He or she will understand that those privately-owned loan institutions go broke right along with their customers. Japan keeping their loan institutions open and their companies funded when under just such a crisis and those alliances discussed above rapidly restructuring their banking systems and economies under this expanding crisis, will be under discussion.

It is understood that America's Federal Reserve is an arm of government and the trail blazed by Japan, really the only option, will be taken. But this crisis will be different than all others in history, including Japan's. Three times—after WWI, in the depth of the Great Depression of the 1930s, and after WWII—the monopoly system avoided its overthrow only by a hair. This time, with half the world industrialized—but divided into various centers of capital—and the yet-unindustrialized other half fully aware, there should be no way to save it.

The scope of this crisis and the need to totally restructure the economy requires more than a bank holiday as declared by President Roosevelt on March 6, 1933. The fiction of the Federal Reserve being privately owned must be ended through buying up its stock. As the federal government has guaranteed most major loans and the banks go bankrupt right along with their clients, the rules of monopoly capitalism are that society owns those banks. Social ownership of the banking system needs to be and, through nationalization of the bankrupt banking system, can quickly be, made official.

Before going into the simplicity of using the power of a *socially-owned* banking system to stop an economic crash in its tracks and reorganize an inefficient unequal economy to one that is highly efficient with full and equal rights for all, we must point out that current powerbrokers understand the process very well. They were using these principles to prevent financial and economic collapses well before Japan put them into practice.

The one-day stock market collapse of 22.6% in 1987 was nearly double the October 29th crash which heralded the Great Depression. Wall Street was paralyzed. Banks were told to keep loaning money to those bankrupt brokerages and the government guaranteed everything. The same quasi money creation features were implemented to resolve the 1982 Savings and Loan scandal, the 1990 Citibank bailout, the 1994 Mexico crisis that threatened U.S. banks, the Asian currency crisis of 1997-98, Long-Term Capital Management's bankruptcy crisis in 1998, and the stock market crash of 2000-2001.[a]

However that money was being created to protect the monopoly system, not the people per se. Under such protection, the imbalances became greater and greater and, theoretically, the day has arrived when they can no longer be shored up.[b] The goals must be the greatest good for the greatest numbers—food, fiber and shelter for everybody, protecting the savings and equities of the maximum number of people, and establishing an efficient economy.

It has been analyzed by this president's advisors that, with the banking system under social ownership, money can be created to stop the economic collapse in its tracks, the economy can be restructured, and prosperity can be quickly reestablished. With that vision, our courageous president and frightened Congress nationalizes the banks and a decree is issued for every adult without a job and without other income or resources (husbands, wives, and

---

[a] Robert Kuttner, "Cant and Recant," *The American Prospect* (January 2006) pp 34-37. After the financial collapse of 1997, South Korea invested heavily in education and leading technologies and they are poised to recover. Those efforts are replays of Germany's and Japan's historic and intense investments to break past Britain's and America's patent monopolies. Our suggested approach to modernization of the undeveloped world are only such policies applied cooperatively regionally—even world-wide—as opposed to competitive investments in individual nations. Once inventors are paid well with their inventions in the public domain, competition will be more intense then under current monopoly structures and final consumer costs will drop by roughly half.

[b] As we analyze the crazy quilt of banking within a monopolized economy, it is obvious that a banking system can be balanced anywhere from highly efficient, to massively corrupt, to its current extreme monopolized inefficiency. Today's economies are far more out of balance than they were in 1929, the collapse started six or seven times, but massive infusions of money stopped them. The unavoidable collapse will arrive when other nations develop the financial, economic, and military power to checkmate the imperial centers' financial, economic, and military depredations around the world.

singles) to apply to their bank or credit union for a monthly subsistence based on single households receiving 75% that of married couples and an allowance for each dependent. The loan institution will put their account's electronic transfer number on that application. That form will include testimony, under oath, that they have no income or resources. Upon signing—and on the 1st of each month thereafter until receiving their first *full paycheck* when reemployed—subsistence funds will be computer-deposited into those accounts. That person would walk out with funds in the bank to cover food, fiber, and shelter for that month and each month thereafter, until employed, those debit card and check-accessible funds will be deposited. Those who would be against this would be so out of sync with events they will be few and irrelevant.

With this first break from Western *rule of law* as structured over the past 700 plus years, all are now fed, clothed, and housed and the worst aspect of the crisis—a cold and hungry citizenry—is under control. Spending of those subsistence funds will increase demand and start stabilizing the economy. Once agreements have been reached to control money flows across national borders, any shortage of circulating money for subsistence payments' continued funding or repairing economic infrastructure can—as we have addressed—be created.

Inflation threats due to too much circulating money are easily handled. If required reserves of 3% are increased to 6% in step with money creation doubling reserve deposits, the circulation of money is reduced by half and the money supply remains the same. A 30% increase in reserve deposits (created money) will require a mandated reserve increase to possibly 4% to maintain the same money supply. However, both money and investment confidence will have been destroyed in the economic collapse, creating inertia, increasing those required reserves will be only after the economy has returned to normal and threatens to inflate. Once the advantages of created money and bond repayments building and maintaining infrastructure are understood, the proper level of money creation and money destruction (higher required reserves) for maximum economic efficiency can be calculated. [a]

In such a crisis, a *socially-owned* banking system can very closely target the destination of money. Both the initial distribution of *created money* and destruction of any surplus—if necessary—through increased mandated reserves, along with careful choices for loans, are tools to focus the destination and final owners of money. Both deflations and inflations can be avoided and the only crisis will be from natural disasters (see footnote, p. 23).

When the poorer regions of the world are first developing, and remembering that it can only be done if their currency cannot be spent outside their borders (a dual currency system), their infrastructure and even major industries can be built with created money. With the understanding that higher reserve re-

---

[a] Those calculations will come up against the appropriated wealth bond problem discussed below. Allied or federated regions of the undeveloped world, creating money for both infrastructure and industry, will require higher mandated reserves.

quirements permit higher levels of money creation, it is possible to operate those developing economies at very high levels of money creation and money destruction.

Financial structures between nations will be in crisis. The current insistence on free flows of money is only part of controlling the *wealth producing process*. As addressed above, the nations of Asia are conscious and will be restructuring their banking systems under their own—or a regional—currency. But those banking systems must be protected against cross-border flows of money.

A world trading currency under control of one nation (the dollar) or one bloc of nations (the Euro) puts others at the mercy of that nation or bloc of nations. This president initiating negotiations to protect each region from rapid money flows across borders will be the flickering beginnings of a true international currency for a peaceful federated earth. Going to an international currency for world trade and retaining trading currencies that can be spent only within economic regions creates a dual currency system whose money is valid only within the borders of each region and a world currency valid for trade between regions. Which is, of course, what we have now except America is in charge of the international trading currency, there are no cross border controls, and leaving an imperial power in control of the world's trading currency is an open invitation for financial destabilizations within the alliances we are addressing as crucial for the world's final break for freedom.

We will assume those negotiations led to establishing a true Bank for International Settlements (an honest World Bank) overseeing that dual currency system. Only if internal currencies are valueless outside a trading bloc can a region rapidly develop and its currency and economy be protected. A world currency would be created for trades between nations. As the money of a properly-structured world bank will be only blips on a computer, there will be no paper currency, thus no risks of counterfeiting or black market exchanges. The "flickering beginnings" of a world federation with a world central bank will have become a steady glow.

Having addressed control of the flow of money across borders so regions can create money and rapidly develop, we return to the collapsed American economy which has just been stabilized by creating money for subsistence payments to the unemployed, for restarting the economy, and for economic structural changes we have yet to address. All that requires control of cross border money flows as we just addressed.

With the old powerbrokers keeping a low profile and an appreciative citizenry paying close attention, this president realizes that lobbyists can no longer block insurance and universal health care being reformed into a human right (as Massachusetts is now (2006) considering). Faced with the unchallengeable logic of better service at half the price, those secondary monopolies will quickly be legislated, or voted by referendum, out of existence. The once cold and hungry citizenry are now warm, well fed, and their insurance and health care costs (paid through payroll deductions) have dropped, or will drop, by half. With food, fiber, and shelter for each citizen secure, crime will drop rapidly.

The genie will be out of the bottle and it cannot be put back. The advantages and efficiencies of a *socially-owned* banking system, universal health care, and insurance as aright will be so obvious that the citizenry will be looking forward to a continued restructuring to full and equal rights. A dialog on abandoning the monopoly system *structured in law* for the past 700 plus years will be on-going world-wide. The wastefully-used insurance offices being turned to productive use—even as all citizens are fully insured at lower cost—will enter that discussion as an example of the great efficiency gains that are possible.

Considering an entire generation will have to be reeducated—though restructuring should start immediately—rationalizing health care will take time.[a] But, with that discussion now mainstream, the legal foundation for universal health care, for ascertaining the safety and usefulness of every food additive and drug, and for broad establishment of permaculture will be secure.

By this time the citizenry worldwide—having been listening close to the on-going drama in America—will understand Henry George's key concept: Human labor did not produce land (resources), nature offers it all, and a rightful share for each can be had through society collecting resource (land) rents. All other taxes disappear as those resource rents and bank profits—along with created money—are expended on running governments and building and maintaining economic infrastructure.

As this is their field of study, surely this president will, if he or she had not already done so, bring Georgists in for advice. When the citizenry learn that other taxes will disappear as the purchase price of land drops to zero, society collecting resource rents (land rent)—the primary thesis of Henry George—will be an easy sell and that will pass by law or referendum. The mother of all monopolies will be eliminated,[b] all will be receiving their share of the wealth produced by nature, and—for the first time in history—an honest capitalist society will have been established.

As opposed to the *excluding* social structures designed by monopolists the past 700 plus years, under the principles of *inclusive rules of law* as designed by Henry George, all taxes will be quaint history (Social Security and universal health care are insurances). The equal sharing of jobs, a reasonable ratio be-

---

[a] This will take a full restudy of nutrition and drugs without input or interference by food or drug companies and providing the citizenry with the knowledge to take control of their own health. Remember deaths go down when doctors go on strike. Both deaths and food costs will drop rapidly when the processed food craze is understood and avoided.

[b] Land as the mother of all monopolies is obsolete. This treatise proves that monopolization of both banking and technologies are equally as powerful and damaging to an economy. We have addressed above the elimination of the monopolization of technology as the key to developing the impoverished world. Thus patent monopolies have adverse effects equal to either land or banking monopolies.

tween higher and lower paid labor, and an analysis of the economy requires an accounting system. Social Security and universal health insurance payroll and self-employed deductions, along with business required to annually file their profits and production figures, provide that accounting data.

Assuming created money financed bonds for foundation economic frameworks, whether governments, infrastructure, or any other social needs are financed through resource rents, banking profits, or created money protected against inflation through flexible required reserve levels is immaterial. The cost of each is built into the price of products, services, and bond payments and each will—through their every day purchases and relative to their standard of living—be paying their share. The savings possible under an economy fully restructured to Henry George's *rules of law*, including his powerful economic and financial engine creating investment funds replacing appropriated values capitalized into huge blocs of capital, are so enormous that money to fund this *peaceful* society will be in plentiful supply.

As all the above is taking place, accountants experienced in real estate will be assessing the value of all property before and after the financial collapse. The price mechanism of capitalism had measured those values but those old monopoly-created values and the 60% of the current blocs of capital created to buy and sell those capitalized appropriated values were not legitimate then and are not legitimate now. But protection of honestly-earned savings mixed with those monopoly values requires reduction in debts at the same ratio as the rationalization (collapse) of property values. Part of the roughly 60% of finance capital has already disappeared due to the financial collapse and erasure of revalued debts (the discussion three paragraphs below). That which has moved on to other investments is dealt with further below.

Under these *inclusive* principles, land values are now zero but the *use values* are as valuable as ever and the renewed titles to land (resources) will require paying resource rents to society. With property reassessment ongoing, this president proceeds to clear up titles to all property and—with the greatest good for the greatest number in mind—restore the financial health of the citizenry. With current values assessed and with previous owners having first rights, the land under all homes, all farms, all mines, and all industries shall be listed as available to the current owners (previous owners if property had been foreclosed upon) through paying monthly resource rent. Considering those resource rents are offset by all taxes eliminated, the land under homes and small businesses will—relative to today's tax structure—be utilized at no net increase in cost. It must be emphasized that the property owner has all rights to that land except the right to retain, or collect, a private tax (land rent).

With the *use value* of land paid to society as resource rents, land values are zero as soon as those laws are enacted. As *use values* have replaced monetized (capitalized) values, loans against land must be erased from the records and that against structures revalued to current assessed values. Justice demands that debts against structures be revalued in the same proportions.

Original owners—including former owners of foreclosed properties—will have first rights. Acceptance of that new title with its revalued debts obligates owners to pay monthly resource rent to society and, if a debt is owed, make payments on *value adjusted* mortgages (debts against land erased and that against structures revalued). If 50% of loan value was backed by the land before the crisis, that 50% loan value is erased. If homes and structures (separate from the land) were half paid for before the collapse, the remaining loan will be discounted to 50% those structure's current value. Auto and other loans would be similarly restructured. Paid-for property would not be affected except that landowners would owe monthly resource rent to society.

Those with more than one home, or other resources, will not be receiving subsistence payments until those resources have been consumed. That rule would not apply to an owned business in which that person is directly employed and which is temporarily idle due to the crisis. Such productive resources would be entitled to protection and support from the *socially-owned* banking system in the same manner as these suggestions for protection of title to homes.

One's home ownership rights under a *socially-owned* banking system, while restructuring, should not go beyond funding for one home. Under the financial crisis, most second homes or investment properties carrying debt will have been repossessed by the loan institutions. Assuming a rental home had been repossessed, those renting will be first in line to purchase those homes and financing will be available. This *socially-owned* banking system, being not-for-profit, has replaced trillions of dollars in uncollectable debts with collectable debts at the same debt/equity level as before the collapse.

A private bank can write off only a modest amount of loans before they are bankrupt. Under Henry George's powerful financial engine—since all values are real—*socially-owned* banks would write off far fewer loans in normal times than a private bank. However, when stabilizing a crisis such as we are now addressing, a *socially-owned* bank can erase all debt that is necessary. The process is simple and the rights of all can be protected while stabilization of a severe crisis simply is not viable under private banking. Protecting borrowers would be in direct conflict with a private banks purpose of maximizing profits and protecting their own assets.

With the citizenry understanding the monopoly system they previously were unaware existed, and with property rights of the maximum number of people secure, this is the time to tackle the doubling of consumer costs due to patent monopolies. Explanations to the citizenry on how consumer prices are at least twice that necessary will make those legal changes imperative. Whether by Congressional action or referendum, those patent laws will change to paying inventors well and placing patents in the public domain. When that law is fully in place, eighty-five percent of the casinos known as stock markets will be idle. The resources and talented labor previously battling within equity markets over who shall claim the enormous wealth produced by technology will be available for truly productive use.

Current patents will be in force for up to 20 years. Transferring technology to undeveloped regions in trade for access to resources while letting them run out within the developed world, will give corporations those 20 years to unwind from their monopoly positions. When unwound, their production /distribution capacities will be intact but they will no longer be appropriating wealth through monopolization. As the gains and protections of society as a whole are obvious, the same will happen simultaneously in other countries.

The wealthiest nations have greater dependence upon developing world resources. Rising centers of capital will be rapidly transferring technology in trade for resources. All will recognize that Western *rule of law*—monopolization patterned after aristocratic law—had effectively collapsed and they will adjust accordingly.

Monopoly values of corporations are primarily capitalized values of wealth appropriated through *exclusive* title to nature's wealth and technologies, the monopolization process. These are all big boys fully believing in the system they had created and which had now crashed. As most those values had been appropriated from productive labor over the years and that *rule of law*—now proven as a system of theft—has been abandoned, nothing is owed there.[a] The economic collapse plus the loss of monopoly values will drop the value of many corporations below their debt values. As the original private banks will have been holders of 1st mortgages, the now *socially-owned* banks will own most of those corporations and the looming elimination of patent monopolization, along with the economic crisis, would, as in all great crashes, collapse many stock values to that of wallpaper. As private property and free enterprise should be maintained, distributing shares to labor and management within those corporation as market-value loans, with those loans to be repaid along the principles of the subchapters "Accumulation of Capital under Henry George's *inclusive rule of law*" (chapter 1) and "Investment and Job Opportunities" (chapter 5) would resolve that equitably. With its own workers the new owners—along the lines of those subchapters—those industries will be operated efficiently.

By the same debt revaluation formulas as above, the modest market values acknowledged in those payments would be distributed among what few previ-

---

[a] The simplicity of inflation and deflation control proves that inflations were due to conscious decisions. An example is the current, 2005, housing bubble. Money had to be created to buy and sell those doubled values. It is well understood that borrowing against the values created by the housing bubble was the buying power that rescued the stock market which had collapsed 40%. So that housing bubble was planned event utilizing created money to rescue the stock market which only creates another imbalance that has to be weathered. All such maneuvers protecting power and wealth disappear when an honest banking system fully funds the real economy and the many games in the ethereal world of high finance intercepting massive wealth are history.

ous creditors are still standing. As in all economic collapses, those values will be low to nonexistent. It will be up to the new manager/owners to operate a productive/profitable company and rebuild values. For that purpose and for new entrepreneurs, a subdivision within the *socially-owned* banking system would fund those major industries and businesses. Since this banking system has the power to point created money to areas in need while simultaneously holding required reserves high enough to destroy surplus buying power and maintain a steady money supply, and each industry or business being responsible for their debts, conservative funding would not be a problem. Risk loans to cover expansions and new enterprises will be available at interest rates high enough to cover risk.

The many subdivisions of financial empires within the ethereal world above the real economy will have collapsed when the economy crashed. The *socially-owned* and controlled banking system will keep the real economy operating while—along the guidelines laid out below—those many methods of intercepting wealth within that vapory world that are reducing economic efficiency can wither on the vine. Most are financial empires built capitalizing the appropriated values of monopolization, that roughly 60% of America's unneeded finance capital that we keep mentioning. Except that they were unearned, a large share is invested in honest production which we address below in the discussion on bonds. But a large share also circles in the ethereal land of high finance looking for more ways to lay claim to wealth produced by others. Most those intangible ethereal values disappear in an economic collapse and with it those appropriated blocs of capital.

A great hue and cry will go up that these blocks of capital are necessary to operate an efficient economy. That warning will be muffled as the economy, pulled by the mighty engine of Henry George capitalism, doubles the efficiency of the economy. Once full and equal rights are established a slim, trim, "real" economy will replace the highly-inefficient laissez-faire economy which had evolved into a crazy quilt of methods to intercept the wealth produced by productive labor. Each of those best and brightest who once owned and operated those niches within a monopolized economy will be guaranteed a "productive" job. There will be no need to carve out a survival territory (or a financial empire) within the economy. Those who see opportunities for truly productive use of capital will have a job or investment capital by alerting bank managers to those investment needs. An alert citizenry and those within the banking system will recognize scams and paying those well who spot criminal or inefficient uses of finance capital will keep an economy operating at maximum efficiency.

With a *socially-owned* banking system, what we have laid out philosophically can be done. It cannot be done under a private banking system because that *rule of law* is designed for maximum rights to monopolists and minimum rights for all others. In each financial crisis, the relative wealth of deeply entrenched monopolists increase as the entire nation goes broke. If your property is half paid for, the creditor owns half and you own half. But when a financial crisis hits—values drop, the creditor owns it all, and you own nothing. Instead of claiming what is properly your equity, a *socially-owned* banking system can rebalance debts to match value collapses and protect everyone's honestly-earned equity. However, it has no responsibility for protecting unearned wealth within the old *rule of law*. A large share will have disappeared in the above collapse and revaluations. We address the remaining unearned wealth in the bond discussion below.

The citizenry should be alerted that the goal of restructuring the *rule of law* established by Western power brokers over the past 700 plus years, which caused this—and all past—economic crises, to Henry George's *rule of law* with a quality life for all while working only 2 to 3 days a week. Though it can also be done under socialist or communitarian principles,[a] his philosophy retains a capitalist system while eliminating monopolies.

Recognizing the security of titles to land with a purchase price of zero through paying resource rents to society, noting the efficiencies and equality of a *socially-owned* banking system, with the properties and equities of the maximum number protected, with universal health care and insurance as a human right, with the promise of the respect and security of a productive job, and all this now part of the social dialog, a mandated reduction of the workweek to create a highly-efficient economy will be an easy sell.

Among those large numbers of unemployed will be people well qualified to calculate the number of productive jobs in a fully rationalized, efficient, economy. Let's say their calculation matched ours—2.5 days work per week for each employable citizen. From that calculation, Congress would pass and a President would sign, or a voter referendum would authorize, a reduction of the work week by that 50%. A productive job for each is now guaranteed.

Subsistence payments continuing as wages during the first one or two months, or more, of employment/learning period will readjust the workforce smoothly. Highly skilled jobs (pilots, railroad engineers, etc.) will take substantially longer. A few skills (scientists) may take years to rebalance the workforce but that and a stable money supply can be seamlessly accomplished.

There are people that are much more productive than others but not so productive as to justify the current wide disparity in pay. There will be exceptions (an Einstein, an Oprah Winfrey, a president, and a few others) but serious researchers have concluded that a differential in pay no greater than 4 to 1 is reasonable. Through raising the wages of the lower paid, this badly needed social adjustment should be put into effect simultaneously with sharing those

---

[a] In either case it is possible to create money for both infrastructure and industry and control the consumer money supply through higher mandated reserves. As the many possibilities leave monopolists out of the loop while maintaining the efficiencies of money, this has not been used within the American economy. This author's calculations are that these options will, measured in money units but valued in productive labor units, lower product and service costs by half.

productive jobs. Poverty within this economy is now history. We have stated consistently that the cost of products and services would drop roughly the same 50% as hours worked. Thus living standards will be approximately the same as before the collapse.

While the economy is being restructured, *primary-created money* should be spent for building and maintaining basic infrastructure. That money, as did the subsistence money, circulates and returns as reserve deposits (savings) available for loans. At the start of this crisis, banks may be unable to pay out cash but that crisis within a crisis will quickly subside as all checks against *adequate bank balances* within this *socially-owned* banking system are honored. With debts restructured, property titles secure, with honoring of all adequate bank balances proving a *socially-owned* banking system automatically has 100% reserves, and with buying power in consumer pockets, the economy has nowhere to go but forward.

There will be other problems to resolve but, once the banking system is under social ownership and monopolies are eliminated, those are all solvable. The key is that most will have lost everything as the economy collapsed and everyone comes out of the economic crisis with secure title to homes and businesses, secure jobs, and equal and adequate pay. Those full and equal rights create an economy that—so long as monopolies and inefficient social structures are avoided—will maintain stable and secure values for millenniums. After historic past economic collapses, citizenry distrusted banks and were afraid to go into debt. This, potentially the worst of all collapses in history, would be so short, and security restored so quick, the citizenry will soon spend and save normally.

We have analyzed WiFi as so efficient that it has the potential of destabilizing the entire world monopoly system. It is observing that possibility that led to this analysis of the least traumatic way to restructure to a peaceful and prosperous world. So we allow the communications industry as quickly restructuring to a fully WiFi wired world along the lines of chapter 5 (communications). Phone, cable, TV, and radio monopolies, as well as 85% of the brick, mortar, and labor of the education system and possibly 60% the infrastructure of retail industry, disappear.

With the old power structure totally discredited and thus without a political voice, alert and moral *managers of state* and a frightened Congress[a] or voter referendum would pass the necessary restructure laws as laid out above. With a citizenry enjoying the security and higher quality of life of these restructurings,

---

[a] In the crisis of the 1930s, the legislators were just that frightened which is what permitted the passage of many laws giving Americans rights taken for granted today (Social Security, Unemployment Insurance).

constitutional and other legal challenges will be quickly set aside by national referendums.[a]

Only under a *socially-owned* banking system can you quickly provide subsistence payments to a cold and hungry citizenry and simultaneously restructure debts and the entire economy. It is that quick alleviation of the crisis and rapid restructuring which alerts a citizenry to the full and equal rights possible by abandoning the monopoly system so carefully structured the past 700 plus years. For centuries economic classics have told us that this is the best of all possible systems. Until an alternative example has been put in place, most will be unaware those monopolies even exist. Besides the classics, that misguided *belief system* is due to monopolists funding justifying philosophers (primarily through the spin of think tanks) in step with establishing, and as a part of maintaining, the monopoly system. That explains suppression of the world's breaks for freedom the past 60 years. If any example of full and equal rights for all ever successfully established itself, the monopoly system would have stood exposed and would have collapsed.

An efficient world economy requires each region producing most of their consumer needs. Part of restructuring the American economy to those specifications will be rebuilding regional industries that were sent overseas. Creating money for those industries, along with that for building infrastructure, will increase the economic pulse.

That is why undeveloped regions of the world require a regional currency acceptable only within the borders of an economically viable alliance. With a regional currency, money to build both industry and infrastructure can be created and that—plus resources and labor—are the fundamentals for wealth production. That foundation of an industrial economy, plus the wealth produced, backs the created money and its circulation operates the economy.

Necessary adjustments will be made after an analysis of how these monopoly laws evolved over the centuries. The conclusion can only be that they were *rules of law* put in place undemocratically to lay claim to wealth produced by others and those huge blocs of capital invested in bonds are—beyond the roughly 40% which were honest earnings and savings—appropriated wealth.[b]

---

[a] We fully recognize that the powerful have put many blocks to changes, constitutional and legal, in their *rule of law*. Theoretically any substantial change will take years and each will have many roadblocks. But a broad economic collapse will not be normal times. If an alert leader can quickly provide security to a cold, hungry, and panicky citizenry with promises of total security for the foreseeable future few legislators or judges would dare stand against it.

[b] With former powerbrokers powerless in a crisis threatening to break into a full revolution, under *socially owned* banks, debts within internal economies can be canceled. Bonds and treasuries held by financial institutions of other countries will require negotiation. The variables are so great that how that plays out can only be determined at that time. A just settlement will require sacrifices from all parties.

Thurow's explanation that "patient savings and reinvestment has little or nothing" to do with generating large fortunes bears repeating:[4]

> at any moment in time, the highly skewed distribution of wealth is the product of two approximately equal factors—instant fortunes and inherited wealth. Inherited fortunes, however, were themselves created in a process of instant wealth in an earlier generation. *These instant fortunes occur because new long-term disequilibriums (sic) in the real capital market are capitalized in the financial markets....* Those who are lucky and end up owning the stocks that are capitalized at high multiples win large fortunes in the random walk. Once fortunes are created, they are husbanded, augmented, and passed on, not because of "homo economicus" [economic man] desires to store up future consumption but because of desires for power within the family, economy, or society.[5]

Bonds are the final sanctuary for appropriated wealth. While all other values are collapsing, interest rates fall and the values of earlier-issued bonds with higher interest rates rise. A doubling of bond values as real property values crash can be a quadrupling in relative values.

Just as aristocracy's titles to land was for centuries the proverbial elephant in the living room denying all others the right to enjoy their full and equal rights, that elephant's children—the share of that 60% of those huge blocs of capital once buying and selling capitalized appropriated values that have moved to other investments—are still preventing full realization of rights.

As we laid out the simplicity of eliminating monopolization within each sector of an economy through restructuring to Henry George's *inclusive rule of law*, we pointed out that appropriated values were no longer there because they had been transformed into *equally-shared use values*. But for centuries the money realized from selling those capitalized appropriated values had been moving into other investments, some into productive industries addressed above in which those appropriated values have disappeared and some into bonds in which those values, both honestly earned and appropriated, have increased.

We will break through the complexities of millions of transactions through a simple example: If John Jacob Astor had given 100 year leases on Manhattan Island, instead of selling it off piecemeal; those hundreds of billions of dollars in today's value would belong to his ancestors. If those ancestors still held title to that land as the economy was restructured to society collecting the land rent, values tied to land will vanish. But if they had sold that property before that restructuring, the new owners and the banks holding the mortgages would take that loss while Astor family money will be safely invested somewhere else. As it most likely would be, we will assume they invested in bonds.

Instead of those hundreds of billions of dollars going to Astor's descendants, those monopoly profits were shared among the tens of thousands of people who bought and sold property on Manhattan Island the past 150 years. A large share was reinvested, a large share went for extravagant living, and another large share provided a comfortable life without the expenditure of labor

That spent for high living and a life without labor have largely been wasted. That spent for entrepreneurial investment is a *relatively* efficient aspect of *subtle monopoly capitalism*. Most loaned out at interest is also properly invested. But both the profits and the interest on that unearned wealth have to be paid for by the very people from whom that finance capital was first appropriated. And it will be paid for again and again, on into perpetuity, even when those profits are productively reinvested.

Within the *rule of law*, as structured, those monopoly profits are properly invested. But current titles to nature's wealth and technologies—derived directly from aristocratic property rights and fine-tuned for the past 700 plus years as Western *rule of law*—are unequal, inefficient, and unethical. That marks a substantial share of properly-invested funds as unearned wealth. So we have moral investors functioning within an unethical system. Those unearned blocs of capital create problems for a final restructuring to an efficient, productive economy with full and equal rights for all. Even though an economy is restructured, those huge blocs of capital that were created only to buy and sell capitalized values of appropriated wealth and are now invested in bonds—unethically earned yet morally invested—are both perpetuating the cycle of unearned wealth and blocking investment of honest savings and created money.

Example: we addressed above how the need for safe investments for these blocs of appropriated wealth led bankers to ignore the potential efficiencies of fractional reserve banking to create money for highways, railroads, water systems, sewers, WiFi communication, libraries, parks, etc. Financial efficiency was ignored to provide a safe place to invest appropriated wealth.

Until those huge blocs of appropriated capital are addressed, the same problem still exists in a restructured economy. Investing that unearned wealth in property would inflate values. As per above, investing in bonds would deny society the right to create money to build infrastructure, and higher mandated reserves so as to reduce inflation when creating money for those purposes would penalize honestly earned savings. So it is impossible to restructure to an efficient economy without directly addressing those huge blocs of wealth which were unethically earned but ethically invested.

How do we resolve the conundrum of moral investors amassing wealth within an unethical system? The appropriated wealth represented by unearned values in banking, land, technology, communications, insurance, health care, the legal system, etc., have been eliminated by the above restructuring to the *inclusive rules of law* of Henry George. Having no choice, those invested directly in those monopolies have taken their loss and—still having a secure life—they can philosophize on their experience within what they did not realize, but the alert will now understand, was an unequal and inefficient *rule of law*.

But the unearned money which has been spirited away to the safety of bonds has yet to be dealt with. Like the proverbial elephant in the living room, others cannot exercise their rights so long as that beast—appropriated wealth invested in bonds—is still there.

In a complete revolution heads roll, property is confiscated, and a new *rule of law* is put in place. Considering the French Revolution lasted only 26 years before aristocracy once more ruled, revolutionary changes within Western civilizations has been—as addressed in chapter 2—more from four accidents of history than serous overthrows of governing systems.

Those four accidents were: the vast expanses of land within America did not permit establishing aristocratic law, those gained rights blowing back onto Europe, those same gains in democratic rights forcing power brokers to give more rights (usually during economic or political crisis), and the Cold War suppression of the world's breaks for freedom forced massive sharing of wealth both with internal citizenry as supporters and soldiers and with allies necessary to stop fast expanding socialism.

Within those four political frameworks there were massive numbers of high quality people working to expand rights to all people and many rights were gained. But they are illusory. Shut off the wealth appropriated from the rest of the world, retain the residual feudal monopolistic *rule of law*, and Western economies would—in the form of a few financial aristocrats and an impoverished citizenry—shrink to the aristocratic structure from which it never really successfully evolved. That, of course, is the coming collapse we are describing in this thesis and outlining a path to a productive and prosperous world economy as opposed to the aristocratic monopoly system powerbrokers will be fighting to preserve.

Throughout those several centuries of struggles the citizenry were told—through the classics we now realize were only justifying a system of theft—that they had full and equal rights and current *rule of law* was structured for maximum economic efficiency. We have thoroughly documented that the monopoly system in place for centuries is inefficient to the extreme and the rights we thought we had attained were only the enormous efficiency gains of technology (of which less than half its potential reached the people) and from the massive wealth appropriated from the periphery of empires.

Up to this point, all losses of unearned wealth due to restructuring the economy were within monopoly capitalism's *rule of law*. By restructuring to utilize Henry George's mighty economic and financial engines, most citizens quickly came out of the crisis with a quality life and more secure than before the crash.

Monopolists knew what they were doing when they created those laws, entrenched wealth invested in bonds cannot be legally displaced within current *rule of law*. We are determined that any theoretical restructuring we do will be within those rules. Therefore we will only describe the problems and leave it up to the newly restructured society to decide how to solve the conundrum of honest investing of unearned wealth within the rules of a corrupt system.

The problem is rather straightforward: (1) Those huge blocs of capital created through capitalizing annually appropriated values are mixed in with honestly earned wealth. (2) The citizenry from which that wealth was appropriated must pay off those bonds and other investments over and over in perpetuity. (3) Those massive blocs of unearned wealth—needing secure havens for investment—deny society the right to create debt-free money.[a] (4) The entire process reduces the efficiency of an economy and places it at a disadvantage in trades with efficient economies.[b]

If an economy had not been monopolized, the first essential social infrastructures would have been built with debt-free created money. Investment integrity may or may not require that later infrastructures incur a bonded debt even if built with created money. Once a region is fully developed, payments from earlier bonds going right back into infrastructure would be a continual circulation of that first created money. In that efficient economy, citizens need never have owed money for building infrastructure to anyone except themselves.

A large share of the money currently invested in bonds is the capitalized values of wealth appropriated through the monopoly structure. Entrenched unearned wealth is today's remnant of the aristocratic system sitting there preventing change just as its predecessors have done for centuries. A truly free and democratic society can resolve that problem. Societies that did so were all overthrown or contained (the Soviet Union, Yugoslavia, Cuba, Indonesia, Chile, and many more) and branded as dictators and worse. It is enough to point out that—even though under attack and embargoed for decades—Cuba has high-quality universal health care, education equal to the best in the world, their citizenry discuss and vote directly on laws and their constitution, over the next 10 years they will return sight to 4.5 million blind Latin Americans, and they have medical teams working and teaching in many impoverished countries. That is only a snapshot of what can be done through policies of full and equal rights as opposed to policies of monopolization. We assume the citizenry of the newly restructured economy can chart their way past that minefield of unearned wealth honestly invested in bonds and, because a resolution can only be outside of current *rule of law*, leave resolving it to them.

There will be derivatives that will—after the shakeout and like bonds—place title to much of the nation's wealth into the hands of very few people. Most derivatives ($12.5 trillion worth in 2006 and rising fast) in the ethereal world of high finance are little more than schemes for appropriation of wealth through complex forms of short term titles (claims on wealth). Under full and equal rights, money earned matches values created and there are no needs for those shenanigans supposedly insuring investments. Along the same lines as changing the rules when the Hunt brothers had the silver market cornered—which saved the market and came close to bankrupting the Hunts—these un-

---

[a] Money can still be created but that excess will unbalance investments markets. The massive levels of created money today would appear to discredit this position. But that money is being created for all the wrong reasons, wars and protection of the monopoly system.

[b] Those disadvantages being resolved for centuries through worldwide control of resources and the *wealth producing process* are addressed in this author's simultaneously released *Economic Democracy: A Global Strategy for World Peace and Prosperity.*

earned wealth accumulations can be, and must be, set aside. The only difference between the Hunt brother's almost successful cornering of the silver market and entrenched wealth in bonds is that the silver crisis was current and something could be done about that while that appropriated successfully for decades or centuries through exclusive titles to nature's wealth and technologies is firmly in the name of current owners and there is no way to challenge that under current law. The derivatives problem, like the Hunt brothers cornering of the silver market, is current and that can be resolved along the guidelines of that previous crisis. Just as the Hunt brothers had to relinquish their claims to enormous unearned wealth, so should those final derivative holders.

Once the principles of full and equal rights are in place under Henry George's *inclusive rules of law*, operation of an economy will be simplicity itself. There need be no taxes beyond payroll deductions for Social Security and universal health care and they are insurances, not taxes. Remembering that oil, minerals, and communication spectrums are included, resource rents and banking profits will operate governments and provide many social services. In a region's earlier development, created money will finance bonds to build infrastructure (roads, railroads, WiFi communications, water systems, sewers, etc.). There are other ways besides financial accountability to assess use of and conserve resources. When built with created money, water, electricity, and natural gas can have low charges up to a proper amount for an efficient home, higher charges above that, and very high charges for excessive usage. A mature economy will fund infrastructure and maintenance out of both created money and payments on earlier infrastructure bonds. A society's savings, the level of required reserves, and, at times, the necessity for financial accountability will determine the line between debt-free and bonded infrastructure.

Keeping the value of one's currency in line with the currency of other nations is important. As addressed above, this requires an international currency with its own central bank (a bank for international settlements under the control of a democratic world government). Until regions are developed, blips on computers at this World Bank will replace current international trading currencies. While exports and imports are sold and purchased in the international currency, each allied region will have full control of money within their borders. With that currency having no value outside their borders, their banking systems can create money to build infrastructure and industries and rapidly develop an internal economy.

As shown by the example of the current American economy—which is at least 50% wasted capital, labor and resources—an economy can, for limited periods, balance anywhere. We have structured our theoretical economies with full and equal rights which will stay in balance forever. Once regional economies are developed and efficient, currency values between regions will balance. Until that time, trade between regions must be managed; that is what trading resources for technology and establishing regional and international currencies were, in this example, all about.

Once each region is sustainably developed, its labor equally as productive and equally paid, all currencies will be relatively equal and could be, and maybe should be, made interchangeable. If the dual currency structure is working at maximum efficiency, a democratic world governing body may decide that it is too valuable for controlling cross-border flows of drugs, illegal harvesting of resources, and simply for keeping a finger on the pulse of the world and resolving problems before they get out of hand.

Primary-created money can install WiFi and build bridges, highways, city streets, water systems, sewers, parks, libraries, etc., and, in newly developing regions, even loaned to build industry. The circulation of that *primary-created money* will operate the economy. As the economy matures, more and more infrastructure and all industry will be from savings and less and less from created money. To maintain the desired money supply, it will be balanced by creation of money and higher or lower required reserve levels.

With full and equal rights (elimination of those monopolies, equal pay for equally-productive labor, sharing those remaining productive jobs, and elimination of *plunder by trade*)[6] each dollar of earnings matches each dollar of value in the market. There are no appropriations of what was earned by others so there are no air pockets (those huge blocs of capital created by capitalizing the value of annually appropriated wealth) within the newly-created/restructured economies, and thus no inflations or deflations (see footnote, p. 23). A society with full and equal rights—perhaps for the first time in modern history—will have been created. It can be done, and any region that first sets that example most likely would, be copied worldwide.

For the world to become peaceful, for poverty to be eliminated, and for protection of resources and the environment, something similar to what we lay out has to happen in a seamless web worldwide. With modern communications informing the world, that can happen.

Assuming sharing of technology in trade for access to resources has been agreed upon, a part of the surplus labor and resources within the wealthy world released by the rationalization of monopolized economies (that 50% of the economy which is wasted) should be turned to installing satellite and solar panel WiFi communications throughout the developing world. WiFi installs fast with a minimum level of skilled labor and low-tech regional labor should be trained and so employed. Labor for intermediate technologies should be trained, should work as apprentices and—when fully trained—take over those jobs. As they are educated and trained, local labor will take over the highly skilled jobs. They will train apprentices who, when trained and employed, will train more apprentices. Under such policies, and remembering that in an efficient developed economy employed labor hours do not need to exceed 2 to 3 days per week, any labor force can rapidly expand..

As WiFi is being installed, students will be trained to operate their low-cost, school-system-provided, laptop computer. Recorded classes on all subjects will be prepared in whatever is chosen as a universal language (it does not have to be English but probably will be). Those recorded lectures and documentaries will be translated into the languages of each region. If the world community is serious, WiFi installations, recordings on all subjects for all classes, and local scholastic testing stations will be operational within a developing region within five years of a decision to install an efficient communication/education system. Education would be available as fast as WiFi is installed.

As motivated students will breeze through classes at 2 to 3 times the speed of brick and mortar schools, some will be ready for college courses before WiFi across an allied region is fully in place. Within 15 years all will be literate, within 20 years a population will be fully educated, and within 40 years their education level will be relatively equal to the best in the world. With tests showing one of the world's highest scholastic levels, Cuba has already proven this.

Simultaneous with establishing a modern educational system, resources will be mapped and power systems, industries, railroads, ports, airports, roads, etc., planned. As energy is the resource in shortest supply, special attention must be given to solar and other renewable energies. Permaculture and three dimensional orchard farming will create a secure food base while protecting—actually rebuilding—the soil and the environment.

The money previously spent on war can be turned to fulfilling the agreement to trade technology and training for access to resources. A few crucial factories can be built early on with created money and others necessary for a balanced economy brought on stream as the population becomes educated and trained. Appendix II outlines how master home builders can be trained and industries to provide windows, trim, and furnishings built.

Those factories, homes, and industries that emerge to provide services, consumer products, and wages to those modernizing that region will be the wealth that backs the newly-created money.

Looking to the future, care must be exercised to create high values. Comfortable rammed earth homes with ceramic interiors that will last for hundreds of years can be built for little more than, and in some regions cheaper than, the cost of mobile homes that have a lifespan of less than 30 years.

Driverless, almost risk free, electric-rail pod systems can be built in moderate-to-heavily populated areas that can provide transportation at less than half the cost of automobiles. As fuel prices rise, those energy-efficient systems will be providing cheap comfortable transportation in populated areas throughout the world.[7] Heathrow Airport in England will have a test run in 2008.

The entire process will require management and oversight by a fully democratized United Nations or its replacement. Those alliances are the embryonic formations of a peaceful federated earth. That world legislative body will replace negotiations overseeing the equal sharing of the world's resources. As opposed to the federation of the United States, the European Union, and China centuries ago—all of which became powerful but internally unequal—a federation of the earth with full and equal economic rights,—as we are suggesting—will maintain peace, tranquility, equality, and a quality life for millenniums.[a]

A very quick summary: Aristocracy's theft of the land used in common was recognized as theft and fought against. But the unorganized common people were overwhelmed and they became serfs forced to hand over half or more of what they produced to the aristocratic lords of the land. (Note that today half of labor's production is still appropriated.) When sheep produced more money than serfs, the enclosure acts gave *exclusive title* to that later lord of the land and denied the common people even those meager rights.

Each step in the early privatization of the commons was recognized as a theft and fought against. Compliant philosophers (we know them today as the classics) justified that theft.[b] The principle of amassing unearned wealth through exclusive titles to nature's wealth and technologies was applied to every sector of the economy. As fast as a technology came on stream, *exclusive titles* were—primarily through the patent system and stock markets but also by license—bestowed on those in position to take advantage of the opportunity. Over time, rental values going to those holding title to natures wealth and technologies or a license to practice within a monopolized system (banking, insurance, medical care, law) were accepted as normal.

That those *exclusive titles* had been designed to lay claim to unearned wealth was forgotten and titles and licenses to practice within monopolized systems were accepted as proper. The enormous rewards (your name in history, promotions within the system, very well paid, etc.) for producing and practicing a philosophy that protected the system were so great and the penalties (beheadings in those early centuries—today extreme difficulties in finding employment, ostracized to the fringes, and pay almost non-existent) so damaging that few stood up and the pure theft of *exclusive titles* severely compromising economic efficiency became accepted as highly efficient and any who would suggest different were easily ignored.

---

[a] Note how the elimination of monopolization of technology permits the rapid and low-cost development of poor regions of the world. Protecting the many forms of monopolization has been the cause of war and poverty for millennia. Even our earliest forefathers were battling over resources (territory). It is time to eliminate all forms of monopolization and share this world in peace.

[b] In *A Perplexed Philosopher*, Henry George describes how Herbert Spencer, the leading thinker of the late 17th century, no doubt after reading his *Progress and Poverty,* believed fully in society collecting land rent. He simply was not let back into polite society until he recanted those views. That peer pressure has successfully kept the system protected for several hundred years. Most professors and intellectuals know in advance they will be ostracized if they seriously challenge the fundamentals of the system. Those who do are marginalized to the fringes. It seems only revolutions will break through a firmly entrenched *belief system.*

That principle of theft of others' wealth was the very essence of world trade from the beginning and—with the exception of those who were added to that alliance to stop fast expanding socialism (South-east Asia)—still is today.

If a challenging philosophy gained credence it would be suppressed by massive financial and economic power (embargoes) or covert and overt warfare. Those massive inflictions of violence were carried out under barrages of propaganda as to those under assault being dictators and genocidal murderers.

The truth of the matter was that, until successfully suppressed, the living standards rose rapidly in each nation that broke free and gained control of their resources and destiny. A massive power structure based upon the theft of others' wealth did not dare let other nations or their own citizens see the potential gains of economies based upon rights of people to their share of the rental value of resources and rights to the production of their own labor.

The propaganda has been so intense that few realize they could be living a life beyond their fondest dreams while working half their current hours. Under a system of full and equal rights, all would have rights to a piece of land (a home). That home could, through WiFi, communicate with any other home in the world. All could be educated over that communication system to whatever level they wished at almost no cost. Three-dimensional orchard permaculture would permit bringing fresh vegetables and fruits from the garden each day or delivered from Southern climes during the winter. The local mall would carry groceries and small consumer items. At half the price, expensive items would be ordered over the Internet. Laws and constitutions would be discussed and voted on over that communication system (participatory and direct democracy). Each person would be electronically identified (eye and thumbprint scans, etc.) so there can be no cheating. (Privacy aside, a society with full and equal rights would have almost no crime and big brother would have been done away with anyway.) Many jobs—recording, accounting, and communicating—can be handled from home.

As monopolies *structured in law* are eliminated, everybody has rights to land, rights to medical care, rights to a quality retirement, rights to educate oneself as far as one wanted to go, the right to know of and discuss laws to be passed, the right to vote on those laws, and on and on. Each region of the world, each country, each region of a country, each community, and each entrepreneur has rights to finance capital. Just as inequality has been structured into past constitutions and law, virtually everything required for an efficient, equal, and honest community can be put into constitutions or law as a right. The right to a belief (religion) balanced by a right not to believe requires a constitutional separation of church and state.

Quoting from our introduction emphasizes how rapidly the impoverished world could develop under the principles of full and equal rights. Even as resources and the environment are protected, poverty can be eliminated in 10 years and a quality life for all can be provided in less than 50 years:

> The infrastructure necessary for the developing world to be efficient appears expensive. But that is only true if built by outside contractors. All costs above resource rent values are labor costs and we thoroughly document that most resources are within their borders and such rents properly go into the social fund. Machinery and infrastructure built by a region's own companies and trained labor creates wealth equal in value to the price of that labor (which is their own), interest on industrial capital (stored labor and those factories should be built with local labor), and resource rent (which comes from their regional resources). As labor spends their wages for their living and governments spend resource rent and banking profits to run governments and essential services, all those values, except that spent for imports, are a region's circulating buying power.
>
> Train labor, build industries to scale for a region, build construction equipment with those industries, build that infrastructure, and the cost to a region is primarily importing modern tools for those factories. Those undeveloped regions have most of the world's natural resources and all manufactured wealth is processed from natural wealth. So, although it is necessary that the banking system be *socially-owned*, developing a region is primarily creating money to train and employ a region's own labor force to build the necessary infrastructure. That infrastructure and the wealth produced backs both newly created and circulating money. Current *exclusive titles* to nature's resources and technologies and the many other monopolies copied after those original excessive rights *structured in law* deny that simplicity to the world.

Preventing every aspect of this from happening is what wars and struggles of all kinds have been about and still are today.

Again we must point out that the customs, *belief systems*, and *rules of law* of cultures seldom permit a radical structural change as laid out in this theoretical model. However, it has happened and it will happen again. But those past revolutions were carried out by too few people compared to the power of the countries still firmly controlling the world. Historic power centers did not dare let the world's citizenry see a society with substantially more rights and freedoms. Much of the history of the past 50 years has been the suppression of just such potentially freer people. This is why we focused on the importance of a large enough share of the world breaking free. Only when their numbers are large enough (through alliances) will a countervailing power be in place that can challenge current powerbrokers and demonstrate to the world a truly free, peaceful, and productive social structure.

Make no mistake about it; though no one can predict the outcome, a worldwide populist revolt has already started. With the dispossessed of one region in full contact with those of other regions, this should be an uncontainable upheaval. After all, if imperialism cannot militarily contain 26 million Iraqis, how can they contain three billion people worldwide allied together to become free?

Thus, since all sincerely want peace, we have laid out the possibilities, and the outline, of a peaceful, velvet revolution. Just as we are aware that the world is unlikely to fully break free from the strangle hold of monopoly capitalism's *rule of law,* we recognize that other societies have other methods of monopolizing power, wealth and rights, many lacking the economic engine effect of monopoly capitalism, and those systems will be just as difficult to reform as those of the West.

So it will be a long struggle. Some societies may try socialist or communitarian economic structures. For those economies to be efficient, four rules must be followed: (1) Society must collect all resource rents and utilize those funds to operate governments, federal, state, and local. (2) A *socially-owned* and operated banking system must create money to build infrastructures and, in the initial stages of development, crucial industry.[a] Required reserves must be managed to maintain the proper level of buying power. (3) Inventors must be well paid and all patents placed in the public domain. (4) Each region, each state, each community, and each entrepreneur has a constitutional right to finance capital.

Those four points are easiest to understand as Henry George's *rule of law,* his mighty economic engine.

---

[1] Alfred W. McCoy, *A Question of Torture: CIA Interrogation from the Cold War to the War on Terror* (New York: Henry Holt and Company, 2006).

[2] Ian Bremmer, "Who's in Charge in the Kremlin" World Policy Journal (Winter 2005/06), p.3.

[3] Taylor, *Fall of the Dynasties,* chapters 17--19

[4] Lester C. Thurow, Generating Inequality (New York: Basic Books, 1975). p. 149.

[5] Ibid, p. 154, (emphasis added).

[6] Smith, Economic *Democracy: A Grand Strategy,*

[7] keywords: PRT International, LLC, John E. Anderson.

---

[a] Actually all infrastructure and industry can be built and maintained with created money and mandated reserves can be raised high enough to maintain stable, as opposed to inflationary, buying power. But such an economy would have no finance capital amassed from savings and no financial or efficiency accountability, so we stayed with Henry George's mighty, and accountable, economic engine.

Appendix I: Myths in Monetary Theory

Under required reserves in fractional reserve banking mandated by law, private banks cannot, and do not, create money. What really happens is bankers have control of the Federal Reserve and create massive sums of money for the wrong purposes. Remove those corrupt bankers, eliminate the monopolies which consume that money, then create money for productive purposes, and you have an efficient economy. There still remains the myth of paying off debts destroying money, the myth of the need for 100% reserves, and the myth of debts being money.

Logic proves that paying off debts does not destroy money (as stated by both the Federal Reserve and money theorists). If you took in cash to pay off a $10,000 loan, the bank is not going to burn that money. They are going to put it in their vault right alongside their other cash. If you pay by check, those funds are debited from one reserve account and credited to that bank's reserves either within that bank or at the Federal Reserve.

What they mean to say is, unless that money is loaned back out, the money supply is reduced. Yes, when loans are paid off and that money is not loaned back out the money supply is reduced and if all loans were paid off there would be no deposits beyond the initial *primary-created money*. That money has been destroyed is only appearances. All that is missing is the circulation of money which creates what is known as "the money supply." As the money supply shrinks the economy slows, values collapse, debts become unpayable, and then is when money is destroyed.

By keeping her banks running even when they were technically bankrupt, Japan has shown how to avoid the destruction of money. A minimum level of Japan's *primary-created money* has been destroyed and those bankrupt banks, maintaining their loan policies, have kept most money loaned out (much of it to America). That which is not circulating is sitting there, available, in reserve accounts.

Early 100% reserve theorists suggested that the government print currency and use it to buy up treasuries and other debt instruments of banks. Each dollar on deposit was to be matched by a dollar in cash in the bank's vaults. This was to guarantee depositors that the cash they had on deposit could always be redeemed. Later variations of 100% reserves had the banks borrowing or purchasing enough currency from the Treasury to match all deposits.

There are severe contradictions here. (1) When banking first starts there would be no debt instruments to buy up. (2) The government earning interest on those debt instruments instead of the banks, or the bank paying interest on the money loaned them by the government to keep in their vaults, would be a massive drain on banks which would have to be paid for by higher interest rates. This would effectively be a tax paid by every citizen. (3) The government backing the many forms of debt the banks would turn over to the government in trade for enough currency for 100% reserves is a monopolist's dream come true. The government would be guaranteeing their unearned wealth. (4) Eliminate those monopolies, have society operate those banks, pay equally for equally-productive labor, share the remaining productive jobs, and each dollar earned and/or deposited will represent true value (*use value*) within the economy. There will be no inflations or deflations due to too much money chasing too few goods, there will be no runs on banks, and there will be no need for reserves beyond that mandated by the Federal Reserve for a balanced economy. The 100% reserves would be already in place by values purchased matching the value of money paid. Even if there was a run on a bank, which there would not be, all checks or debit card usage against deposits would be honored and the citizenry would soon learn their money was safe. As their job is to keep the money supply in balance and they can do so by either creating or destroying money, a *socially-owned* banking system automatically has 100% reserves. Private banks do not have those automatic reserves, a central bank—by the rules—cannot create it for them on demand, and destroying money would be—to them—akin to suicide.

The myth of debt money: Money is just what we have described it, circulating *primary-created money*. A debt is just that a debt. Money flows through the economy in the process of producing, distributing, and purchasing. Though it may be sold to a different owner, a debt just sits there waiting to be paid off and the equity pledged backs loaned reserve accounts.

On the other hand, the meaning of debt money as money created to provide loans to buy and sell monopoly values is, as described throughout this treatise, valid.

Though we have outlined an efficient economy that would operate on roughly 60%, possibly 70%, less borrowed money, debt is an essential feature of a modern economy. Mandated reserves, managed by a Federal Reserve authorized to create money for economic infrastructure and essential social services, is pure gold.

Unless it is a gift, virtually no one starts life with adequate finance capital; it must be earned or borrowed. Earning takes a long time whereas borrowing takes minutes. As soon as that finance capital is borrowed gifted people can put their talents to work producing with the efficiency laid out throughout this book. This is why rights to finance capital for regions of the world, for countries, for regions within countries, for states, for communities, and for entrepreneurs are so important.

Appendix II: A Practical Approach for Developing Poor Nations & Regions

Let's design an emerging-nation development plan utilizing cheap, broadly-available resources. Almost all countries have traditional, fireproof, earthen-material homes hundreds of years old. Most developing nations have large numbers of unemployed labor quite capable of building in the traditional ways and who can build high-quality earthen homes cheaply. Firing the inside of earth homes creating ceramic walls and floors opens an unlimited potential of beautiful, clean, easily maintained—yet cheap—housing. Some regions traditionally use other building materials such as stone, straw-bale, timber, bamboo, etc.

Local master-craftsmen can train the apprentice home builders, and these newly-trained practitioners can teach others on the job. The teachers would be paid, and the workers' pay would be their training as master home builders. For example, assuming five workers to a crew on an adobe or rammed earth home, every 3 or 4 houses built will result in five more master builders, rapidly expanding the home building project. Other building materials will require differing periods of training to produce master craftsmen, but the principle is the same. (See Hassan Fathy's book, "Architecture for the Poor," for an inspiring account of the method that was used to create a total-process system of adobe construction in Egypt.) Having designed and built sustainable housing and major architectural projects in many countries, Phil Hawes (philhawes@theriver .com) is an internationally known expert.

Additional industries are necessary to produce doors, windows, plumbing and electrical systems, flooring, roofs, and furniture. These industries will also expand rapidly.

Though these homes will be built cheaply, they have full *use value*. As some projects mature, the labor will be paid, while in others the master-builder will train volunteer workers to build more homes for themselves, family, and friends, and are thus paid indirectly, but paid well.

Since real value is being produced utilizing local and regional resources, primary money can be created by any nation, or region, up to the value of those homes, businesses and inventory. Created money is the proper financial source to utilize a nation's own resources to build the industries, regional businesses, and inventory necessary to service a developing community.

Simultaneous with building homes, a country or region must develop a prosperous agriculture. Permaculture fruits, nuts, berries, tubers, and vegetables work will with eco-village housing. Commercial farms, equipment, and the food produced have value and—as it is locally produced—money can be created for that development as well. All resources should be processed locally into high value-added products both for regional consumption and export. As economic activity and production increases, community values rise, and buying power increases to purchase the new production.

So long as countries or regions are utilizing local resources, money can be created to build industries and infrastructure. Correctly guided, this can even include higher-tech industries for manufacturing such energy producing equipment as wind generators, small hydro generation units, and photovoltaic cells. These can convert the naturally occurring, non-fossil fuel forces of wind, waterpower, and sunlight into electrical energy. It is possible to train ambitious local inhabitants to assemble electronic equipment, such as TVs and computers, which can provide a free education via satellite and solar powered WiFi.

However, a developing country or region will soon need technology and industries that—unless the revolution we addressed throughout this book has taken place—are firmly under the control of the imperial centers. It is at this point that regions must ally together to negotiate with the imperial centers to trade access to resources for access to technology. To not ally together would result in the locally created wealth being transferred to those imperial centers via unequal pay for equally-productive labor. Local resources will be purchased far below their full value, resulting in the familiar inevitable debt traps for the developing regions. The key is cheap, quality, local production of social infrastructure.

Taxing nature's wealth as per Henry George's *rule of law* (chapters 1 through 5) prevents capitalized values and protects the entire nation from having those values attached to repay debts. HG taxing principles are essential both for economic efficiency and protection against creditor nations laying claim to a weak nation's wealth. The *use value* is still there but society collecting resource rents and interest on loans prevents those values from being capitalized, keeps them out of the hands of creditors, and thus those values are forever kept in trust for a nation's citizens.

By all classes being available via satellite or WiFi and studied on home TV, it is possible for the developing world to educate their citizens for 5-15% the cost of conventional brick and mortar schools. Not only would the youth become well educated, so would many older citizens. WiFi wiring those emerging nations would give the talented access to jobs and markets in the highly developed world.

Currency values can only remain stable if a country's productive capacity is efficient and stable. So a country needs to develop infrastructure cheaply and efficiently and the above building of quality homes and support industries cheaply is an example but only a start.

With technology and markets monopolized, high technology industrializing is more problematic. The key is maximum production of high-value-added products rather than selling raw resources. Example: an oil producing nation has the option of refining its oil, producing plastics, etc. The monopolies of wealthy nations are so powerful that such industries will require trading alliances or full federations between weak nations, a step toward the full federation of all nations.

Stevia is 30 times sweeter than sugar, is cheap to produce, cheap to process, and it does not have the health damaging effects of sugar. William Hayward (<haywardwj@execs.com>) has containers filled with Stevia plants, processing equipment, and instructions ready to ship anywhere in the world. Africa also has a couple indigenous sweet plants that may replace sugar. The gains to a society both financially and in health care substituting any one of these sweeteners for sugar is huge.

Most important is sharing with other developing nations the various ways to protect their wealth from being claimed by speculators of wealthy nations.

Hopefully these nations can ally together to build their infrastructures and protect themselves from monopoly capital. As this simple development plan is put together, other areas of utilization of local labor and resources will become visible.

Bibliography

101 Famous Thinkers on Owning Earth (New York: Schalkenbach Foundation);

Aaron, Craig. "Sun, Sand and Spectrum Policy." *In These Times*, September 19, 2005

Aptheker, Herbert. *The American Revolution.* NY: International Publishers, 1985.

_____. *The Colonial Era.* 2nd ed. New York: International Publishers, 1966.

_____. *Early Years of the Republic.* New York: International Publishers, 1976.

Bandler, Richard, and John Grinder. *Frogs Into Princes.* Moab, UT: Real People Press, 1979.

Bagdikian, Ben. *Media Monopoly.* Boston: Beacon Press, 1983.

———. *Media Monopoly.* Boston: Beacon Press, 1987.

Banco, Anthony. "Playing With Fire." *Business Week* (September 16, 1987).

Baran, Paul A., and Paul M. Sweezy. *Monopoly Capital.* London: Monthly Review Press, 1968.

Barnet, Richard. *The Lean Years.* New York: Simon and Schuster, 1980._

_____. *The Alliance.* New York: Simon and Schuster, 1983.

_____. *The Rockets' Red Glare: War, Politics and American Presidency.* New York: Simon and Schuster, 1983.

_____. "Lords of the Global Economy." *The Nation* (December 19, 1994).

_____. and John Cavanagh. *Global Dreams: Imperial Corporations and the New World Order.* New York: Simon and Schuster, 1994.

Beard, Charles A. *An Economic Interpretation of the Constitution.* New York: Macmillan Publishing Co, 1941.

Berlan, Jean-Pierre. "The Commodification of Life." *Monthly Review* (December 1989).

Bernstein, Merton C., Joan Brodshaug Bernstein. *Social: The System That Works.* New York: Basic Books, 1988.

Bhagirath Lal Das, *WTO: The Doha Agenda: The New Negotiations on World Trade.*
London:: Zed Books, 2003.

Bishop, Abraham. *Georgia Speculation Unveiled.* Readex Microprint Corporation,
1966.

Blaug, Mark. *Great American Economists Before Keynes.* Atlantic Highlands, NJ: Humanities Press International, 1986.

Breckinridge, S. P. *Legal Tender.* New York: Greenwood Press, 1969.

Brown, Michael Barratt. *Fair Trade.* London: Zed Books, 1993.

Boorstein, Edward. *What's Ahead? - - - The U.S. Economy.* New York: International Publishers, 1984.

Borsodi, Ralph. *Inflation.* Great Barrington, MA: E.F. Schumacher Society, 1989.

Budiansky, Stephen. "An Act of Vision for the Third World." *U.S. News & World Report* (November 2, 1987).

Chase, Stuart. *The Economy of Abundance.* New York: The Macmillan Company, 1934.

_____. *Men and Machines.* New York: The Macmillan Company, 1929.

_____. *The Tragedy of Waste.* New York: The Macmillan Company, 1925.

Clark, William R. *Petrodollar Warfare, Oil, Iraq, and the Future of the Dollar.* Google Search

Cohen, Carl, ed. *Communism, Fascism, Democracy.* New York: Random House, 1962.

Conine, Ernest. "U.S. Should Take a Tip from Canada." *Missoulian* (Apr. 2, 1990).

Dacey, Norman F. *How to Avoid Probate.* Updated. New York: Crown Publishers, Inc., 1980.

Daly, Herman E. *Steady-State Economics.* San Francisco: W.H. Freeman 1977.

_____. John B. Cobb Jr. *For the Common Good.* Boston: Beacon Press, 1989.

_____. Salah El Serafy, editors. *Population, Technology, and Lifestyle.* Washington DC: Island Press, 1992.

Dentzer, Susan. "The Coming Global Boom." *U.S. News & World Report* (July 16, 1990).

Desmond, Edward W. "Japan's Trillion-Dollar Hole." *Time* (April 8, 1996).

_____. "The Failed Miracle." *Time* (April 22, 1996).

Diamond, Jared. *Collapse: How Societies Choose to Fail or Succeed.* New York: Penguin, 2005.

_____. *Collapse: How Societies Choose to Fail or Succeed.* New York: Penguin, 2005.

_____. *Guns, Germs, and Steel: The Fates of Human Societies.* NY: W.W. Norton, 1999.

_____. *The Third Chimpanzee: The Evolution and Future of the Human Animal.* New York: HarperCollins, 1992.

Dorgan, Byron, Senator. *The North Dakota REC* (May 1984).

Echeverria, Durand. *The Maupeou Revolution.* Baton Rouge: Louisiana U Press, 1985.

Fathy, Hassan. "Architecture for the Poor. Google search.

Faux, Jeff. "The Austerity Trap and the Growth Alternative." *World Policy Journal* (Summer 1988).

Fawthrop, Tom. "Havana, Operation Miracle" (*The Scotsman*, Google search).

Feagin, Joe E. *The Urban Real Estate Game.* Engelewood Cliffs, NJ: Prentice-Hall, 1983.

Fingleton, Eamonn. *Unsustainable: How Economic Dogma is Destroying American Prosperity.* New York: ThunderMouth Press, 2003.

Foner, Philip S. *Labor and World War I.* New York: International Publishers, 1987.

_____. *Abraham Lincoln: Selections From His Writings.* New York: International Publishers, 1944.

_____. *From Colonial Times to the Founding of the American Federation of Labor.* New York: International Publishers, 1947.

_____. *From the Founding of the A.F. of L. to the Emergence of American Imperialism.* New York: International Publishers, 1982.

"Four of 10 Hospital Stays are Unneeded." *The Missoulian* (Nov. 13, 1986).Fuchs, Victor R., PhD.,.

Gaffney, Mason, Fred Harrison. *The Corruption of Economics: With The Development of Democracy, Mind Control Became the Urgent Need: Neo-Classical Economics Was the Tool.* London: Shepheard-Walwyn, 1994.

Galbraith, John Kenneth. *Economics in Perspective.* NY: Houghton Mifflin, 1987.

_____. *Money.* New York: Houghton Mifflin, 1976.

_____. "*Which Capitalism for Eastern Europe.*" Harpers (April 1990).

_____. and Stanislav Menshikov. *Capitalism, Communism, and Coexistence.* Boston: Houghton Mifflin Company, 1988

George, Henry. *Progress and Poverty.* New York: Robert Schalkenbach Foundation,1981.

_____. *A Perplexed Philosopher.* New York: Robert Schalkenbach Foundation, 1965.

_____. *Protection or Free Trade.* New York: Robert Schalkenbach Foundation, 1980.

Gephardt, Richard, speech at Wharton School of Economics.

Goldhaber, Michael. *Reinventing Technology.* New York: Routledge & Kegan Paul, 1986.

Gowan, Peter. *The Global Gamble.*: New York: verso, 1999.

Grant, Phil. *The Wonderful Wealth Machine.* New York: Devon-Adair, 1953.

Greider, William. *One World Ready or Not.* New York: Simon and Schuster, 1997.

_____."Annals of Finance." *The New Yorker,* (November 9, 1987; Nov. 16, 1987; November 23, 1987).

_____. *The Education of David Stockman and Other Americans.* New York: New American Library, 1986.

_____. "The Money Question." *World Policy Journal* (Fall 1988).

_____. *Secrets of the Temple.* New York: Simon and Schuster, 1987.

_____. *Who Will Tell the People?* New York: Simon and Schuster, 1992.

Hahn, James S., A.B. "How Does Canada Do It." *The New England Journal of Medicine* (Sept. 27, 1990

Harrison, Fred. *Boom Bust: House Prices, Banking and the Depression of 2010.* London: Shepheard Walwyn, 2005.

Hartzok, Alanna. *The Earth Belongs to Everyone.* www.ied.info/. The Institute for Economic Democracy, 2006.

Henry George School. New York. gopher://echonyc.com:70/11s/Cul/HGS.

Henry George Foundation of America. 2000 Century Plaza, #238, Columbia, MD. 21004.

Herman, Edward S, "The Assault on Social Security." *Z Magazine* (Nov. 1995).

Henwood, Doug. *Wall Street.* New York: Verso, 1997.

_____. "Clinton and the Austerity Cops." *The Nation* (November 23, 1992).

_____. "The U.S. Economy: The Enemy Within." *Covert Action* (Summer 1992).

Himmelstein, David Steffie Woolhandler, Dr. Ida Hellander, *Bleeding the Patient: The Consequences of corporate Health Care.* Common Courage Press, 2001.

Hixson, William F. *It's Your Money.* Toronto, Canada, COMER, 1997.

_____. *Triumph of the Bankers: Money and Banking in the Eighteenth and Nineteenth Centuries.* Westport, Conn.: Praeger, 1993.

Hufton, Olwen. *Europe: Privilege and Protest.* Ithaca, NY: Cornell U Press, 1980.

Hudson, Michael, Baruch A. Levine. *Privatization in the Near East - The Story of Power.* Cambridge: Harvard University, 1996.

Hunt, E. K., Howard J. Sherman. *Economics.* New York: Harper & Row, 1990.

Hurwit, Cathy. "A Canadian Style Cure." *Dollars and Sense* (May 1993).

Iglehart, John K. "Health Policy Report: Germany's Health Care System." *The New England Journal of Medicine.*

Illich, Ivan, *Medical Nemisis.* New York: Harmony Books. 1984.

Impoco, Jim, Jack Egan, Douglas Pasternak. "The Tokyo Tidal Wave." *U.S. News & World Report* (September 17, 1990).

Johnson, Chalmers. *Blowback: The Costs and Consequences of the American Empire.* New York: Henry Holt & Company, 2000.

_____. *The Sorrows of Empire: Militarism, Secrecy, and the End of the Republic.* New York:

Johnson, Haynes. "Teflon 80s Bear Striking Resemblance to 'Giddy 20s,' *The Missoulian* (March 25, 1987), reprinted from *Washington Post.*

Josephson, Matthew. *Robber Barons.* New York: Harcourt Brace Jovanovich, 1962.

Kennedy, Paul. *The Rise and Fall of the Great Powers.* New York: Random House, 1987.

"Kids in the Cuckoo's Nest." *Utne Reader* (Mar./Apr. 1992).

Kilmer, Jeanie, "Public Power Costs Less." *Public Power Magazine* (May/June 1985).

Kindleberger, Charles P. *Manias, Panics, and Crashes.* New York: Basic Books, Inc., 1978.

Korten, David. *When Corporations Rule the World.* West Hartford, CT: Kumarian Press and San Francisco: Berret-Koehler, 1995

Krehm, William. *Price in the Mixed Economy: Our Record of Disaster.* Toronto: Thornwood Publications, 1975.

Kropotkin, Petr. *Mutual Aid.* Boston: Porter Sargent Publishers Inc., 1914.

_____. *The Great French Revolution.* New York: Black Rose Books, 1989.

_____. *The State.* London: Freedom Press, 1987.

Kuttner, Robert. "Cant and Recant," *The American Prospect* (January 2006)

Kurtzman, Joel. *The Death of Money.* New York: Simon and Schuster, 1993.

_____.*The Decline and Crash of the American Economy.* New York: W.W. Norton, 1988.

Lacey, Robert. *Ford.* New York: Ballantine Books, 1986.

Lambert, Angela. *Unquiet Souls.* New York: Harper & Row, 1984.

Lee, Katherine J. "Justice Has Broken Down." *Americans For Legal Reform* 4:2 (1985).

Levy, Steven. "Bills New Vision," *Newsweek*, November 27, 1995.

Longworth, Richard C. *Global Squeeze: The Coming Crisis of First-World Nations.* Chicago: Contemporary Books, 1999.

Lyon, Peter. *To Hell in a Day Coach.* New York: J. B. Lippincott Company, 1968.

Mackay, Charles. *Extraordinary Delusions and Madness of Crowds.* 2nd. ed. New York: Farrar Straus and Giroux, 1932.

Makin, John H., *The Global Debt Crisis* . New York: Basic Books, 1984.

Manchester, William. *The Glory and the Dream.* New York: Bantam Books, 1988.

Martin, Edward Winslow. *History of the Grange Movement.* New York: Burt Franklin, 1967.

Marx, Karl. *Capital*, 3 vols. edited by Frederick Douglas. New York: International Publishers, 1967.

McCoy, Alfred W. *A Question of Torture: CIA Interrogation from the Cold War to the War on Terror.* New York: Henry Holt and Company, 2006.

McHugh, Robert. "Money Supply versus Interest Rate Policy," *Comer*, January 2006.

Mead, Walter Russell. *Special Providence: American Foreign Policy and How it Changed the World* . UK: Routledge, 2002.

_____. "After Hegemony." *New Perspective Quarterly*, (1987).

_____. "American Economic Policy in the Antemillenial Era." *World Policy Journal*, (Summer 1989).

_____. "The Bush Administration and the New World Order." *World Policy Journal* (Summer 1991).

_____. *Mortal Splendor.* Boston: Houghton Mifflin Company, 1987.

_____. "Saul Among the Prophets." *World Policy Journal*, (Summer 1991).

Metcalf, Lee, Vic Reinemer. *Overcharge.* New York: David McKay, 1967.

Milko, George. "It's Hassle Free Down Under." *Americans for Legal Reform* 6:3 (1986).

Miller, Christian, "Wall Street's Fondest Dream: The Insanity of Privatizing Social Security," *Dollars and Sense* (November/December 1998).
Mirow, Kurt Rudolf, *Webs of Power* (Boston: Houghton Mifflin, 1982)
Modern Money Mechanics (MMM, http://landru.i-link-2.net/monques/mmm2.html),
Moffitt, Michael. "Shocks, Deadlocks, and Scorched Earth: Reaganomics and the Decline of U.S. Hegemony." *World Policy Journal* (Fall 1987).
_____. *The World's Money*. New York: Simon and Schuster, 1983.
Moret, Leuren. "A death Sentence Here and Abroad, The Trojan Horse of Nuclear War." Google Search
Mumford, Lewis. *The City in History*. New York: Harcourt Brace Jovanovich, 1961.
_____. *Pentagon of Power.* New York: Harcourt Brace Jovanovich, 1964, 1970.
_____. *Technics and Civilization.* New York: Harcourt Brace Jovanovich, 1963.
_____. *Technics and Human Development.* New York: Harcourt Brace Jovanovich, 1967.
Murphy, R. Taggart. *The Weight of The Yen.* New York: W.W. Norton, 1996.
Murray, Charles, Herrnstein, Richard J.. *The Bell Curve: Intelligence and Class Structure in American Life.* New York: Free Press, 1994.
_____. *Losing Ground.* New York: Basic Books, 1984.
Nadudere, Dan. *The Political Economy of Imperialism.* London: Zed Books, 1977.
101 Famous Thinkers on Owning Earth, New York: Robert Schalkenbach Foundation, no date.
Owen, Wilfred. *Strategy for Mobility.* Westport, CT: Greenwood Press, 1978.
Parenti, Michael, *Power and the Powerless.* New York: St. Martin's Press, 1978.
Perkins, John. *Confessions of an Economic Hit Man.* (San Francisco: Barrett-Kohler, 2004.
Phillips, Kevin. *Boiling Point: Democrats, Republicans, and the Decline of Middle Class Prosperity.* New York: Random House, 1993.
_____. *The Politics of Rich and Poor.* New York: Random House, 1990.
_____. *American Dynasty: Aristocracy, Fortune, and the Politics of Deceit in the House of Bush.* New York: Penguin Books, 2003.
Pilzer, Paul Zane. *Unlimited Wealth.* New York: Crown Publishing, 1990.
Polanyi, Karl. *The Great Transformation.* Boston: Beacon Press, 1957.
Prados, John. *The Presidents' Secret Wars.* New York: William Morrow, 1986.
_____. *The Presidents Secret Wars*, revised. Warwick: Elephant Paperbacks, 1996.
_____. Prados, John. *The Hidden History of the Vietnam War.* Chicago: Elephant Paperbacks, 1995.
_____. *Keepers Of The Keys A History Of The National Security Council From Truman To Bush.* New York: William Morrow, 1991.
Public Power Directory and Statistics for 1983. Washington, DC: American Public Power Association, 1983.
Quinn, T. K. *Giant Business: Threat to Democracy.* 3rd. ed. New York: Exposition Press, 1954.
Rasell, Edie. "A Bad Bargain." *Dollars and Sense* (May 1993).
Renard, George, *Guilds in the Middle Ages.* New York: Augustus M. Kelley, 1968.
Richter, Paul. "Commodity Marts Face Fraud Fallout." *Los Angeles Times*, Quoted in the Missoulian (July 4, 1987).
Robinson, Donald. "The Great Pacemaker Scandal." *Readers Digest* (Oct. 1983)
Rodell, Fred. *Woe Unto You Lawyers.* Littleton, CO: Fred B. Rothman & Co., 1987.

Rousseau, Jean Jacques. "A Discourse on the Origins of Inequality." *The Social Contract and Discourses.* New York: Dutton, 1950.

Routh, Guy. *The Origin of Economic Ideas.* Dobbs Ferry, NY: Sheridan House, 1989.

Sale, Kirkpatrick. *Human Scale.* First Peregree printing. New York: G. P. Putnam and Sons, 1982.

Sally Jesse Raphael Show (May 30, 1988). Patient Advocates Bill Johnson and Tom Wilson.

Samuelson, Robert. "The Great Global Debtor." *Newsweek* (July 22, 1991).

Schalkenbach Foundation, 41 East 72nd St., NY, NY 10021 (212-988-1680).

Schiller, Herbert I. *Information and the Crisis Economy.* Boston: Oxford University Press, 1986.

———. *Communications and Cultural Domination.* White Plains, NY: M. E. Sharp, 1976.

———. "The Information Superhighway: Paving over the Public." *Z Magazine* (Mar. 1994).

———. *Mind Managers.* Boston: Beacon Press, 1973.

Schlosstein, Steven. *Trade War.* New York: Congdon and Weed, 1984.

Schor, Juliet B. "Workers of the World Unwind." *Technology Review* (November/December 1991).

_____. *The Overworked American.* Basic Books, 1991.

Seldes, George. *Even the Gods Can't Change History.* Secaucus, NJ: Lyle Stuart, 1976.

———. *In Fact.* New York: Lyle Stuart, Inc., 1968.

———. *Never Tire of Protesting.* New York: Lyle Stuart, Inc., 1968.

———. "The Roman Church and Franco," *The Human Quest* (Mar.-Apr., 1994).

Shealy, Tom. "The United States vs. the World: How We Score in Health." *Prevention* (May 1986).

Shiva, Vandana. *Stolen Harvest: The Hijacking of the Global Food Supply.* Cambridge: South End Press, 2000.

Smith, Adam. The Wealth of Nations. New York: Random House, 1965.

"Smith, Adam" (George J.W. Goodman). *Supermoney.* NY: Random House, 1972.

_____. *Nightly Business Report*, PBS (June 17, 1987).

Smith, J.W. *Economic Democracy: A Grand Strategy for World Peace and Prosperity.* www.ied.info/. the Institute for Economic Democracy, 2006.

_____. *Economic Democracy: The Political Struggle of the Twenty-First Century*, updated and expanded 4th edition, www.ied.info/. the institute for Economic Democracy, 2005.

_____. *WHY?: The Deeper History Behind the September 11th, Terrorist Attack on America.* updated and expanded 3rd edition. www.ied.info/: the Institute for Economic Democracy, 2005.

_____. Cooperative Capitalism: A Blueprint for Global Peace and Prosperity. updated and expanded 2nd edition. www.ied.info/. the Institute for Economic Democracy, 2005.

_____. The World's Wasted Wealth 2. the Institute for Economic Democracy, 1994, www.ied.info/.

Spencer, Herbert. *Social Statics.* Schalkenbach Foundation, 1850 unabridged ed.

Swann, Robert. *The Need for Local Currencies.* Great Barrington, MA: E.F. Schumacher Society, 1990.

Tabb, William. *The Amoral Elephant: Globalization and the Struggle for Global Justice in the Twenty-First Century.* New York. Monthly Review Press, 2001.

Taylor, Edmond. *The Fall of the Dynasties:: The Collapse of the Old Order, 1905-1922,* New York: Dorset Press, 1989.

Thoren, Theodore R., Richard F. Warner. *The Truth in Money.* Chagrin Falls, Ohio: Truth in Money Publishers, 1994.

Thurow, Lester C. *Head to Head: The Coming Economic Battle Among Japan, Europe, and America.* New York: William Morrow, 1992.

_____. "Falling Wages, Failing Policy." *Dollars and Sense* (September/October 1996).

_____. "The Crusade That is Killing Prosperity." *The American Prospect* (March/April 1996).

_____. *Dangerous Currents.* New York: Random House, 1983.

_____. *Generating Inequality.* New York: Basic Books, 1975.

_____. "Investing in America's Future." *Economic Policy Institute*, C-Span Transcript. (October 21, 1991).

_____. *The Future of Capitalism: How Today's Economic Forces Shape Tomorrow's World.* England, Penguin Books, 1996.

_____. Thurow, Lester, *Building Wealth: The New Rules for Individuals, Companies and Nations in a knowledge Based Economy.* New York: HarperCollins, 2000.

Tobin, Eugene M. *Organize or Perish.* New York: Greenwood Press, 1986.

Train, John. *Famous Financial Fiascoes.* New York: Clarkson N. Potter,1985.

Tokar, Brian. *Redesigning Life? The Worldwide Challenge to Genetic Engineering.* London: Zed Books, 2001.

Tucker, George. *The Theory of Money and Banks Investigated.* New York: Greenwood Press, 1968.

Vidal, Gore. "The National Security State: How To Take Back Our Country." *The Nation* (June 4, 1988).

Weisman, Alan. "Columbia's Modern City." *In Context* 42 (1995).

_____. *Nothing Wasted, Everything Gained:.*" Mother Jones (March/April, 1998).

Wessel, James, Mort Hartman. *Trading the Future.* San Francisco: Institute for Food and Policy Development, 1983.

Weil, Robert. "Somalia in Perspective: When the Saints Go Marching In." *Monthly Review* (Mar. 1993).

Wild, Rolf H. *Management by Compulsion.* Boston: Houghton Mifflin Company, 1978.

Windishar, Anne. "Expert: 20% of Gifted Kids Drop Out," *Spokane Chronicle*, January 7, 1988, p. B7.

Winters, Rebecca. "From Home to Harvard," *Time*, September 11, 2000, p. 55.

Wolf, Eric R. *Europe and the People Without History.* Berkeley: University of California Press, 1982.

Zarlenga, Stephen. *The Lost Science of Money: The Mythology of Money – the Story of Power..* Valatie, NY: American Monetary Institute, 2002.

Zinn, Howard. *A People's History of the United States.* New York: Harper Colophon, 1980.

_____. *Terrorism and War.* New York: Seven Stories Press, 2002.

_____. *The Politics of History.* Chicago: University of Illinois Press, 1990.

_____. *The Twentieth Century.* New York: Harper & Row, 1984.

Index

accumulation of capital, 30-34, 49-50, 61, 77, 83, 121
Africa, 75-76, 97, 101, 120, 125-28, 130, 173
AlJazeera, 104, 127
America; 60% of finance capital wasted, 7, 11-12, 40, 154; 9% of land deeded to railroads, 65; Bill of Rights, 51, 73; Civil War, 21; Declaration of Independence, 47; Homestead Act, 49; joined forces with imperial nations, 121; lost moral high ground, 12, 121, 140; Revolution, 6, 15, 21, 47, 77; robber barons, 48, 50, 65, 83; wildcat banking, 28
Americans with Disabilities Act (ADA), 96
Argentina, 127, 128
ASEAN, 126
Asian currency crisis, 147
Astor, John Jacob, 48, 50, 158
Australia, 126, 128
Bandler, Richard, 95
bankruptcies, 21, 39, 82, 94, 98, 146-47, 152, 169
Baruch, A. Levine, 50, 56
Bolivar, Simon, 127
Bolivia, 75, 124, 126, 144
Bolton, John, 140
Borsodi, Ralph, 110
Bowles, Samuel, Gordon, and Weiskopf, 110
Brazil, 61, 127-28
Britain; aristocratic law, 49
Enclosure Acts, 5-6, 46, 165
outlawed printing money in colonies, 15; WW I & II, 123, 128;
Brunei, 126
Bush; President GW, 39
Bush, President HW, 139
Cambodia, 126
Canada, 95
Cantillon, Richard, 50
Central American Free Trade Agreement (CAFTA), 128
Central Asia, 124-25, 138, 140
Chase, Stuart, 68-69, 71, 110
Chavez, Hugo; 128; Bolivarian Revolution, 127
Chicago Board Options Exchange, 82
Chile, 127, 161
China, 18, 62, 66, 124, 126-28, 139, 141, 143, 164; cars, 62, 124, 142; euros, 128; Industrial Revolution, 84, 120; opium, 49
satellites for developing world, 127, 142; trade with developing world, 128, 140-41, 145; UN, 139, 141; WW II, 120
Churchill, Winston, 43
Citibank bailout, 147
Clark, William R., 141
Cold War, 55, 123, 129, 160
Collins, Marva, 116, 117
Columbia, 127
Committee on Monetary and Economic Reform (COMER), 19
Conflict Resolution Law, 94
Confucius, 51
constitutions, 4, 10, 73, 77, 132, 140, 156, 161, 166, 168
Crédit Mobilier, 65
Cuba, 94, 161; direct democracy, 4
one of highest scholastic levels, 164; treat 4.5 million blind Latin Americans, 75
Dacey, Norman F., 93
deflation, 11, 15, 79, 153
democracy; imperial, representative, participatory, direct, 4, 166

Democracy Now, 104, 126
derivatives, 82-84, 161
Diamond, Jared, 143
Doha round, 129, 140
Duke of Bedford, 46
Westminster, 46
East African Community, 128
East Asian Summit (EAS), 126-27, 129
Economic Hit Man (EHM), 126
Ecuador, 127
Edison, Thomas A., 69
Egypt, 68, 171
Einstein, Albert, 51, 155
Eisenhower, President Dwight, 51
Europe, almost lost, 123; City States, 120; European Union (EU), 128, 139, 164
Euros, 125, 128
Fathy, Hassan, 171
Federal Reserve, 18-32, 36-37, 91, 125, 146, 169, 170
federation of earth, 7, 10, 37, 41, 118, 121, 128-29, 138, 143, 148-49, 164, 173; Provisional World Parliament, 40
Fletcher, Governor Benjamin, 47
Ford, Henry, 51, 62, 69, 73-74
fractional reserve banking, 20,-29, 36-37, 136-37, 159, 169
France, 18, 50, 71, 81, 94, 123, 139
Franklin, Benjamin, 15
Free Trade Area of the Americas (FTAA), 128
French Revolution, 6, 125, 159
Furman, Rosemary, 93
Gaffney, Mason, 52, 54
Galbraith, John Kenneth, 51
Gates, Bill, 105
Gaviotas community, 76
General Agreement on Trades and Services (GATS), 128
George, Henry, 1-3, 6-14, 32, 41-44, 47-57, 62, 64, 69, 71, 79, 84, 86, 90, 99, 111, 121-22, 130-37, 145-46, 150-62, 165, 168, 172
Germany, 45, 76, 120, 123, 129, 139, 147
gold standard, 15
goldsmiths, 20
Gorz Andre, 110
Graham, Dr. David, 96
Great Depression, 38, 81, 145, 146-47
greenbacks, 21
GroundSwell, 145
Habsburg, 19
Harrison, Fred, 52, 54, 145
Hartzok, Alanna, 5
Hawes Phil, 171
Hayward, William, 173
hedge funds, 82
Hess, Rudolf, 123
Himmelstein David & Steffie Dr. Ida Hellander, 96
Hong Kong, 83
Hudson, Michael, 56
India, 120, 126, 128-29, 140, 141, 145; caste system, 7; oil Central Asia, 124, 127; protect indigenous knowledge, 75
Indonesia, 126, 128, 143, 161
industrial capital, 10-11, 17, 20-21, 31, 36-37, 40, 46, 52, 59-67, 105-06, 131, 141, 167
Industrial Revolution, 6, 72-73, 84
Indymedia, 104
inflation, 11, 23, 28-29, 36, 38, 79, 151, 153, 159
initial price offerings (IPO), 77
INN Report, 104
International Monetary Fund (IMF), 128
Iran, 125, 128
Iraq, 121, 124, 138-41, 146
Ithica Hours, 38
Japan, 36, 94, 126, 128, 139-47, 169
capital accumulation, 34, 49

embargoed, 123; oil Central Asia, 127; operating 65% of capacity, 61; protection of, 76
reject rules of capitalism, 52, 146
Jefferson, Thomas, 51
Josephson, Matthew, 48, 65
Kaiser Wilhelm, 76, 120
Kenya, 97, 128
Keynes, John Maynard, 51, 80
King George V, 76, 120
Koran, 41
Krehm, William, 19
Kropotkin, Petr, 45, 46, 52
Laos, 126
Latin America, 75-76, 101, 127-28, 161
Law, John, 80, 81
Leisler, Jacob, 47
Lefmann, Ole, 2
LET Systems, 38
Libya, 4
Link TV, 104, 113, 144
Locke, John, 47, 50
Lord Cornbury, 47
Lyon, Peter, 48, 65
Mackay, Charles, 80-81
Malaysia, 126, 128, 143
Martin, Professor Glen, 40, 65
Melman, Seymour, 110
Mercosur alliance, 127
Mexico crisis, 147
Middle Ages, 49, 93
Mill, John Stuart, 51
Mirabeau the Elder, 50
Modern Money Mechanics (MMM), 22
Moffit, Michael, 61
money; circulation of, 22-28, 36, 61, 132, 169; commodity money, 15-16, 24; money supply, 10, 12, 20, 23-29, 36, 67, 77, 130, 148, 154-55, 163, 169; primary created, 10-11, 20-28, 32-39, 156, 163, 169-70; Savings and Loan scandal, 147
Morales, President Evo, 126
Mosaic, 104
Multilateral Agreement on Investments (MAI), 128
Mumford, Lewis, 110
Muslim, 124-26, 139
Myanmar, 126
Nath, Kamal India's Trade Minister, 129
New Zealand, 94, 126
Newcastle Philosophical Society;, 51
North American Free Trade Agreement (NAFTA), 128
Open Market Operations, 26
Organization for Economic Cooperation & Development (OECD), 129
Owen, Robert, 19
Paine, Thomas, 51
Paraguay, 127
Penn, William, 50, 51
Perkins, John, 126
permaculture, 133, 164, 166, 171
Peru, 127
Philippines, 126
Physiocrats, 50-51, 53
populist, 38, 127
propaganda, 166
Queen Victoria, 76, 120
Rand Corporation, 95
Reagan, President Ronald, 55
rent seeking, 3, 6, 46, 90, 99, 135
required reserves, 18, 23-24, 28, 36-37, 148, 155, 159, 168
Ricardo, David, 50-53
Rifkin, Jeremy, 110
Ripley, C.M., 71
Rodell, Fred, 92, 93
Rothschild, 20
Rousseau, Jean Jacques, 44
rule of law, 3-13, 32, 35, 41, 47-49, 51-52, 59, 63, 69, 76, 90-91, 101, 103, 123, 128-29, 132-33, 136, 141-48, 153-55, 158-61, 168, 172

Russell, Bertrand, 110
Russia, 124, 127-28, 134, 139-41, 145; Ruble, 82
Sally Jesse Raphael Show, 95
Saudi Arabia, 138
Schalkenbach Foundation, 51
Schor. Juliet, 110
Sinclair, Upton, 110
Singapore, 126
Skype, 103
Smith, Adam, 51, 54, 62, 74, 76, 108
Social Security, 10, 55-56, 89-92, 150, 156, 162
socialism, 13, 145-46, 155, 168
South Africa, 94, 120
South America, 81, 125-30
South Korea, 62, 126, 128, 143, 147
South Sea Bubble, 81
Southeast Asia, 7, 18, 76, 124-25, 144
Soviet Union, 18, 65-66, 123, 129, 139-40, 161
Spencer Herbert, 51, 165
Sperry, Thomas, 51
Spinoza, 50
Statute of Merton, 1235, 5
stock market crash, 61, 76, 81, 83, 86, 89, 98, 121-22, 125, 128, 135, 141, 144-48, 151-54, 156, 160
Stockman, David, 55
Taiwan, 128, 143
Tanzania, 128
Telesur, 127
Thailand, 62, 126
Thurow, Lester, 78
Tikopia Island, 143, 144
Time Dollars, 38
Tocqueville, Alexis de, 1
Twain, Mark, 44, 51
Uganda, 128
unemployment insurance, 89
Union Pacific Railroad, 65, 67
United Nations, 97, 138-41
Charter, 140; Security Council, 138-41; World Food Program, 97
universal health care, 10, 56, 89, 94, 96-97, 136, 149-50, 155, 161-62
Uruguay, 127
US Treasury, 22, 26-28, 32, 36, 37, 53, 169
Veblen, Thorstein, 68, 110
Venezuela, 75, 124, 127-28, 144
Vidal, Gore, 55
Vietnam, 126
Voice over Internet Protocol (VoiP), 103
Wall Street, 74, 147
WiFi, 64, 66, 101-12, 117-18, 133, 135, 142, 144, 156, 163-66, 172
10% the capacity for 10% the cost, 73
Winfrey, Oprah, 104, 155
World Bank, 128, 162
World Trade Organization (WTO), 128, 129
World War I, 15, 76, 114, 120, 123-24, 128-29, 145, 146
World War II, 15, 18, 33, 36, 38, 68, 76, 120-29, 138-40, 145, 146
World War III, 125, 126
Zambia, 97
Zarlenga, Stephen, 10, 13, 41

About the Author

With a PhD. in political economics from Union Institute and University, J.W. Smith has presented these concepts in 10 countries. This is his 6th book on the causes and cures of world poverty.

The Indonesian University System appears to have named their "Centre for Economic Democracy Studies" after his Magnum Opus, *Economic Democracy: The Political Struggle of the Twenty-First Century*. That book has been translated and is in use in Indonesian classrooms.

Three books are in print in India: WHY? A deeper History of the September 11th Terrorist Attack on America was accepted by a Book of the Month Club.

University research libraries have been a primary market for this author's work and all have seen use in the university classroom.

Until he wrote this book, Smith felt his moving Henry George's philosophy across the full economic spectrum was almost certainly his most important contribution to economic theory.

Smith not only takes a different view from most economists on how economies are currently structured and how they should be structured, his views on money firmly challenges accepted aspects of monetary theory.

He now thinks his melding of Henry George philosophy with the exposure of Western economic classics as justifications for unjust and unequal *rules of law* rather than philosophies for economic efficiencies is equally important.

We think many will agree: The restructuring of *exclusive title* to nature's wealth to *conditional title* eliminating those huge blocs of monopolized capital, the reforming of those appropriated values into relatively *equally-shared use-values*, and the doubling of economic efficiency is quite persuasive.

Paying through PayPal or mailing us a receipt of your purchase of one of our books, will automatically register you as a member. Those in the developing world are automatically registered by simply emailing us they wish to be a member. Go to www.ied.info/ resources.html or www.ied.info/ for further updates. Please join us:

The Institute for Economic Democracy
Global peace and sustainable development equals peace and prosperity for all
1st World, $30/Students, $10/3rd World free
www.paypal.com/, account: ied@ied.info www.ied.info/

International Philosophers for Peace

1st World, $30/Students, $10/3rd World free

Developing a just social, economic, & political basis for peace and human well-being

www.paypal.com/, account: ippno@ippno.org www.ippno.org/

Institute on Word Problems

Creating a world order of peace, justice, and freedom

1st World, $30/Students, $10/3rd World free

www.paypal.com/ - account: gmartin@radford.edu

www.worldproblems.net

Action Institute for Literacy and Human Resource Development

1st World, $30/Students, $10/3rd World free

Education through Project Learning Communities (PLC)

www.paypal.com/, account: plc@ailahurd.org

www.ailahurd.org/

The Hour Money Institute for Global Harmony

1st World, $30/Students, $10/3rd World free

Dedicated to establishing an hour of work as the money unit worldwide

www.paypal.com/, hourmoney@hourmoney.org

www.hourmoney.org/

Network On Democracy Over Empire

1st World, $30/Students, $10/3rd World free

Dedicated to egalitarian democracies replacing the global imperial system

www.paypal.com/, accounts: wdavis@kent.edu

www.altedavis.info/

Global Issues (www.globalissues.org)

A very active supporter but does not take donations at this time

Rights are available for publishing in your region, in English or translations, www.ied.info/.

ied@ied.info

We are available to present these concepts to your class or group. www.ied.info/.

ied@ied.info

Printed in the United States
60400LVS00001B/82-165

9 780962 442346